OFFICE-HOLDERS IN MODERN BRITAIN

I
Treasury Officials
1660–1870

OFFICE-HOLDERS
IN MODERN BRITAIN

I

Treasury Officials
1660-1870

compiled by

J. C. SAINTY

UNIVERSITY OF LONDON
INSTITUTE OF HISTORICAL RESEARCH
THE ATHLONE PRESS
1972

Published by
THE ATHLONE PRESS
UNIVERSITY OF LONDON
at 4 Gower Street, London WC I
Distributed by
Tiptree Book Services Ltd
Tiptree, Essex

© *University of London* 1972

0 485 17141 4

Printed in Great Britain by
WESTERN PRINTING SERVICES LTD
BRISTOL

Preface

The progress of British historical studies has long been impeded by the lack of lists of office-holders. Even where such lists exist they are often incomplete or inaccurate and fail to provide the kind of information that enables the student to relate the offices themselves to their institutional background.

It is with the object of remedying this situation that the present series *Office-Holders in Modern Britain* has been devised. The immediate purpose of the series, which is in the course of preparation at the Institute of Historical Research, is to provide lists of the officials who served in the departments of the central government between the Restoration and 1870. Each volume will contain a short introduction discussing the development of the department with which it is concerned and notes explaining the various offices and grades within the department as well as lists of appointments and an alphabetical list giving details of the periods of service of each official.

Part of the original research for this first volume was undertaken by Mr D. M. Gransby. The material was checked, supplemented and re-arranged by Mr J. C. Sainty, who also wrote the introduction and the explanatory notes. The Institute of Historical Research is extremely grateful to him for making such useful information available in so convenient a form.

A. G. DICKENS

Acknowledgements

I am grateful to the many librarians and archivists who have helped to make this work possible. I am particularly indebted to Dr Henry Roseveare for his unfailing encouragement at all stages in the preparation of the lists.

J. C. S.

Contents

Abbreviations

Add.   Additional
app.   appointed, appointment
Bart.   Baronet
BM   British Museum
c.   circa
cr.   created
d.   death, died
dis.   dismissed
ed.   edited, edition
f., ff.   folio, folios
HC   House of Commons
Hon.   Honourable

kt., ktd.   knight, knighted
MI   Monumental inscription
MS, MSS   manuscript, manuscripts
occ.   occurrence, occurs
pd.   paid
pt.   part
Rept.   Report
res.   resigned
ret.   retired
succ.   succeeded
TM   Treasury minute
vac.   vacated office, vacation of office

References

IN MANUSCRIPT

British Museum, London

Add. MS 34736	West Papers.	Loan 29/456/12	Harley Papers.
Add. MS 35597	Hardwicke Papers.		

Christ Church, Oxford
Evelyn Papers

Public Record Office, London

AO 3/1101–5	Declared Accounts: Treasury Solicitor.
C 66	Patent Rolls.
C 75	Surrender Rolls.
E 197/8	Exchequer Seal Office: Cash Book 1803–35.
E 403	Patent Books of Auditor of Receipt.
LS 13/231	Poll Tax Assessment 1689.
PC 2	Privy Council Registers.
PRO 30/8/231	Chatham Papers.
Prob 8	Prerogative Court of Canterbury: Probate Act Books.
Prob 11	Prerogative Court of Canterbury: Registered Copies of Wills.
T 1	Treasury Papers.
T 29	Treasury Minute Books.
T 38/436–85	Treasury Fee Books.
T 38/552	Account Book of W. Cotton 1820–9.
T 41	Treasury Salaries 1794–1856.
T 48/63	Various Papers and Accounts 1726–51.
T 48/64	Rough Account Book 1738–58.
T 53	Warrants relating to Money.
T 54	Warrants not relating to Money.
T 60	Order Books.
T 64/67	Accounts of New Year's Gifts 1742–55.
T 64/126	Minutes of Commissioners of Public Accounts 1702–3.
T 90/16	Royal Commission on Courts of Justice 1815. Returns and Examinations: Exchequer and Exchequer Chamber 1822.
T 90/142–4	Chancellor of Exchequer: Day Books 1761–1806.

Treasury, London

AB, i–iv	Arrangement Books containing copies of Treasury minutes and other material relating to appointments, remuneration and office organisation 1805–87.

WORKS IN PRINT

Baxter, *Treasury* S. B. Baxter, *The Development of the Treasury 1660–1702.* London 1957.

Chamberlayne, E. and J. Chamberlayne, *Angliae (Magnae Britanniae) Notitia ;*
  Present State *or the Present State of England (Great Britain).*

Court and City Reg. *Court and City Register.*

CTB *Calendar of Treasury Books.* 32 vols., 1660–1718. London 1904–69.

CTBP *Calendar of Treasury Books and Papers.* 5 vols., 1729–45. London 1897–1903.

CTP *Calendar of Treasury Papers.* 5 vols., 1557–1728. London 1868–89.

15th Rept. on *Fifteenth Report of Select Committee on Finance 1797.* Reports
  Finance of Committees of House of Commons 1797–1803, xii.

Gent. Mag. *Gentleman's Magazine.*

Hist. Reg. Chron. *Historical Register . . . Chronological Diary.*

Lond. Mag. *London Magazine and Monthly Chronologer.*

Luttrell, *Hist.* N. Luttrell, *A Brief Historical Relation of State Affairs from*
  Relation *September 1678 to April 1714.* 6 vols. Oxford 1857.

Miège, *New State* G. Miège, *The New State of England.*

Namier, *Structure* L. B. Namier, *The Structure of Politics at the Accession of*
  of Politics *George III.* 2nd ed. London 1957.

New Companion *The New Companion to the London and Royal Calendars or Court and City Register.* London 1808.

Rept. on Misc. *Report of Select Committee on Miscellaneous Expenditure 1848.*
  Expenditure (HC 1847–8, xviii.)

Royal Kal. *The Royal Kalendar.*

2nd Rept. on Fees *Second Report from Commissioners for Enquiring into Fees in Public Offices 1786.* (HC 1806, vii.)

Secret Service *The Secret Service Expenses of Charles II and James II,* ed.
  Expenses J. Y. Akerman. Camden Soc. 1851.

Thomas, *Notes of* F. S. Thomas, *Notes of Materials for a History of Public*
  Materials *Departments.* London 1846.

Times *The Times.*

Todd, *Parliamentary* A. Todd, *Parliamentary Government in England.* 1st ed. 2 vols.
  Government London 1867–9.

Note on Editorial Method

This volume is designed to make available lists of the officials who served in the Treasury between the Restoration in May 1660 and the reorganisation of the establishment which was initiated in May 1870. The material is presented in four parts: an introduction, lists of appointments, periodic lists of officials and an alphabetical list of officials. The purpose of the introduction is to provide a short account of the institutional development of the Treasury during the period in order that the various offices and grades may be related to their general context. The lists of appointments give the dates of appointments to these offices and grades. They are preceded by introductory notes which bring together information concerning such matters as the method of appointment, remuneration and the relevant statutes and Treasury minutes. The periodic lists enable the complete establishment to be seen at selected dates.

The alphabetical list is not intended to be a biographical index. Its purpose is confined simply to providing summarised accounts of the offices held by each individual within the Treasury during the period. No information has been included unless it is directly relevant to this purpose. Thus dates of death are included only if the individual in question was in office at his death. Appointments to offices outside the Treasury have been ignored unless they occasioned, or can reasonably be held to have occasioned, the departure of the official from the Treasury. In general the accounts of the careers of the 'political' officials, the Treasurer, Chancellor of the Exchequer, Commissioners and the Secretaries, have been confined to a simple statement of their periods of service in these offices; information concerning resignations and retirements is provided only in the case of those holding 'permanent' offices. Where an individual held an additional office within the Treasury such as a private secretaryship, which was not directly related to the ordinary course of promotion, the details of his period of service in this additional office have been placed in a separate paragraph. A similar course has been adopted in the case of Chancellors of the Exchequer who were also Commissioners. The accounts of the careers of those who were in office in May 1870 have not been continued beyond this date.

All references have been concentrated in the alphabetical list except in the case of the Commissioners where they are included in the relevant list of appointments. Where printed calendars of manuscript material exist they have been used as authorities provided that the calendaring is sufficiently full. Peers and holders of courtesy titles have been indexed under their titles. In the case of changes of name or status, appropriate cross-references have been inserted. Unless otherwise noted, information concerning peers and baronets has been taken from the *Complete Peerage* (ed. G.E.C. 2nd ed. 13 vols. London 1910–59), the *Complete Baronetage* (ed. G.E.C. 5 vols. Exeter 1900–6) and Burke's *Peerage*.

Certain conventions have been adopted for dating appointments. The year is taken to have begun on 1 January throughout the period. In the case of those offices which were conferred by an instrument, whether this took the form of letters patent under the great seal, Treasury constitution or Treasury warrant, the date is that of the instrument. Where appointment was by Treasury minute, it is that of the minute. For reasons that are given in the relevant introductory notes these conventions have been modified in the cases of the Chancellor of the Exchequer from 1782 and the First Lord from 1827. The task of determining the periods of service of the 'political' officials presents considerable difficulty particularly in the nineteenth century when their appointments were frequently canvassed in newspapers and elsewhere several days before the date of their formal entry into office. For the sake of consistency the latter date has been adopted throughout the period. All officials are taken to have remained in office until the appointment of their successors unless there is clear evidence to support the selection of an earlier date. Where there is no indication of the date of the appointment of an individual, his period of service is dated by reference to the time during which he received a salary or other remuneration or, failing this information, by reference to the earliest and latest date at which he is found occupying a particular office.

Introduction

At the Restoration the Treasury had little of the character of a settled institution. It largely lacked permanent records and established routines of business. As far as personnel was concerned the Treasurer or the Treasury Board had a general authority over a collection of salaried officials—a Serjeant at Arms, a Messenger of the Chamber and four Messengers of the Receipt—but their origins antedated the development of the Treasury office in its modern sense and they were, in any case, of relatively small importance. Apart from a Solicitor the only other official belonging to the Treasury at that time was the Secretary.

Although he received no instrument of appointment and no salary from public funds, the Secretary had by 1660 become indispensable to the exercise of the functions of the Treasury. His duties were already sufficiently onerous to require the assistance of Clerks. For the earlier part of the reign of Charles II there is no evidence to suggest that these Clerks had any expectation of remaining in employment after their masters had left office. This fact goes far to explain the lack of material concerning the recruitment, remuneration and general organisation of the clerical staff during this period. No records dealing specifically with these questions survive that are earlier in date than the reign of William III and it is doubtful whether many were ever created. One can learn of the names and activities of Clerks only incidentally from documents dealing with matters on which they happened to be engaged. Thus, while it is clear that such Clerks as Charnock, P. Lloyd and Fleetwood played an important part in the work of the Treasury, only an approximate idea can be formed of the limits of their periods of service. The sources of their remuneration and their standing relative to their colleagues are obscure. In all probability they did not regard their position as anything more than temporary. Such evidence as there is suggests that they looked for financial security not in a permanent career in the Treasury but in making use of the influence of their patrons to acquire profitable offices elsewhere.[1]

While it is right to stress the fluidity of the organisation of the Treasury office during the reign of Charles II, it should also be recognised that there were at the same time factors making for continuity and permanence. One of these factors was the growing complexity of the work undertaken by the Treasury. It became increasingly important to retain the services of Clerks who had acquired the specialised knowledge necessary for the efficient dispatch of business. Of comparable significance was the fact that the Treasury was in commission for a substantial part of the reign. Under a Treasurer there was a tendency towards informality in the conduct of business, but the existence of a Board necessitated the introduction and maintenance of settled procedures, which in their turn required the services of a body of Clerks familiar with the usual forms.

Perhaps the earliest indication that the Clerks of the Treasury had received recognition as a distinct body is the allocation to them of new year's gifts from the King. Payments of the relatively small sum of £25 are recorded for the years 1674–5 and

---

[1] For the careers of some of the Clerks during this period, see Baxter, *Treasury*, 214–39.

1677–8 but, since they are made to the Clerks collectively, they are of no assistance to an understanding of the organisation of the office.[2] From 1679 the Clerks received periodic payments from the secret service for travelling charges. Until 1690 these payments are recorded simply as totals although, as the sums differ in each case, it is clear that they were made up of particular amounts based on individual claims.[3]

The principal source of the remuneration of the Secretary and the Clerks were the office fees. These were payable on instruments prepared in the Treasury authorising such actions as the issue of money or the grant of offices. An important development in this context was the introduction of a permanent arrangement for the division of these fees. This arrangement apportioned two thirds of the product to the Secretary and one third to the Clerks and was to be observed until the introduction of fixed salaries in 1782. It is uncertain when this arrangement was made. The earliest surviving list of receipts of Treasury fees covers the years 1679 to 1685 during the period of Guy's first secretaryship.[4] This list discloses no information about the remuneration of Clerks. However, in the next surviving lists, which give details of the fees which fell to Gwyn, Guy's associate between April 1685 and December 1686, the monthly totals are divided, Gwyn taking two thirds and the Clerks one third.[5] It is conceivable that this apportionment had its origin in 1685 and that Guy, when making the arrangement for Gwyn to receive certain of the office fees, took the opportunity to make permanent provision for the Clerks. The lists for 1685–6 do not indicate who were the recipients of the one third share nor the basis on which it was apportioned.

The earliest document to throw any light on this question is the assessment for poll tax for Whitehall and St James's made in July 1689. In addition to the Commissioners, Secretary and Office Keeper (described as Under Clerk), this gives the names of six Clerks. Five of these, Glanville, Evelyn, Squibb, Langford and Lowndes are assessed at a common rate. The remaining Clerk, Powys, is assessed at a lower rate.[6] This document should be read in conjunction with that recording the payment made from the secret service on 4 February 1690 to the Clerks and other officers of the Treasury for coach hire.[7] As already stated earlier payments of this kind are recorded simply as totals. The entry in this case, however, lists fourteen recipients with payments at differential rates. One of the recipients was the Office Keeper and another the Serjeant at Arms. Three can be identified with reasonable certainty as Messengers. The remaining nine, with the exception of Southworth whose name does not occur elsewhere, are known from other evidence to have been Treasury Clerks. Five of them, Squibb, Lowndes, Langford, Glanville and Evelyn, received payment at the rate of 13s 4d a day and four, Southworth, Powys, Tilson and Taylor, at 10s a day. This evidence, taken in conjunction with that available for the years after 1695, would appear to support the identification of the five Clerks paid at the higher rate with the Chief Clerks, whose special position was defined by their right to equal shares in one third of the office fees. If this supposition is correct, the four Clerks paid at the lower rate would be equivalent to the later Under Clerks. In this connection it is significant that the second edition of Miège's *New State of England*, which appeared in 1693 and contains the first published account of Treasury officials, lists five 'First' Clerks.[8]

---

[2] *CTB*, iv, 277; ibid. v, 834.   [3] *Secret Service Expenses*, 7, 20, 29, 66, 79, 97, 114, 141, 176, 210.
[4] Baxter, *Treasury*, 272–4.   [5] T 38/436; totals printed in Baxter, *Treasury*, 274–5.
[6] LS 13/231 p. 13.   [7] *CTB*, xvii, 553–4.
[8] Miège, *New State* (1693), pt. iii, 404; all subsequent editions of Miège's work contain lists of Treasury officials. Chamberlayne's *Present State* began to include such lists only from the twenty-first

The fact that Evelyn is said to have bought his chief clerkship in 1690 suggests that these posts were already well established by this date. The circumstances surrounding this transaction are obscure but it can reasonably be said that purchase would not have been contemplated unless the right to a share in the profits of the office had already been clearly defined.[9]

While the outlines of the later structure of Treasury organisation can already be discerned before 1695 it was not until William Lowndes became Secretary in that year that the surviving evidence is of a kind to make possible the study of the careers of individual Clerks in any sort of detail. The relevant material is at first confined to two principal types of record: the accounts of the office fees and the accounts of the secret service. The former are made up monthly and cover the period 1695 to 1715.[10] A number are missing but the series is sufficiently complete to provide a basis for generalisation. Each account contains a list of sums paid in by the Clerks and others. The total receipts are apportioned, in accordance with the principle already described, to give two thirds to the Secretary and one third to be divided equally amongst a fixed number of Chief Clerks. In 1695 and 1696 this number was five. No accounts survive for 1697 but when they resume in 1698 the number had been reduced to four at which level it remained until 1834.[11]

The accounts mention several Clerks who had no share in the third of the office fees. These can reasonably be identified as Under Clerks. They also record the payment of fixed salaries to two or three such Clerks between 1695 and 1713, the amounts required being met by proportional abatements in the dividends of the Secretary and Chief Clerks. It may be that the practice of paying such salaries in this way was in operation on a wider scale before 1695.[12] This possibility derives some support from the fact that from this date a number of Under Clerks began to receive regular salaries from the secret service. While it is conceivable that this development represents an entirely new departure, the more likely explanation would appear to be that these salaries were simply transferred from the fees to public funds. If this surmise is correct, the arrangement may have been part of a bargain made by Lowndes on his entry into office whereby, in return for the abolition of certain 'Gratuities' and the establishment of a fixed table of fees approved by the King, the crown undertook to assume responsibility for the bulk of the Under Clerks' salaries.[13] After 1695 even the few salaries that were paid from the fees were in each case eventually transferred to the secret service. The number of Clerks receiving salaries from these sources between 1695 and 1714 varied from seven to ten. The most usual salary was £50. Some Clerks

edition (1704). The information contained in these publications, while not without value, is often at variance with the evidence in Treasury sources.

[9] *Memoirs of John Evelyn*, ed. W. Bray, 2nd ed. (1819), i p. xxii. While the Evelyn MSS at Christ Church, Oxford, have a few items referring to the younger Evelyn's period at the Treasury, including his father's account of his dismissal in 1691, they do not appear to contain any evidence to support Bray's assertion that the office had been purchased. The Treasury condemned the practice of selling clerkships in TM 16 March 1722 (T 29/24, pt. ii, 152).

[10] These accounts are amongst the Treasury Papers. The totals between 1695 and 1701 are printed in Baxter, *Treasury*, 276–82.

[11] See, however, the petition of the 'Four Chief Clerks of the Treasury' endorsed 'Read Aug. 1696' (*CTP 1557–1696*, 543).

[12] See the case of Dorney (*CTB*, v, 1348).

[13] TM 24 April 1695 (*CTB*, x, 1369); see also Lowndes' evidence to the Commissioners of Public Accounts in Nov. 1702 (T 64/126 pp. 232, 264).

received this at once; others after having served for a period at £40. Between 1704 and 1709 successive editions of Chamberlayne's *Present State* list three Clerks paid at the latter rate as 'Supernumeraries' but this designation is not found in the Treasury records at this date.[14] From 1696 to 1714 the secret service accounts also record payments to Chief and Under Clerks to reimburse them for the amounts they had paid in taxes, thus providing an additional means of identifying them.[15]

After 1714 the nature of the evidence is such as to make possible more confident statements about the personnel of the Treasury than is the case for the earlier period. The principal additional source to become relevant is the series of minute books of the Treasury. Before 1714 the minutes record practically no decisions concerning the appointment, promotion or remuneration of those in the employment of the office. Thereafter entries dealing with these questions occur with increasing frequency.[16] Not too much significance should be attached to this development. There was a general tendency for the minutes to become fuller after 1714. Their silence on establishment matters before this date should not be taken as evidence that the Treasurer or the Board were unaware of or unconcerned with developments in this field. Nevertheless the very fact of recording the relevant decisions in a permanent manner had the effect of creating a body of precedent and stabilising the structure and conventions of the office.[17]

In October 1715 the Board called for 'a list of the clerks, under clerks, doorkeepers, messengers and other officers of the Treasury'. It was delivered on the 17th of the month and the Board, after replacing the Office Keeper, ordered the rest of the officers to remain in their employments. The list itself is appended to the minutes for that day and is of considerable interest since it apparently represents the first conscious attempt which the Treasury made to define the rather heterogeneous group of officials who constituted the establishment in its wider sense.[18] The list, which also contains details of salaries, may be summarised as follows:

2 Secretaries
4 Chief Clerks

[14] In some cases the names of Clerks occur in the accounts of the fees before they begin to receive salaries which may mean that they began their service in the office as supernumeraries.

[15] This practice appears to have arisen following the petition of the Chief Clerks of 1696 which sought this privilege; see p. 3 n. 11. Later the reimbursements were made out of the incidents; see also *2nd Rept. on Fees*, 55.

[16] Appointments of Under Clerks began to be recorded in the minutes in 1718; those of Secretaries and Chief Clerks were not regularly so recorded until 1730 and 1742 respectively. The appointments of certain officials of the Treasury were embodied in instruments. The Treasurer and Commissioners of the Treasury, the Chancellor and Under Treasurer of the Exchequer, the Serjeant at Arms and the Messengers of the Receipt (until 1825) were appointed by letters patent under the great seal. The Solicitors, the Messenger of the Chamber, the Office Keeper and the Keeper of Papers were, at various times, appointed by Treasury constitution.

[17] As a general rule all minutes were entered in the minute books until 1849. Thereafter many that were considered of relatively small importance were excluded. After 1859 the books contain practically no material relating to establishment matters. From 1805 'Arrangement Books' were kept by the Treasury into which minutes and other documents concerning appointments and the organisation of the office were transcribed. For the purpose of these lists the Arrangement Books have been used as the principal source for the years 1860–70.

[18] TM 13 and 17 Oct. 1715 (*CTB*, xxix, 296, 297–8). There is a similar list dated 6 June 1711, amongst the Harley MSS (BM Loan 29/45B f. 12/259). I am grateful to Mr Thomas K. Moore for drawing my attention to this document.

9 Under Clerks
3 Under Clerks for keeping accounts
1 Office Keeper
1 Doorkeeper
1 Sweeper
1 Bag Carrier
4 Messengers of the Receipt (and 3 deputies)
1 Messenger of the Chamber
1 Letter Carrier (also deputy Messenger of the Chamber).

Although the Treasury office was to grow continuously during the eighteenth century its basic structure, illustrated by this list, was to remain fundamentally unchanged until the reform of 1782. A general survey of its nature and functions during this period may therefore be appropriate.

At the head of the office were the Secretaries. Apart from the special arrangement of 1685–6 whereby Gwyn undertook the Irish business of the Treasury, there was only one Secretary until 1711. In that year a second secretaryship was created. This officer shared the two thirds of the office fees equally with his colleague and was, like him, usually a member of the House of Commons. However, while the senior secretaryship was held on what amounted to a permanent tenure until 1752, changes in the holders of the junior post were frequent and reflected alterations in the political complexion of the Board. It was not until the second half of the eighteenth century that the senior secretaryship came to be governed by similar considerations and the right of succession from the junior to the senior position was established. Arrangements for the division of responsibilities between the Secretaries must have been made from the first. They were not, however, the subject of Treasury minutes. A memorandum of about 1783 is the first document to deal specifically with this question.[19] It was unusual for Secretaries to be promoted from within the office. Apart from William Lowndes (1695) the only Clerks to achieve this distinction were Taylor (1714), Bradshaw (1767) and, after a period of retirement, C. Lowndes (1765).[20]

The four Chief Clerks ranked next in the structure of the office. Appointments to these offices were normally made from amongst the active Under Clerks, usually on the basis of seniority.[21] On five occasions between 1695 and 1782 appointments were made from outside the office. The appointments of Thomas (1713) and Kelsall (1714) appear to have been dictated by considerations of patronage alone. In the remaining cases—Postlethwaite and Yeates (1759) and Bradshaw (1761)—the same considerations undoubtedly applied, but the individuals in question seem to have owed their preferment at least as much to their special qualifications for the posts.[22] Once appointed

---

[19] Memorandum on office organisation in Chatham MSS (PRO 30/8/231); for the distribution of duties in 1804, see Thomas, *Notes of Materials*, 17.

[20] In 1782 E. Chamberlayne was nominated a Secretary but died before actually entering office.

[21] H. Fane was appointed from the place of seventh Under Clerk in 1742. On three occasions Under Clerks were recorded as having declined promotion; see TM 22 Dec. 1761 (T 29/34 p. 207), 18 Aug. 1767 (T 29/38 p. 451), 22 Feb. 1776 (T 29/45 p. 53). For the question of active Under Clerks, see below.

[22] Thomas was Private Secretary to Treasurer Oxford; Kelsall was appointed at the age of twenty-one; Postlethwaite was the author of a *History of the Public Revenue* (1759); Yeates was a Clerk in the House of Commons and was responsible for the drafting of parliamentary bills for the Treasury; Bradshaw had been First Clerk in the War Office.

the Chief Clerks enjoyed a secure tenure, generally remaining in office until death or voluntary resignation.[23] So far as the functions of the Chief Clerks were concerned the manner in which they received their remuneration, by freeing them from immediate dependence on particular types of business, made it possible for them to develop a general view which was important to their fulfilment of the role of advisers to the Secretaries and the Board which they exercised until 1805. Particular areas of responsibility were assigned to individual Chief Clerks although, when occasion arose, each was expected to be ready to undertake any of the business of the office.[24]

The year 1714 witnessed an alteration in the position of the Under Clerks. Down to the death of Queen Anne their salaries were provided from the secret service. Following the accession of George I, they were transferred to the civil list. No radically new principle was involved in this development. The salaries continued to be borne by public funds as they had been since 1695. So far as the internal organisation of the Treasury was concerned, however, the change was not without significance. Few formalities were involved in the disbursement of the secret service funds by the Secretary of the Treasury. Payments from the civil list, on the other hand, involved the preparation of a quarterly warrant to the Auditor of the Receipt, which required the authorisation of the Board. This procedure had two important consequences. In the first place, the warrant, being a formal document, listed the recipients in order of seniority. Secondly, the necessity for periodical authorisation enabled the Board to keep their identity and remuneration continuously under review. The Clerks who received salaries from this source constituted the 'establishment' in the sense in which it was usually understood in the eighteenth century. So defined the term never comprehended the whole clerical staff of the Treasury. It excluded, for example, the Chief Clerks and also the Clerks in the Revenue Department, unless they happened to draw salaries from the civil list. Nevertheless it was a concept of some value since it provided the yardstick by reference to which the Board was accustomed to measure the effects of changes in the number of Clerks employed in the office.

The number of Clerks on the establishment varied. Beginning at nine in 1715, it had doubled by 1761. Thereafter it rose rapidly, reaching a peak of twenty-seven in 1773. Until 1733 the three most senior Clerks enjoyed salaries of £100, while the rest received £50. From that year £100 was the normal salary for all. With rare exceptions Clerks were placed at the bottom of the salary warrant on their appointment to the establishment. They enjoyed a secure tenure and rose upwards on the principle of strict seniority, a convention which received specific endorsement in a minute of 1757 which laid down 'that the Under Clerks rise according to seniority as has been usual in the office . . .'.[25] Finally when they had reached first place they became eligible for the offer of a chief clerkship. Although they might, from time to time, be given special tasks to perform, the principal function of the Under Clerks was the preparation of instruments authorising expenditure. The business undertaken by each Clerk was settled at successive 'divisions'. It was not until 1776 that these divisions were regu-

---

[23] Only Leheup was dismissed (1755). W. Lowndes and Burnaby, who retired in 1759 to make way for Postlethwaite and Yeates, were both granted pensions (T 29/33 p. 218). C. Lowndes was allowed to retain the office of Keeper of Papers, probably as a means of providing him with a pension, on his resignation in 1762 (T 29/34 p. 232).

[24] TM 18 Nov. 1714 (*CTB*, xxix, 30–2), 31 July 1759 (T 29/33 pp. 218–19).

[25] TM 27 July 1757 (T 29/32 p. 475). The dismissal of Under Clerks was rare. The following cases are recorded: Martin (1722), Plaxton (1758), Chowne (1772) and H. Webster (1782).

larly approved by the Board and recorded in the minutes. Before this date there is no consistent body of evidence on which to base detailed study. Nevertheless there is enough information to indicate the general principles which operated. Following each change in the composition of the group of Clerks involved, a re-arrangement of the work took place under the general authority of the Secretaries. Categories of business were grouped together and allocated to particular Clerks with the object of ensuring that those with the greater seniority received the larger income from fees. These fees were personal and distinct from those which were carried to the common fund that provided the remuneration of the Secretaries and Chief Clerks.[26]

Apart from the Clerks whose activities have just been described it was usual for the establishment to accommodate a number of individuals whose membership of the Treasury office was purely nominal. This seems to be accounted for by the Board's reluctance to dismiss Clerks who, for a variety of reasons, were unable or unwilling to undertake any duties. Evidence on this question is fragmentary. The career of E. Webster is, however, instructive. A Clerk from about 1691, there seems little doubt that he ceased to play an active part in the work of the office after his appointment as Chief Secretary to the Lord Lieutenant of Ireland in 1717. Yet he remained on the establishment and continued to receive a salary of £100 from the civil list until his death in 1755.[27] His was, perhaps, an extreme case but it was not without parallel.[28] In a different category were those Clerks in the Revenue Department who were placed on the establishment as a means of augmenting their salaries from the customs.

Supernumerary Clerks may conveniently be considered at this point. These may be defined as those Clerks who were appointed with the expectation, either express or implied, of being placed on the establishment, although not necessarily at the next vacancy. The minutes during this period describe them indifferently as 'Supernumerary' and 'Extraordinary'. This creates a certain amount of confusion, since the latter term came to have a distinct meaning as will be seen in due course. Although they may have existed at an earlier date, the appointment of Supernumerary Clerks is recorded for the first time in the minutes in 1736. It was not until 1756, however, that they became a regular feature of the office. From this year it was usual for Under Clerks on the establishment to begin their service in the Treasury as Supernumerary Clerks.

The establishment was eventually regulated by a minute of 22 February 1776 which is of considerable importance since it represents the first step in the direction of a comprehensive reform of the office.[29] It had three main objects. The first was to dispense with the services of those individuals who were unable or unwilling to take an active part in the business of the Treasury and to ensure that the office was staffed by a body of working Clerks. The second was to provide a proper training for Clerks by arranging the business 'in such Manner that in future every Clerk may from his Entry

[26] TM 22 Feb. 1776 (T 29/45 pp. 55–6); for a division of 23 Nov. 1752, see T 48/64; for a list of 'Perquisites' of about 1760, apparently representing the expected yield of fees to particular Under Clerks, see BM Add. MS 34736 f. 121.

[27] For Webster, see *Hist. Reg. Chron.* (1717), ii, 20, TM 14 May 1717, 6 Sept. 1721 (*CTB*, xxxi, 16; T 29/24, pt. ii, 92) and BM Add. MS 34736 f. 105. He was passed over for promotion to a chief clerkship in 1724, 1738, 1742 and 1752 and was not included in the division of the latter year.

[28] De Grey was not included in the division of 1752 and was not considered for promotion to a chief clerkship in 1761. For the position of Schutz, see BM Add. MS 34736 f. 121. For the case of Beldam, held in 1762 to have been 'a clerk to the Duke of Newcastle, not the Treasury', see BM Add. MS 35597 f. 96.

[29] T 29/45 pp. 53–8.

into the Office be regularly instructed, and go through every Branch as he shall be promoted'. Finally it was laid down that for the future the considerations governing the promotion of Clerks should be their 'Ability, Attention, Care and Diligence . . . and not their Seniority'. With these objects in view the Board 'superannuated' four Clerks, leaving twenty-one places on the active civil list establishment. Seven of these places were reserved for the Clerks in the Revenue Department who continued to receive the £100 annuities as contributions towards their remuneration. The business of expenditure was divided up amongst the remaining fourteen Clerks. The granting of retiring allowances to the four superannuated Clerks was the beginning of a regular practice whereby the Treasury pensioned off those of its staff who were incapable of carrying out their duties in person.[30]

Immediately following the Under Clerks in the list of October 1715 are the 'under clerks for keeping accounts'. In order to place them in their context, some account must be given of the origin and development of the Revenue Department. Although it always formed part of the Treasury organisation in its wider sense, the Revenue Department had specialised functions which resulted in its remaining outside the ordinary establishment until 1834. As its name implies its basic function was the preparation of accounts of the revenue. The first indication that the Treasury was keeping such accounts is to be found in March 1681 in the payment from the secret service 'For keeping private accompts of the several branches of His Majesties Revenue' for the half year beginning in March 1680. This is the first of a series of payments from public funds which were made necessary by the fact that the service rendered gave rise to no fees. Beginning at £50 the annual rate was raised to £150 in 1685.[31]

Until 1688 the charge for this service formed part of the Treasury incidents received by the Secretary. At the accession of William III, however, the payments were transferred from the secret service to the customs and directed to a particular Treasury Clerk, Taylor, who may in consequence reasonably be regarded as the first identifiable Chief Clerk of the Revenue.[32] There is no evidence to indicate whether Taylor found it necessary to employ additional Clerks to assist him in the preparation of the accounts. It is, however, noteworthy that his successor, Tilson, was allowed to retain the £50 annuity from the secret service which he had received as an Under Clerk after his promotion to a chief clerkship about 1697. When in 1709 his allowance from this source was raised to £150, it was described as being paid 'for making up the accounts of the public revenues and defraying the charge he is at for clerks and other incidents in carrying on and performing that service'. Tilson's payment from the secret service in 1712 specifically refers to 'myself and two clerks'.[33]

It is clear, therefore, that the Revenue 'Department' had already been in existence in an embryonic form for some time before its Clerks were given formal recognition in the minute of October 1715. It is, however, impossible to give a complete account of

[30] This practice attracted the favourable comment of the Commissioners on Fees of 1786 (2nd Rept. on Fees, 55). Before 1776 no such allowances were granted to Under Clerks, presumably because they were usually permitted to remain on the establishment until death, whether they were active or not. The practice with regard to Chief Clerks was different since, as a general rule, they were required always to exercise their functions in person. See p. 6 n. 23.

[31] Secret Service Expenses, 25, 31, 44, 52, 64, 71, 80, 85, 94, 100, 108, 114, 120, 127, 136, 140, 148, 150, 168, 174, 183, 190, 201, 210.

[32] CTB, viii, 2151; ibid. ix, 19. The bulk of the charge of the Revenue Department continued to be borne by the customs until 1831 when the salaries were transferred to the annual estimates.

[33] CTB, xxviii, 466–7, 491.

the department during the first half of the eighteenth century since the minutes do not always record the appointments of the Clerks employed in it and the salary warrants name only the Chief Clerk without specifying his colleagues. In 1714 a sum of £260 a year was made available from the customs for the remuneration of the Revenue Clerks.[34] Down to 1725 the recipient was Frecker, an Under Clerk on the establishment, later promoted to a chief clerkship. In that year the number of Under Clerks had been reduced to two, who were said to be 'very diligent and give double the attendance of any other in the office, their business requiring them so to do, now having but 50 per annum each'.[35] Probably as a means of alleviating their lot the decision was made to transfer the annual payment from the customs to Beresford, the senior Under Clerk, to share with his colleague. In the light of subsequent events it is clear that this decision had the effect of underlining the differentiation of the Revenue Department from the ordinary establishment. In 1726 a clerk on the establishment was appointed to assist in the business of the department with 'such other of the Under Clerks as are little employed'[36] but there is no evidence to indicate that this arrangement remained effective. Probably of more significance was the reverse process whereby Revenue Clerks were transferred to the active establishment.[37] In 1745 the department was composed of four Clerks. After 1752 their number was progressively reduced. In 1757 the remaining two were placed formally on the establishment as a reward for their 'industry and fidelity'. At the same time the Board directed that 'two of the Junior Clerks (on the establishment) be appointed by the Secretaries to do business in the Accomptants Office in order thoroughly to understand that branch of business'.[38]

From 1758 it appears to have been accepted that the needs of the Revenue Department would be best served by the employment of a distinct group of Clerks. The number of such Clerks increased rapidly, reaching seven in 1767 at which level it remained with only minor variations until the department was fully absorbed into the Treasury office in 1834. From 1762 it was the rule for all of them to be members of the establishment in the formal sense of receiving £100 salaries from the civil list. From that date it was rare for a Clerk to be recruited directly, appointments usually being made from amongst the Supernumerary Clerks or the Clerks already on the establishment. Once appointed they almost invariably remained in the department for the rest of their service in the Treasury. This convention received explicit confirmation in 1776 when it was laid down that 'the Revenue Office . . . should be kept as a distinct and separate department' and that 'the Persons named as Revenue Clerks (are) to succeed in that Office only'.[39]

The list of 1715 concludes with a group of officials who constituted the subordinate staff of the Treasury. The first is the Office (or Chamber) Keeper. This office originated about 1667 and its duties included the custody of the Treasury chambers and the provision of the usual necessaries. Out of his annual allowance he paid salaries to the Doorkeeper and the Sweeper. During the eighteenth century the two latter posts gradually rose in standing and profitability. The office of Doorkeeper had by 1763 become a sinecure, its duties being exercised by deputy. That of Sweeper, dignified successively by the designations 'Necessary Woman' and 'Housekeeper' came to involve responsibility for a number of inferior domestic staff. In 1762 a distinct House-

---

[34] Ibid. xxix, 628.
[35] BM Add. MS 34736 f. 105.
[36] TM 3 May 1726 (T 29/25 p. 173).
[37] Plaxton (1754) and Kerrick (1755).
[38] TM 11 Oct. 1752 (T 29/32 p. 71), 27 July 1757 (ibid. p. 475).
[39] TM 22 Feb. 1776 (T 29/45 p. 57).

keeper was appointed to take care of the rooms, known commonly as the 'Levée Rooms' which had been transferred to the Treasury from the office of the Secretary of State for the Northern Department.

Finally there were the Messengers whose history is complex and to some extent obscure. The four Messengers of the Receipt were technically officers of the lower Exchequer and received their basic salaries as such. Having been originally attached to the Treasurer they came under the general authority of the Board. However, their offices were of great antiquity and at the Restoration conformed closely to the classic proprietary pattern. They were appointed for life and enjoyed the right of exercising their functions by deputy. The evidence suggests that the Treasury did not succeed in obtaining much useful service either from them or from their deputies even after 1689 when they were made theoretically more amenable to direction by having their tenure altered from life to pleasure. The situation of the Messenger of the Chamber was in some ways comparable to that of the Messengers of the Receipt. Until the early part of the eighteenth century he was employing a deputy although later he became a working official with useful functions.

For the most part these officials constituted an intractable and largely useless legacy from the past and, in order to obtain efficient service, the Treasury was obliged to employ additional Messengers. During the reign of William III there were normally two such Messengers receiving regular salaries. One of these was usually also the deputy of the Messenger of the Chamber and appears as such in the list of 1715. The place of the other had by that year been taken by the Bag Carrier whose particular function was to attend the Secretaries at the House of Commons. In the course of time the Office Keeper's civil list bill on which the salaries of these officials were normally carried was increased by the addition of further charges. In 1717 a salary was made available for the post of Assistant to the Office Keeper and Messengers, or Bookranger. Further salaries were provided which, although originally intended for working Messengers, had by 1772 been absorbed by the four Messengers of the Receipt, the Messenger of the Chamber and the deputy Doorkeeper, who appear to have regarded them simply as supplementary perquisites of their offices. The Treasury was, therefore, thrown back on the expedient of employing a distinct body of Messengers who were paid weekly out of the incidents. In 1786 two of these were permanently attached to the Joint Secretaries.

The only officials belonging to the Treasury in 1715 who were not included in the list of that year were the two Solicitors who, in view of their special functions, remained apart from the ordinary structure of the office. The older solicitorship dated from the Restoration. In 1696 the duties were divided and a second office created. After 1716 the older office gradually became a complete sinecure while the holder of the second took over the whole of the work. An assistant solicitorship existed between 1685 and 1689 and between 1722 and 1730 but did not become established on a regular basis until 1746.

Between 1715 and 1782 changes in the organisation of the Treasury can largely be explained in terms of the development of offices already in existence. There were few innovations. In 1726 a Keeper of Papers was appointed. Although this post had useful functions attached to it, its effectiveness was limited by the fact that it was allowed to pass into the hands of deputies, the principals treating it simply as an additional source of income. In 1742 an act of Parliament disqualified the Clerks of the Treasury, together with the subordinate officials of a number of other departments, from membership of the House of Commons.[40] In 1769 the Treasury appointed a Counsel to undertake the drafting of its parliamentary bills and an Agent to supervise their passage through the House of Commons.

The year 1782 witnessed a major reform of the Treasury office. A minute of 30 November began by reaffirming the principles laid down in that of February 1776 and went on to introduce further changes.[41] In the first place it established fixed salaries for the Secretaries and the Clerks. The amounts in each case were settled after an examination of their receipts in representative years of peace and war. Provision was made for the charge of the salaries to be borne by the existing fee fund from which the Secretaries and Chief Clerks had received their dividends, augmented by the personal fees which had previously been taken by the Under Clerks for their own use. In the event of the product of the fund proving insufficient, the salaries were to suffer proportional reductions.

The reform paved the way for a reorganisation of the business of expenditure. The earlier arrangement by which the number of divisions had varied according to the number of clerks participating in the business was replaced by six fixed divisions in which its distribution was unaffected by changes in personnel. The new divisions were each manned by two Under Clerks who received the designations Senior and Junior Clerk.[42] The grouping of the various items of business was, however, still governed by the expected yield of the fees. This fact was reflected in the salaries of the Senior and Junior Clerks which, although of fixed amounts in each case, varied according to the division in which they served.

Under the new arrangements the number and functions of the Chief Clerks remained unaltered. There was no change in the position of the Clerks in the Revenue Department who had, as already indicated, always received their remuneration in the form of fixed salaries. The active civil list establishment continued to consist of twenty-one places, of which seven were reserved for the Revenue Clerks and twelve for the Senior and Junior Clerks. There remained two Clerks, of whom one was appointed Copying Clerk and the other was apparently left without specific responsibilities. A Receiver of Fees was appointed but no alteration was made in the number or functions of the subordinate staff.

In 1786 the Treasury office was investigated by the Commissioners on Fees. Their second report, which includes the examinations of forty-six of the staff, contains much valuable information. In general the Commissioners professed themselves satisfied with the state of the office and praised the reforms introduced in 1782. No action was taken on the report until 1793. In that year an order in council gave effect to such of their recommendations as were acceptable to the Treasury.[43] The Treasury rejected a proposal that one of the Joint Secretaries should be placed on a permanent tenure and made ineligible for Parliament and also a suggested reduction of one in the number of Chief Clerks. On the other hand, it accepted an arrangement for the payment of

---

[40] 15 Geo. II, c 22. The following were members of the Commons while holding clerkships in the Treasury: Shaw (1685), Kelsall (1791–34) and Tilson (1727–34). Bendish was a candidate in 1710 (Luttrell, *Hist. Relation*, vi, 541, 543). Pennington (1745) and H. Fane (1757) relinquished their clerkships on election. E. Webster was a member of the Irish parliament of George I.

[41] T 29/52 pp. 516–24.

[42] In the lists below the Junior Clerks have been designated 'Junior (Assistant) Clerks' in order to distinguish them from the undifferentiated Junior Clerks on the establishment.

[43] *15th Rept. on Finance*, 288–9.

salaries which was more favourable than that introduced in 1782. The effect of this
was that all salaries which had previously been paid to officials of the Treasury from the
civil list were discontinued. The amounts of these salaries were made good from the
customs in the case of the Clerks in the Revenue Department and from the fee fund
in the case of the rest. Deficiencies in the fee fund were not to result in reductions in
salaries but were to be met by payments from the civil list to which any surplus was to
be carried.[44] The Board also agreed to reduce the salaries of certain of the subordinate
staff and, on the expiry of existing interests, to abolish the sinecure solicitorship and
to insist that the holders of the offices of Keeper of Papers and Doorkeeper executed
their duties in person.

Apart from the changes that flowed from the recommendations of the Commissioners of 1786, the main developments in the office between 1782 and the next major
reorganisation in 1805 were occasioned by the rapid growth of business. To deal with
this there was a considerable increase in the number of junior Clerks on the establishment, no fewer than five being added in 1797. In 1798 there was a general salary increase throughout the clerical organisation.[45] A new class of Extraordinary or Extra
Clerks became a feature of the office. This development apparently dated from 1777.
Unlike Supernumerary Clerks, Extra Clerks had, in ordinary circumstances, no
expectation of being placed on the establishment. However, certain of them were
retained in the office on a more or less permanent basis, several ultimately becoming
established. As the Commissioners of 1786 remarked 'They have been found essen-
tially useful in services which before, for want of proper Officers, had been much
neglected'.[46] Together with the Supernumerary Clerks and those established Clerks
who were awaiting promotion to the divisions the Extra Clerks formed a pool of labour
which was principally employed in the copying of documents. Some of them were,
however, assigned to particular work such as the recording of minutes, the registering
of papers and the care of Treasury bills of exchange.

The House of Commons Select Committee on Finance examined the Treasury in
1797. Their report was largely devoted to a review of the changes that had taken place
since 1786. The Committee did, however, recommend the abolition of the practice
whereby certain officers of the Treasury received new year's gifts from other departments. This recommendation was in due course carried into effect.[47]

A minute of 19 August 1805 made a number of important changes in the structure
of the office.[48] In the first place it created the office of Assistant Secretary, a post
whose holder was ineligible for the House of Commons. This development may
have been partly occasioned by an alteration in the relationship between the Joint
Secretaries. While the details are obscure it appears that the beginnings of the process
whereby the Senior Secretary became detached from the departmental work of the
Treasury and devoted his attention exclusively to patronage and the management of

[44] See also Civil List Act 1810 (50 Geo. III, c 117, s 9). Following the Civil List Act 1816 (56 Geo.
III, c 46) estimates of the amount of the deficiency of the fee fund were laid before the House of
Commons and the sums required voted annually. It was not until 1837 that the estimates presented
and the sums voted were described as being for the Treasury itself. The great majority of the fees were
abolished in 1835 (*1st Rept. of Treasury Committee of Enquiry into Fees 1837* (HC 1837, xliv), 176–8).
[45] TM 5 July 1798 (T 29/73 pp. 207–12).
[46] *2nd Rept. on Fees*, 52.
[47] TM 10 Oct. 1797 (T 29/71 p. 235) which also provided that an equivalent amount should be paid
to those Clerks who had received such gifts.
[48] T 29/85 pp. 346–51; see also TM 6 Jan. 1806 (T 29/86 p. 1).

the House of Commons can be traced to the early years of the nineteenth century. Inevitably this had the effect of throwing a greater burden of work on the Junior or, as he was ultimately to be called, the Financial Secretary. In so far as the duties of the Assistant Secretary were not entirely new they involved taking an increasing share in the work formerly undertaken jointly by the two Secretaries. At the same time the Assistant Secretary displaced the Chief Clerks at the head of the permanent staff of the Treasury.

The minute of 1805 went on to introduce alterations in the organisation of the divisions. They remained six in number but the categories of business were redistributed among them on the basis of their affinity rather than their expected yield in fees. The four Chief Clerks were deprived of their generalised advisory functions and placed directly in charge of the divisions. Below them the clerical structure was divided into six Senior, nine Assistant and nine Junior Clerks. A Clerk, ranking as a Senior Clerk, was placed in charge of the minutes assisted by two others. Provision was made for two of the Assistant Clerks to undertake the registering and indexing of current papers. Uniform progressive salaries were established and the rotation of Clerks in the divisions and elsewhere thus facilitated. The Clerks in the Revenue Department, while remaining distinct from the ordinary establishment, were linked in point of rank and salary to the new structure. The class of Supernumerary Clerks was abolished and the temporary character of Extra Clerks carefully defined. Finally the offices of Receiver of Fees and Clerk of the Bills were regulated.

The principles laid down in 1805 continued to govern the organisation of the Treasury until 1834. During this period, however, a number of changes of detail were made. Three new senior posts were created or absorbed into the structure of the office. The first was the Principal Clerk Assistant appointed in 1815 to assist the Secretaries. In due course he was joined by the Auditor of the Civil List (1831) and the Clerk for Colonial Business (1832) who had similar functions when they were not engaged in the particular duties of their respective offices. In 1807 an arrangement was made whereby two senior members of the office acted as Treasury Auditors. In 1812 the work involved in the preparation of returns to Parliament led to the appointment of one of the Assistant Clerks in the Revenue Department to superintend them. This work continued to grow and in 1824 it was found necessary to recruit a Clerk specially to undertake it. In 1816 a Commissariat Department was created which was directly under the authority of the Board but which remained distinct from the ordinary establishment.[49] In 1817 following the consolidation of the English and Irish revenues two Clerks of the Irish revenue were transferred to the Treasury.

A minute of 13 July 1808 introduced a probationary period for newly appointed Junior Clerks.[50] This lasted for three months after which they were to be placed on the establishment if the Board were satisfied of their fitness. The minute went on to lay down as a rule what had generally been observed in practice, that all vacancies in the Revenue Department should be filled from among the Junior Clerks on the establishment. At the same time the establishment was increased by the addition of two Assistant and two Junior Clerks. A further increase in the number of Junior Clerks in 1813 was occasioned by the depletion of the effective establishment due to the employment

---

[49] TM 16 Aug. 1816 (T 29/142 pp. 735-43). The officials of the Commissariat are not included in these lists.

[50] T 29/95 pp. 384-9. For recruitment and probation generally during the nineteenth century, see H. G. Roseveare, *The Treasury: The Evolution of a British Institution* (London 1969), 161-81.

of Clerks as full-time Private Secretaries to the First Lord, Chancellor of the Exchequer and the three Secretaries. At the same time salary scales were improved.[51] In 1821, as a result of parliamentary pressure for economy, the Treasury was obliged to take steps to reduce the size and cost of the establishment. As a result salaries were revised and the number of Junior Clerks reduced.[52]

The abolition of the Receipt of the Exchequer in 1834 occasioned the next major reorganisation of the Treasury. A Paymaster of Civil Services was appointed to undertake some of the functions previously performed by that department. This official was placed under the immediate authority of the Board but he and his staff remained outside the ordinary establishment.[53] The latter was regulated by a minute of 17 October 1834.[54] This made explicit the distinction between those officials who were concerned with matters to be submitted to the Board for decision and those who were responsible for carrying the decisions into effect. In the first category were the Assistant Secretary, the Auditor of the Civil List, the Principal Clerk Assistant and the Principal Clerk for Colonial Business. Under them the work was redistributed in five divisions. The business of expenditure which had formerly been undertaken in six divisions was now allocated amongst four. The fifth took over the responsibilities of the Revenue Department which ceased from this date to have an existence separate from the ordinary establishment. Each of the new divisions was presided over by a Chief Clerk. The rest of the establishment was fixed at five Senior, thirteen Assistant and thirteen Junior Clerks.

The next twenty years witnessed several developments in Treasury organisation. In 1835 a Law Clerk was appointed and the work of registering the books and papers of the office was placed under the immediate direction of an Assistant Clerk with the title of Superintendent of the Registry. In the same year the various Messengers attached to the office were consolidated into a unified structure, divided into three classes and placed under the authority of the Office Keeper. In 1836 the position of the four Messengers of the Receipt and that of the two Messengers attending the Chancellor of the Exchequer were regulated.

Following the report of the House of Commons Select Committee on Miscellaneous Expenditure of 1848 the Treasury set up a committee of its own to investigate the office. As a result of the recommendations of this body the number of divisions dealing with expenditure was reduced from four to two with a corresponding reduction in the number of Chief Clerks.[55] In 1854 the special responsibilities of the division dealing with revenue matters were recognised and entrusted to a Principal Clerk of Finance. In the following year a Treasury Accountant was appointed.

Major changes in the organisation of the Treasury were made by a minute of 4 July 1856.[56] This put an end to the distinction which had existed since the early nineteenth century between permanent officials with general advisory functions and those with specific executive duties. The offices of Principal Clerk Assistant and Principal Clerk for Colonial Business were abolished and the work of the department was redistributed among six divisions, presided over by the Assistant Secretary, the Auditor of the Civil List and four Principal Clerks. The old grades of Chief, Senior, Assistant and Junior Clerk were superseded and the rest of the establishment fixed at ten First Class, six-

---

[51] TM 23 Feb. 1813 (T 29/121 pp. 704–15).   [52] TM 10 Aug. 1821 (T 29/200 pp. 237–55).
[53] TM 30 Sept. 1834 (T 29/357 pp. 677–80). The staff of the department of the Paymaster of Civil Services is not included in these lists.
[54] T 29/358 pp. 317–37.   [55] TM 27 March 1849 (T 29/505 p. 30).   [56] T 29/564 p. 47.

teen Second Class and seven Third Class Clerks. One of the First Class Clerks was given responsibility for the parliamentary accounts and another was placed in charge of the Registry and Copying Department.

In 1859 and 1867 the Assistant Secretary and the Auditor of the Civil List were successively relieved of responsibility for divisions, the number of which was in consequence reduced to four. Both these officers were given more general functions. These were defined in a minute of May 1867 which also changed the title of the Assistant Secretary to Permanent Secretary.[57] In 1860 two Clerks were transferred from the establishment to a newly created County Court Department.[58] In 1861 the supplementary branch of the Treasury was reorganised. This was composed of those who had formerly been known as Extra Clerks. They were at this time seventeen in number and were for the most part concentrated in the Registry and Copying Department. They had for long occupied a rather ambiguous position in the clerical organisation of the office. Their status was now defined and they were divided into three categories to which were attached uniform progressive salaries.

The lists have been carried down to the eve of the reorganisation initiated by the minute of 25 May 1870 which, by introducing the principle of open competition for clerkships and by enforcing a division of labour which enabled the members of the 'superior' establishment to free themselves from routine and concentrate on the formation of policy, largely completed the process of reform and laid the foundations of the modern Treasury.[59]

[57] TM 24 Dec. 1859 (T 29/577 pp. 427–33), 10 May 1867 (AB, iv, 272–6).
[58] TM 6 Jan. 1860 (AB, iv, 88–90).
[59] AB, v, 27. The principles laid down on this occasion were carried into effect by TM 31 Dec. 1870 (ibid. 43). See also Roseveare, *Treasury*, 175–6 and M. Wright, *Treasury Control of the Civil Service 1854–1874* (Oxford 1969), 33–4.

Treasurers and Commissioners of the Treasury 1660–1870

There were formerly two distinct offices of Treasurer.[1] One was that of Lord High Treasurer, a great office of state, which was conferred by the delivery of a white staff; the other was that of Treasurer of the Exchequer which was granted during pleasure by letters patent under the great seal. When the Treasury was held by an individual he was appointed to both offices; when it was in commission that of Lord High Treasurer lapsed. On entering office the Treasurer took oaths in the courts of Chancery and the Exchequer.[2] No such formalities were observed in the case of Commissioners. In 1660 the authority of the Treasury covered England and Wales. It was extended to Scotland in 1707 and to Ireland in 1817 when provision was made for the office granted by letters patent to be known as that of Treasurer of the Exchequer of Great Britain and Lord High Treasurer of Ireland and the Commissioners as Commissioners of the Treasury of the United Kingdom of Great Britain and Ireland.[3]

On six occasions between 1660 and 1714 the office of Treasurer was held by individuals. During the same period it was in commission for rather more than half the time. It has invariably been so since 1714. The commission appointed in 1660 conformed to an earlier pattern and was composed of nine senior Privy Counsellors. In 1667 a new practice was introduced. Thereafter a small number of Commissioners were appointed, not all of whom were necessarily members of the Council. The number was in principle fixed at five between 1667 and 1807. In 1807 provision was made for the Chancellor of the Irish Exchequer to be appointed an additional Commissioner without salary.[4] In 1817 the offices of English and Irish Chancellor were united and two additional Irish Commissioners were appointed.[5] The total number of Commissioners was seven from 1817 to 1823 after which the place of one of the Irish Commissioners was not filled. In 1848 their number was reduced from six to five.[6] It was again raised to six in December 1868. The quorum of the commission varied until 1684. It was fixed at three from that year until 1849 when it was reduced to two.[7]

Formally there was no distinction in the standing of the Treasury Lords. In practice the First Lord acquired an ascendancy over his colleagues from an early date, due to his political prominence and to the fact that he customarily communicated the decisions of the Board to the King. Between 1715 and 1835 it was, except for a brief period in 1743, invariable for the office of First Lord to be combined with that of Chancellor

---

[1] For the functions of the Treasurer and the Board at various times, see Baxter, *Treasury*, 1–67; D. Gray, *Spencer Perceval: The Evangelical Prime Minister* (Manchester 1963), 318–20; J. R. Torrance, 'Sir George Harrison and the growth of bureaucracy in the early nineteenth century', *Eng. Hist. Rev.*, lxxxiii (1968), 60; T. Heath, *The Treasury* (London 1927), 6; Todd, *Parliamentary Government*, ii, 325, 448–51; M. Wright, *Treasury Control of the Civil Service 1854–1874* (Oxford 1969), 47–52.

[2] For an account of Godolphin's entry into office in 1702, see H. Hall, *The Antiquities and Curiosities of the Exchequer* (London 1898), 104–8.

[3] 56 Geo. III, c 98, s 2.   [4] 47 Geo. III, c 20.   [5] 56 Geo. III, c 98, s 14.

[6] TM 15 Aug. 1848 (T 29/524 p. 279).   [7] 12 & 13 Vict., c 89.

of the Exchequer whenever the holder of the former was drawn from the House of Commons. In the course of time effective authority came to be concentrated in the First Lord and the Chancellor, assisted by the Joint Secretaries. Regular meetings of the Board continued to take place until 1856. However, no lists of Lords present was kept after 1809 and the First Lord and Chancellor ceased to attend after 1827. During the nineteenth century the activities of the Junior Lords within the Treasury were increasingly confined to formalities and their main function became that of assisting the Parliamentary Secretary in the management of the House of Commons as government whips. Down to the end of the period covered by these lists, however, the practice was generally observed of appointing one Junior Lord for Scotland and one for Ireland on the understanding that they would, if occasion arose, assist in the business of those two kingdoms. In 1868 a 'Third Lord' (Stansfeld) with special responsibilities for revenue matters was appointed to relieve the Financial Secretary but this experiment was discontinued in the following year.[8]

The salary of the Treasurer was £8000. Ordinary Commissioners normally received £1600 each. Payments were made by the Paymaster of the Forces until 1675 and from the Exchequer thereafter.[9] As the result of an arrangement which apparently originated in 1754 the First Lord enjoyed an additional salary which was designed to provide him with a net income of £5000 a year.[10] In 1831 the salary of the First Lord was fixed at £5000, or £7500 if he held the office of Chancellor of the Exchequer as well. At the same time the salaries of the Junior Lords were fixed at £1200. They were reduced to £1000 in 1851. A salary of £2000 was attached to the office of Third Lord in 1868.[11]

In the lists the periods of office of the Commissioners have been dated by reference to the letters patent except in the case of First Lords after 1827. Strictly speaking the authority of the First Lord, like that of the other Commissioners, derived from the letters patent. However, in the course of time, the increasing prominence of the First Lord as the head of the administration resulted in his being nominated appreciably before the other Commissioners were selected and the letters patent could be sealed. The establishment of the precise date when the First Lord took office is a matter of considerable difficulty since he received no seals and took no oath. Eventually the practice of kissing hands on appointment grew up. Before 1827 there is no consistent record of the occasions on which the First Lord kissed hands. After this date it is possible to observe the procedure followed from the Court Circular, published in *The Times*. It appears that it was the practice for the First Lord to kiss hands on appointment at an audience with the Sovereign immediately before the Council at which his colleagues received their seals of office. It is the date on which this ceremony is explicitly stated to have taken place or on which it can reasonably be inferred to have occurred that has been taken as the date of entry into office of First Lords from 1827. It should be noted that it is not the same as that on which the individual concerned received the

---

[8] TM 28 Dec. 1868 (AB, iv, 336); *Times*, 10 Dec. 1868, 3 Nov. 1869. A 'Financial Lord' with similar responsibilities was appointed in 1873 (*Times*, 8 Aug. 1873).

[9] *CTB*, v, 269; Baxter, *Treasury*, 16–17.

[10] Namier, *Structure of Politics*, 226–7. The additional salary was at first paid out of the secret service but was transferred in 1783 to the civil list (*2nd Rept. on Fees*, 63). The deficiencies in Liverpool's salary were met from special service (T 38/552 pp. 255–85).

[11] TM 15 April 1831 (T 29/316 pp. 259–61), 20 May 1851 (T 29/543 pp. 389–91), 28 Dec. 1868 (AB, iv, 336). In 1831 the charge for these salaries was removed from the civil list to the annual estimates for the Treasury.

Sovereign's command to form an administration which is the date frequently selected for the entry into office of Prime Ministers.

LISTS OF APPOINTMENTS

Treasurers and Commissioners

1660	19 June	Hyde, Sir E.; Ormond, Marquess of; Monck, Sir G.; Southampton, Earl of; Robartes, Lord; Colepepper, Lord; Montagu, Sir E.; Nicholas, Sir E.; Morrice, Sir W. (C 66/2931).
1660	8 Sept.	Southampton, Earl of (C 66/2949).
1667	24 May	Albemarle, Duke of; Ashley, Lord; Clifford, Sir T.; Coventry, Hon. Sir W.; Duncombe, Sir J. (E 403/2463 p. 130).
1669	8 April	Albemarle, Duke of; Ashley, Lord; Clifford, Sir T.; Duncombe, Sir J. (C 66/3107).
1672	2 Dec.	Clifford of Chudleigh, Lord (C 66/3142).
1673	24 June	Osborne, Viscount (E 403/2465 p. 147).
1679	26 March	Essex, Earl of; Hyde, Hon. L.; Ernle, Sir J.; Dering, Sir E.; Godolphin, S. (C 66/3215).
1679	21 Nov.	Hyde, Hon. L.; Ernle, Sir J.; Dering, Sir E.; Godolphin, S.; Fox, Sir S. (C 66/3209).
1684	24 April	Rochester, Earl of; Ernle, Sir J.; Dering, Sir E.; Fox, Sir S. (C 66/3245).
1684	9 July	Rochester, Earl of; Ernle, Sir J.; Fox, Sir S. (ibid.).
1684	26 July	Rochester, Earl of; Ernle, Sir J.; Fox, Sir S.; North, Hon. Sir D.; Thynne, H. F. (ibid.).
1684	9 Sept.	Godolphin, S.; Ernle, Sir J.; Fox, Sir S.; North, Hon. Sir D.; Thynne, H. F. (ibid.).
1685	16 Feb.	Rochester, Earl of (E 403/2468 p. 43).
1687	4 Jan.	Belasyse, Lord; Godolphin, Lord; Dover, Lord; Ernle, Sir J.; Fox, Sir S. (C 66/3290).
1689	9 April	Mordaunt, Viscount; Delamere, Lord; Godolphin, Lord; Capel, Hon. Sir H.; Hampden, R. (C 66/3325).
1690	18 March	Lowther, Sir J.; Hampden, R.; Fox, Sir S.; Pelham, T. (C 66/3335).
1690	15 Nov.	Godolphin, Lord; Lowther, Sir J.; Hampden, R.; Fox, Sir S.; Pelham, T. (C 66/3338).
1692	21 March	Godolphin, Lord; Hampden, R.; Fox, Sir S.; Seymour, Sir E.; Montagu, C. (C 66/3350).
1694	3 May	Godolphin, Lord; Fox, Sir S.; Montagu, C.; Trumbull, Sir W.; Smith, J. (C 66/3364).
1695	1 Nov.	Godolphin, Lord; Fox, Sir S.; Montagu, C.; Smith, J. (C 66/3381).
1696	2 May	Godolphin, Lord;[12] Fox, Sir S.; Montagu, C.; Smith, J.; Littleton, Sir T. (C 66/3386).

[12] Godolphin formally resigned office as First Lord on 31 Oct. 1696 (*CTB*, xi, 67). No new commission was issued but Fox became First Lord on this date.

1697 1 May   Montagu, C.; Fox, Sir S.; Smith, J.; Littleton, Sir T.; Pelham, T.
                 (E 403/2469 p. 108).
1699 1 June   Montagu, C.; Tankerville, Earl of; Fox, Sir S.; Smith, J.; Boyle,
                 Hon. H. (C 66/3413).
1699 15 Nov.   Tankerville, Earl of; Fox, Sir S.; Smith, J.; Boyle, Hon. H.;
                 Hill, R. (C 66/3410).
1700 9 Dec.   Godolphin, Lord; Fox, Sir S.; Smith, J.; Boyle, Hon. H.;
                 Hill, R. (C 66/3415).
1701 29 March   Godolphin, Lord; Fox, Sir S.; Boyle, Hon. H.; Hill, R.; Pelham,
                 T. (C 66/3420).
1701 30 Dec.   Carlisle, Earl of; Fox, Sir S.; Boyle, Hon. H.; Hill, R.; Pelham, T.
                 (C 66/3422).
1702 12 Feb.   Carlisle, Earl of; Fox, Sir S.; Boyle, Hon. H.; Hill, R.; Pelham, T.
                 (ibid.).
1702 8 May   Godolphin, Lord (C 66/3424).
1707 27 June   Godolphin, Earl of[13] (C 66/3462).
1710 10 Aug.   Poulett, Earl; Harley, R.; Paget, Hon. H.; Mansell, Sir T.;
                 Benson, R. (C 66/3477).
1711 30 May   Oxford, Earl of (C 66/3479).
1714 30 July   Shrewsbury, Duke of (C 66/3497).
1714 13 Oct.   Halifax, Lord; Onslow, Sir R.; St. Quintin, Sir W.; Wortley
                 Montagu, E.; Methuen, P. (C 66/3510).
1715 23 May   Carlisle, Earl of; Onslow, Sir R.; St. Quintin, Sir W.; Wortley
                 Montagu, E.; Methuen, P. (C 66/3504).
1715 11 Oct.   Walpole, R.; St. Quintin, Sir W.; Methuen, P.; Finch, Lord;
                 Newport, Hon. T. (C 66/3511).
1716 25 June   Walpole, R.; St. Quintin, Sir W.; Methuen, P.; Torrington, Lord;
                 Edgcumbe, R. (C 66/3514).
1717 15 April   Stanhope, J.; Torrington, Lord; Wallop, J.; Baillie, G.; Mickle-
                 thwaite, T. (C 66/3520).
1718 20 March   Sunderland, Earl of; Aislabie, J.; Wallop, J.; Baillie, G.; Clayton,
                 W. (C 66/3524).
1720 11 June   Sunderland, Earl of; Aislabie, J.; Baillie, G.; Turner, Sir C.;
                 Edgcumbe, R. (C 66/3538).
1721 3 April   Walpole, R.; Baillie, G.; Turner, Sir C.; Edgcumbe, R.; Pelham,
                 Hon. H. (C 66/3544).
1724 2 April   Walpole, R.; Baillie, G.; Turner, Sir C.; Yonge, W.; Dodington,
                 G. (C 66/3555).
1725 27 May   Walpole, Sir R.; Turner, Sir C.; Yonge, Sir W.; Dodington, G.;
                 Strickland, Sir W. (C 66/3558).
1727 28 July   Walpole, Sir R.; Turner, Sir C.; Dodington, G.; Oxenden, Sir G.;
                 Clayton, W. (C 66/3568).
1730 11 May   Walpole, Sir R.; Dodington, G.; Oxenden, Sir G.; Clayton, W.;
                 Yonge, Sir W. (C 66/3580).
1735 19 May   Walpole, Sir R.; Dodington, G.; Oxenden, Sir G.; Clayton, W.;
                 Cholmondeley, Earl of (C 66/3593).

[13] Reappointed following the union with Scotland.

1736 20 May   Walpole, Sir R.; Dodington, G.; Oxenden, Sir G.; Sundon, Lord; Winnington, T. (C 66/3595).

1737 22 June   Walpole, Sir R.; Dodington, G.; Sundon, Lord; Winnington, T.; Earle, G. (C 66/3597).

1740 20 Oct.   Walpole, Sir R.; Sundon, Lord; Winnington, T.; Earle, G.; Treby, G. (C 66/3603).

1741 28 April Walpole, Sir R.; Sundon, Lord; Earle, G.; Treby, G.; Clutterbuck, T. (C 66/3604).

1742 16 Feb.   Wilmington, Earl of; Sandys, S.; Compton, Hon. G.; Rushout, Sir J.; Gybbon, P. (C 66/3611).

1743 25 Aug.   Pelham, Hon. H.; Sandys, S.; Compton, Hon. G.; Rushout, Sir J.; Gybbon, P. (C 66/3613).

1743 23 Dec.   Pelham, Hon. H.; Compton, Hon. G.; Gybbon, P.; Middlesex, Earl of; Fox, H. (ibid.).

1744 26 Dec.   Pelham, Hon. H.; Middlesex, Earl of; Fox, H.; Arundel, Hon. R.; Lyttleton, G. (C 66/3615).

1746 27 June   Pelham, Hon. H.; Middlesex, Earl of; Lyttleton, G.; Bilson Legge, Hon. H.; Campbell, J. (C 66/3619).

1747 23 June   Pelham, Hon. H.; Lyttleton, G.; Bilson Legge, Hon. H.; Campbell, J.; Grenville, G. (C 66/3622).

1749 29 April Pelham, Hon. H.; Lyttleton, G.; Campbell, J.; Grenville, G.; Vane, Hon. H. (C 66/3626).

1754 18 March Newcastle, Duke of; Lyttleton, Sir G.; Campbell, J.; Grenville, Hon. G.; Barnard, Lord (C 66/3642).

1754 6 April   Newcastle, Duke of; Darlington, Earl of; Bilson Legge, Hon. H.; Dupplin, Viscount; Nugent, R. (C 66/3643).

1755 22 Nov.   Newcastle, Duke of; Darlington, Earl of; Lyttleton, Sir G.; Dupplin, Viscount; Nugent, R. (C 66/3649).

1755 22 Dec.   Newcastle, Duke of; Lyttleton, Sir G.; Nugent, R.; Wyndham O'Brien, P.; Furnese, H. (ibid.).

1756 15 Nov.   Devonshire, Duke of; Bilson Legge, Hon. H.; Nugent, R.; Duncannon, Viscount; Grenville, Hon. J. (C 66/3654).

1757 2 July   Newcastle, Duke of; Bilson Legge, Hon. H.; Nugent, R.; Duncannon, Viscount; Grenville, Hon. J. (C 66/3658).

1759 2 June   Newcastle, Duke of; Bilson Legge, Hon. H.; Nugent, R.; Grenville, Hon. J.; North, Lord (C 66/3664).

1759 20 Dec.   Newcastle, Duke of; Bilson Legge, Hon. H.; Grenville, Hon. J.; North, Lord; Oswald, J. (C 66/3666).

1761 19 March Newcastle, Duke of; Barrington, Viscount; North, Lord; Oswald, J.; Elliott, G. (C 66/3674).

1762 28 May   Bute, Earl of; Dashwood, Sir F.; North, Lord; Oswald, J.; Turner, Sir J. (C 66/3684).

1763 15 April Grenville, Hon. G.; North, Lord; Turner, Sir J.; Hunter, T. O.; Harris, J. (C 66/3687).

1765 13 July   Rockingham, Marquess of; Dowdeswell, W.; Cavendish, Lord J.; Townshend, T.; Onslow, G. (C 66/3701).

1766 2 Aug.   Grafton, Duke of; Townshend, Hon. C.; Townshend, T.; Onslow, G.; Campbell, P. (C 66/3707).

1767	12 Oct.	Grafton, Duke of; North, Lord; Townshend, T.; Onslow, G.; Campbell, P. (C 66/3715).
1767	1 Dec.	Grafton, Duke of; North, Lord; Onslow, G.; Campbell, P.; Jenkinson, C. (ibid.).
1768	28 Dec.	Grafton, Duke of; North, Lord; Onslow, G.; Jenkinson, C.; Dyson, J. (C 66/3720).
1770	6 Feb.	North, Lord; Onslow, G.; Jenkinson, C.; Dyson, J.; Townshend, C. (C 66/3725).
1773	12 Jan.	North, Lord; Onslow, G.; Dyson, J.; Townshend, C.; Fox, Hon. C. J. (C 66/3740).
1774	11 March	North, Lord; Onslow, G.; Townshend, C.; Beauchamp, Viscount; Cornewall, C. W. (C 66/3745).
1777	16 June	North, Lord; Onslow, Lord; Beauchamp, Viscount; Cornewall, C. W.; Westcote, Lord (C 66/3765).
1777	15 Dec.	North, Lord; Beauchamp, Viscount; Cornewall, C. W.; Westcote, Lord; Palmerston, Viscount (C 66/3767).
1780	12 Sept.	North, Lord; Westcote, Lord; Palmerston, Viscount; Sutton, Sir R.; Buller, J. (C 66/3781).
1782	1 April	Rockingham, Marquess of; Cavendish, Lord J.; Althorp, Viscount; Grenville, J.; Montagu, F. (C 66/3792).
1782	13 July	Shelburne, Earl of; Pitt, Hon. W.; Grenville, J.; Jackson, R.; Eliot, E. J. (C 66/3797).
1783	4 April	Portland, Duke of; Cavendish, Lord J.; Surrey, Earl of; Montagu, F.; Cooper, Sir G. (C 66/3803).
1783	26 Dec.	Pitt, Hon. W.; Buller, J.; Graham, Marquess of; Eliot, E. J.; Aubrey, J. (C 66/3809).
1786	19 Sept.	Pitt, Hon. W.; Graham, Marquess of; Eliot, Hon. E. J.; Aubrey, Sir J.; Mornington, Earl of (C 66/3830).
1789	10 Aug.	Pitt, Hon. W.; Eliot, Hon. E. J.; Mornington, Earl of; Bayham, Viscount; Apsley, Lord (C 66/3849).
1791	20 June	Pitt, Hon. W.; Eliot, Hon. E. J.; Mornington, Earl of; Bayham, Viscount; Hopkins, R. (C 66/3868).
1793	22 June	Pitt, Hon. W.; Mornington, Earl of; Bayham, Viscount; Hopkins, R.; Townshend, Hon. J. T. (C 66/3891).
1794	7 May	Pitt, Hon. W.; Mornington, Earl of; Hopkins, R.; Townshend, Hon. J. T.; Smyth, J. (C 66/3900).
1797	3 Feb.	Pitt, Hon. W.; Mornington, Earl of; Townshend, Hon. J. T.; Smyth, J.; Douglas, S. (C 66/3934).
1797	3 Aug.	Pitt, Hon. W.; Townshend, Hon. J. T.; Smyth, J.; Douglas, S.; Pybus, C. S. (C 66/3941).
1800	28 July	Pitt, Hon. W.; Smyth, J.; Douglas, S.; Pybus, C. S.; Leveson Gower, Lord G. (C 66/3976).
1800	9 Dec.	Pitt, Hon. W.; Smyth, J.; Pybus, C. S.; Leveson Gower, Lord G.; Addington, J. H. (C 66/3981).
1801	21 March	Addington, H.; Smyth, J.; Pybus, C. S.; Thynne, Lord G.; Bond, N. (C 66/3986).
1802	5 July	Addington, H.; Pybus, C. S.; Thynne, Lord G.; Bond, N.; Addington, J. H. (C 66/4009).

1803   18 Nov.   Addington, H.; Thynne, Lord G.; Bond, N.; Brodrick, Hon. W.; Golding, E. (C 66/4022).

1804   16 May   Pitt, Hon. W.; Lovaine, Lord; Fitzharris, Viscount; Long, C.; Wellesley, Hon. H. (C 66/4025).

1804   7 Aug.   Pitt, Hon. W.; Lovaine, Lord; Fitzharris, Viscount; Long, C.; Blandford, Marquess of (C 66/4029).

1806   10 Feb.   Grenville, Lord; Petty, Lord H.; Althorp, Viscount; Wickham, W.; Courtenay, J. (C 66/4049).

1807   31 March   Portland, Duke of; Perceval, Hon. S.; Titchfield, Marquess of; Eliot, Hon. W.; Sturges Bourne, W. (C 66/4064).

1807   16 Sept.   Portland, Duke of; Perceval, Hon. S.; Foster, J.; Eliot, Hon. W.; Sturges Bourne, W.; Ryder, Hon. R. (C 66/4070).

1807   2 Dec.   Portland, Duke of; Perceval, Hon. S.; Foster, J.; Brodrick, Hon. W.; Eliot, Hon. W.; Sturges Bourne, W. (C 66/4073).

1809   6 Dec.   Perceval, Hon. S.; Foster, J.; Brodrick, Hon. W.; Eliot, Hon. W.; Desart, Earl of; Barne, S. (C 66/4096).

1810   26 June   Perceval, Hon. S.; Foster, J.; Brodrick, Hon. W.; Eliot, Hon. W.; Barne, S.; Paget, Hon. B. (C 66/4103).

1812   6 Jan.   Perceval, Hon. S.; Wellesley Pole, Hon. W.; Brodrick, Hon. W.; Barne, S.; Paget, Hon. B.; Wellesley, R. (C 66/4118).

1812   16 June   Liverpool, Earl of; Vansittart, N.; Barne, S.; Paget, Hon. B. (C 66/4124).

1812   5 Oct.   Liverpool, Earl of; Vansittart, N.; Fitzgerald, W.; Paget, Hon. B.; Robinson, Hon. F. J.; Brogden, J. (C 66/4127).

1813   25 Nov.   Liverpool, Earl of; Vansittart, N.; Fitzgerald, W.; Paget, Hon. B.; Brogden, J.; Lowther, Viscount (C 66/4144).

1813   20 Dec.   Liverpool, Earl of; Vansittart, N.; Fitzgerald, W.; Paget, Hon. B.; Lowther, Viscount; Grant, C. (C 66/4145).

1817   7 Jan.   Liverpool, Earl of; Vansittart, N.; Paget, Hon. B.; Lowther, Viscount; Grant, C.; Maxwell Barry, J.; O'Dell, W. (C 66/4182).

1819   25 March   Liverpool, Earl of; Vansittart, N.; Paget, Hon. B.; Lowther, Viscount; Somerset, Lord G. C. H.; Maxwell Barry, J.; MacNaughten, E. A. (C 66/4209).

1823   10 Feb.   Liverpool, Earl of; Robinson, Hon. F. J.; Paget, Hon. B.; Lowther, Viscount; Somerset, Lord G. C. H.; Maxwell Barry, J.; MacNaughten, E. A. (C 66/4252).

1823   3 May   Liverpool, Earl of; Robinson, Hon. F. J.; Paget, Hon. B.; Lowther, Viscount; Somerset, Lord G. C. H.; MacNaughten, E. A. (C 66/4256).

1826   13 June   Liverpool, Earl of; Robinson, Hon. F. J.; Lowther, Viscount; Somerset, Lord G. C. H.; Mount Charles, Earl of; MacNaughten, E. A. (C 66/4307).

1827   30 April   Canning, G.; Mount Charles, Earl of; Leveson Gower, Lord F.; Eliot, Lord; MacNaughten, E. A. (C 66/4319).

1827   31 July   Canning, G.; Mount Charles, Earl of; Leveson Gower, Lord F.; Eliot, Lord; Fitzgerald, M.; MacNaughten, E. A. (C 66/4324).

1827   8 Sept.   Goderich, Viscount; Herries, J. C.; Mount Charles, Earl of; Eliot, Lord; Fitzgerald, M.; MacNaughten, E. A. (C 66/4326).

1828	26 Jan.	Wellington, Duke of; Goulburn, H.; Somerset, Lord G. C. H.; Mount Charles, Earl of; Eliot, Lord; MacNaughten, E. A. (C 66/4332).
1830	24 April	Wellington, Duke of; Goulburn, H.; Somerset, Lord G. C. H.; Eliot, Lord; Bankes, G.; MacNaughten, E. A. (C 66/4363).
1830	31 July	Wellington, Duke of; Goulburn, H.; Somerset, Lord G. C. H.; Eliot, Lord; Bankes, G.; Peel, W. Y. (C 66/4365).
1830	24 Nov.	Grey, Earl; Althorp, Viscount; Nugent, Lord; Smith, R. V.; Baring, F. T.; Ponsonby, Hon. G. (C 66/4375).
1832	26 Nov.	Grey, Earl; Althorp, Viscount; Smith, R. V.; Baring, F. T.; Ponsonby, Hon. G.; Kennedy, T. F. (C 66/4412).
1834	14 April	Grey, Earl; Althorp, Viscount; Smith, R. V.; Baring, F. T.; Ponsonby, Hon. G.; Graham, R. (C 66/4433).
1834	23 June	Grey, Earl; Althorp, Viscount; Smith, R. V.; Ponsonby, Hon. G.; Graham, R.; Byng, G. S. (C 66/4436).
1834	19 July	Melbourne, Viscount; Althorp, Viscount; Smith, R. V.; Ponsonby, Hon. G.; Graham, R.; Byng, G. S. (C 66/4438).
1834	22 Nov.	Wellington, Duke of; Rosslyn, Earl of; Ellenborough, Lord; Maryborough, Lord; Becket, Sir J.; Planta, J. (C 66/4445).
1834	31 Dec.	Peel, Sir R.; Peel, W. Y.; Lincoln, Earl of; Stormont, Viscount; Ross, C.; Gladstone, W. E. (C 66/4447).
1835	19 March	Peel, Sir R.; Peel, W. Y.; Lincoln, Earl of; Stormont, Viscount; Ross, C.; Nicoll, J. (C 66/4452).
1835	20 April	Melbourne, Viscount; Spring Rice, T.; Seymour, Lord; Ord, W. H.; Steuart, R. (C 66/4454).
1835	20 May	Melbourne, Viscount; Spring Rice, T.; Seymour, Lord; Ord, W. H.; Steuart, R.; More O'Ferrall, R. (C 66/4457).
1836	22 Aug.	Melbourne, Viscount; Spring Rice, T.; Seymour, Lord; Steuart, R.; More O'Ferrall, R.; Parker, J. (C 66/4487).
1837	21 July	Melbourne, Viscount; Spring Rice, T.; Seymour, Lord; Steuart, R.; More O'Ferrall, R.; Parker, J. (C 66/4507).
1839	30 Aug.	Melbourne, Viscount; Baring, F. T.; Seymour, Lord; Steuart, R.; Parker, J.; Wyse, T. (C 66/4596).
1839	6 Nov.	Melbourne, Viscount; Baring, F. T.; Steuart, R.; Parker, J.; Wyse, T.; Tufnell, H. (C 66/4580).
1840	30 May	Melbourne, Viscount; Baring, F. T.; Parker, J.; Wyse, T.; Tufnell, H.; Horsman, E. (C 66/4599).
1841	25 June	Melbourne, Viscount; Baring, F. T.; Wyse, T.; Tufnell, H.; Horsman, E.; Cowper, Hon. W. F. (C 66/4632).
1841	8 Sept.	Peel, Sir R.; Goulburn, H.; Milnes Gaskell, J.; Baring, H. B.; Perceval, A.; Pringle, A. (C 66/4638).
1841	20 Sept.	Peel, Sir R.; Goulburn, H.; Milnes Gaskell, J.; Baring, H. B.; Pringle, A.; Young, J. (C 66/4640).
1844	23 May	Peel, Sir R.; Goulburn, H.; Milnes Gaskell, J.; Baring, H. B.; Pringle, A.; Lennox, Lord A. (C 66/4714).
1845	28 April	Peel, Sir R.; Goulburn, H.; Milnes Gaskell, J.; Baring, H. B.; Lennox, Lord A.; Forbes Mackenzie, W. (C 66/4742).

1845 9 Aug.   Peel, Sir R.; Goulburn, H.; Milnes Gaskell, J.; Baring, H. B.; Forbes Mackenzie, W.; Cripps, W. (C 66/4753).

1846 11 March Peel, Sir R.; Goulburn, H.; Baring, H. B.; Cripps, W.; Carnegie, Hon. S. T.; Neville, R. (C 66/4774).

1846 6 July   Russell, Lord J.; Wood, C.; Ebrington, Viscount; O'Conor, D.; Gibson Craig, W.; Rich, H. (C 66/4784).

1847 6 Aug.   Russell, Lord J.; Wood, Sir C.; Ebrington, Viscount; Gibson Craig, W.; Rich, H.; Bellew, R. M. (C 66/4821).

1847 24 Dec.   Russell, Lord J.; Wood, Sir C.; Gibson Craig, W.; Rich, H.; Bellew, R. M.; Shelburne, Earl of[14] (C 66/4831).

1852 28 Feb.   Derby, Earl of; Disraeli, B.; Chandos, Marquess of; Gordon Lennox, Lord H. G. C.; Bateson, T. (C 66/4956).

1853 4 Jan.   Aberdeen, Earl of; Gladstone, W. E.; Hervey, Lord A.; Charteris Wemyss Douglas, Hon. F. R.; Sadleir, J. (C 66/4980).

1854 8 March   Aberdeen, Earl of; Gladstone, W. E.; Hervey, Lord A.; Elcho, Lord; Fortescue, C. S. (C 66/4985).

1855 12 Feb.   Palmerston, Viscount; Gladstone, W. E.; Hervey, Lord A.; Elcho, Lord; Fortescue, C. S. (C 66/4988).

1855 8 March   Palmerston, Viscount; Lewis, Sir G. C.; Monck, Viscount; Duncan, Viscount; Fortescue, C. S. (ibid.).

1855 17 April Palmerston, Viscount; Lewis, Sir G. C.; Monck, Viscount; Duncan, Viscount; Brand, Hon. H. B. W. (ibid.).

1858 1 March   Derby, Earl of; Disraeli, B.; Gordon Lennox, Lord H. G. C.; Taylor, T. E.; Whitmore, H. (C 66/5000).

1859 16 March Derby, Earl of; Disraeli, B.; Taylor, T. E.; Whitmore, H.; Blackburn, P. (C 66/5003).

1859 23 June   Palmerston, Viscount; Gladstone, W. E.; Knatchbull Hugessen, E. H.; Dunbar, Sir W.; Bagwell, J. (C 66/5005).

1862 26 March Palmerston, Viscount; Gladstone, W. E.; Knatchbull Hugessen, E. H.; Dunbar, Sir W.; White, L. (C 66/5013).

1865 26 April Palmerston, Viscount; Gladstone, W. E.; Knatchbull Hugessen, E. H.; Adam, W. P.; White, Hon. L. (C 66/5021).

1865 13 Nov.   Russell, Earl; Gladstone, W. E.; Knatchbull Hugessen, E. H.; White, Hon. L.; Adam, W. P. (C 66/5022).

1866 7 June   Russell, Earl; Gladstone, W. E.; Bonham Carter, J.; Adam, W. P.; Esmonde, J. (C 66/5025).

1866 13 July   Derby, Earl of; Disraeli, B.; Noel, Hon. G. J.; Graham Montgomery, Sir G.; Whitmore, H. (C 66/5026).

1868 3 March   Disraeli, B.; Hunt, G. W.; Noel, Hon. G. J.; Graham Montgomery, Sir G.; Whitmore, H. (C 66/5033).

1868 6 Nov.   Disraeli, B.; Hunt, G. W.; Hamilton, Lord C. J.; Graham Montgomery, Sir G.; Whitmore, H. (C 66/5036).

1868 17 Dec.   Gladstone, W. E.; Lowe, R.; Stansfeld, J.; Lansdowne, Marquess of; Adam, W. P.; Vivian, Hon. J. C. W. (C 66/5037).

1869 9 Nov.   Gladstone, W. E.; Lowe, R.; Lansdowne, Marquess of; Adam, W. P.; Vivian, Hon. J. C. W.; Gladstone, W. H. (C 66/5041).

[14] Office discontinued by TM 15 Aug. 1848 (T 29/524 p. 279).

First Lord from 1827

1827	20 April	Canning, G.	1852	27 Feb.	Derby, Earl of
1827	3 Sept.	Goderich, Viscount	1852	28 Dec.	Aberdeen, Earl of
1828	22 Jan.	Wellington, Duke of	1855	8 Feb.	Palmerston, Viscount
1830	22 Nov.	Grey, Earl	1858	26 Feb.	Derby, Earl of
1834	16 July	Melbourne, Viscount	1859	18 June	Palmerston, Viscount
1834	17 Nov.	Wellington, Duke of	1865	3 Nov.	Russell, Earl
1834	10 Dec.	Peel, Sir R.	1866	6 July	Derby, Earl of
1835	18 April	Melbourne, Viscount	1868	29 Feb.	Disraeli, B.
1841	3 Sept.	Peel, Sir R.	1868	9 Dec.	Gladstone, W. E.
1846	6 July	Russell, Lord J.			

Chancellor of the Exchequer 1660–1870

The Chancellor of the Exchequer was in origin an official of the court of Exchequer.[1] From 1592 he invariably held the office of Under Treasurer of the Exchequer concurrently. The two offices were granted by distinct letters patent under the great seal dated the same day.[2] They were held on a life tenure until 1676 and during pleasure thereafter. On entering office the Chancellor of the Exchequer took oaths before the Lord Chancellor and in the Exchequer. By the early eighteenth century his connection with the Exchequer court was already tenuous. Nevertheless as late as the nineteenth century there remained certain functions, such as the sealing of instruments, which could only be performed on his authority. As a consequence it was customary, when vacancies in the office occurred, to appoint the Chief Justice of the King's Bench as temporary Chancellor to enable the routine work of the court to be carried on.[3] These temporary Chancellors were not officials of the Treasury and their appointments have been inserted in the following list only in the interests of providing a complete account of the succession to the office.

The functions of the Chancellor of the Exchequer within the Treasury derived from the fact that, as Under Treasurer, he occupied an office which had its origin in the position of deputy or associate of the Treasurer. When the Treasury was in the hands of Commissioners he was one of their number.[4] Between 1714 and 1835, except for a brief period in 1743, he was, unless a member of the House of Lords, also First Lord. After 1835 these two offices have been held separately except for the years 1873–4 and 1880–2. From 1710 it was the custom for the Chancellor to occupy the second place in the Treasury commission when the First Lord was in the House of Lords.[5] In 1817, following the consolidation of the revenues, the Chancellor of the Exchequer of Great Britain was appointed Chancellor of the Exchequer of Ireland and the two offices remained united thereafter.[6] The process by which the effective powers of the Treasury came to be vested in the Chancellor was gradual. The evidence suggests that it was complete by 1839.[7]

The remuneration of the Chancellor was originally derived from a number of

---

[1] For this office generally, see T 90/16 pp. 1–8; Thomas, *Notes of Materials*, 9–16; Baxter, *Treasury*, 32–6; Todd, *Parliamentary Government*, ii, 434–7.

[2] This remained the case until 1885 when the two documents were combined.

[3] From 1721 to 1767 these appointments were made by letters patent under the great seal as follows: Pratt (1721) – C 66/3542; Lee (1754) – C 66/3642; Mansfield (1757 and 1767) – C 66/3657, 3714. Thereafter they were made by delivery of the seals alone as follows: Ellenborough (1806 and 1812) – E 197/8 pp. 38, 125; Tenterden (1827) – ibid. p. 257; Denman (1834) – ibid. p. 325. Except in the case of Pratt (1721) no appointment was made to the office of Under Treasurer in these circumstances.

[4] Temporary Chancellors were not included in the commission.

[5] The only exceptions to this convention occurred in 1754 and 1755 when Darlington, as a peer, was given precedence over the Chancellors.

[6] This arrangement was confirmed by act in 1824 (4 Geo. III, c 7).

[7] Baring stated, with reference to his period of office 1839–41, that the Chancellor 'was the person who was responsible to Parliament for everything done at the Treasury'. (*Rept. on Misc. Expenditure*, pt. i, 419.)

different sources. The patent salaries amounted to £200. From at least 1685 an additional salary of £1600 was paid in consideration of the relinquishment of certain profits and perquisites.[8] The Chancellor also enjoyed fees arising from instruments passed under the Exchequer seal. In 1817 the emoluments of the Irish chancellorship were attached to the office. If the Chancellor was a Treasury Lord he received a separate salary as such. In 1830 the total receipts of the office amounted to £5398. In the following year the former arrangements were superseded by a consolidated salary of £5000 or £7500 when the office was held concurrently with that of First Lord.[9]

In the following list of appointments the date down to and including 1767 is that of the letters patent. From 1782 it is that of the reception of the seals which from this time invariably preceded the issue of the letters patent.

LIST OF APPOINTMENTS

1642	19 July	Hyde, Sir E.	1756	16 Nov.	Bilson Legge,
1661	13 May	Ashley, Lord			Hon. H.
1672	22 Nov.	Duncombe, Sir J.	1757	13 April	Mansfield, Lord[10]
1676	2 May	Ernle, Sir J.	1757	2 July	Bilson Legge,
1689	9 April	Delamere, Lord			Hon. H.
1690	18 March	Hampden, R.	1761	19 March	Barrington,
1694	10 May	Montagu, C.			Viscount
1699	2 June	Smith, J.	1762	29 May	Dashwood, Sir F.
1701	27 March	Boyle, Hon. H.	1763	16 April	Grenville, Hon. G.
1708	22 April	Smith, J.	1765	16 July	Dowdeswell, W.
1710	11 Aug.	Harley, R.	1766	2 Aug.	Townshend, Hon. C.
1711	4 June	Benson, R.	1767	11 Sept.	Mansfield, Lord[10]
1713	21 Aug.	Wyndham, Sir W.	1767	6 Oct.	North, Lord
1714	13 Oct.	Onslow, Sir R.	1782	27 March	Cavendish, Lord J.
1715	12 Oct.	Walpole, R.	1782	10 July	Pitt, Hon. W.
1717	15 April	Stanhope, J.	1783	2 April	Cavendish, Lord J.
1718	20 March	Aislabie, J.	1783	19 Dec.	Pitt, Hon. W.
1721	2 Feb.	Pratt, Sir J.[10]	1801	14 March	Addington, H.
1721	3 April	Walpole, R.	1804	10 May	Pitt, Hon. W.
1742	12 Feb.	Sandys, S.	1806	25 Jan.	Ellenborough,
1743	12 Dec.	Pelham, Hon. H.			Lord [10]
1754	8 March	Lee, Sir W.[10]	1806	5 Feb.	Petty, Lord H.
1754	6 April	Bilson Legge,	1807	26 March	Perceval, Hon. S.
		Hon. H.	1812	12 May	Ellenborough,
1755	25 Nov.	Lyttleton, Sir G.			Lord[10]

[8] Before its transfer to the Exchequer in 1703 the history of this additional salary is obscure. It was paid from secret service 1685–6 and 1702–3 (*Secret Service Expenses*, 121, 139, 146, 153; *CTB*, xxviii, 403, 404, 409, 413; ibid. xviii, 371). The Chancellor also received 'robe money' amounting to £34 13s 4d a year payable at the Great Wardrobe. For Ashley's receipts as Chancellor, see K. H. D. Haley, *The First Earl of Shaftesbury* (Oxford 1968), 154.

[9] T 90/16 pp. 1–8; *Rept. of Select Committee on Reduction of Salaries 1831* (HC 1830–1, iii), 508; TM 15 April 1831 (T 29/316 pp. 259–61). In 1831 the charge for the salary was removed from the civil list to the annual estimates for the Treasury.

[10] Chief Justice of the King's Bench.

1812	23 May	Vansittart, N.	1839	26 Aug.	Baring, F. T.
1823	31 Jan.	Robinson,	1841	3 Sept.	Goulburn, H.
		Hon. F. J.	1846	6 July	Wood, C.
1827	20 April	Canning, G.	1852	27 Feb.	Disraeli, B.
1827	8 Aug.	Tenterden, Lord[11]	1852	28 Dec.	Gladstone, W. E.
1827	3 Sept.	Herries, J. C.	1855	28 Feb.	Lewis, Sir G. C.
1828	26 Jan.	Goulburn, H.	1858	26 Feb.	Disraeli, B.
1830	22 Nov.	Althorp, Viscount	1859	18 June	Gladstone, W. E.
1834	2 Dec.	Denman, Lord[11]	1866	6 July	Disraeli, B.
1834	10 Dec.	Peel, Sir R.	1868	29 Feb.	Hunt, G. W.
1835	18 April	Spring Rice, T.	1868	9 Dec.	Lowe, R.

[11] Chief Justice of the King's Bench.

Secretaries 1660–1870

Having originated as the personal servant of the Treasurer, the Secretary of the Treasury had by the Restoration acquired functions which were essential to the conduct of the business of the office.[1] Apart from a special arrangement in 1685–6 when Gwyn acted as additional Secretary for the Irish business of the Treasury, there was only one Secretary until 1711 when a second secretaryship was created on a permanent basis.[2] The right of nomination to the offices rested formally with the Treasurer or the Board.[3] The Secretaries did not receive instruments of appointment, their entry into office being marked only by their being called in to take their seats at the Board. These events were not regularly recorded in the minutes until 1730.[4]

The tenure of the offices was never formally defined and varied considerably at different periods. Between 1660 and 1695 it was relatively insecure, new appointments usually being made whenever there was a change of Treasurer or a substantial alteration in the composition of the Board. From the time of Lowndes' appointment in 1695 until the death of Scrope in 1752 the tenure of the secretaryship which they held was in practice permanent and unaffected by political changes. The tenure of the second secretaryship, on the other hand, was from the first precarious, new appointments usually being made whenever there was a change of First Lord. After 1752 it was the general rule for both Secretaries to retire with their political patrons. Until that year the Secretary with permanent tenure enjoyed precedence over his colleague. Thereafter a new practice was introduced in accordance with which the Junior Secretary succeeded as a matter of course to the senior office when it fell vacant.[5] This practice continued to be generally observed until 1830 after which, with the development of distinct parliamentary and financial secretaryships, it ceased to operate. The adoption of the terms Parliamentary and Financial as opposed to Senior and Junior Secretaries was never specifically authorised by the Treasury and is impossible to date with precision. For the purposes of these lists the year 1830 has been selected as being less open to objection than any other.[6]

[1] For the Secretaries and their functions, see Thomas, *Notes of Materials*, 16–17; Baxter, *Treasury*, 167–203; D. M. Clark, 'The Office of Secretary to the Treasury in the Eighteenth Century', *American Hist. Rev.*, xlii (1936–7), 22–45; A. Aspinall, 'English Party Organisation in the Early Nineteenth Century', *Eng. Hist. Rev.*, xli (1926), 396–7; *The Correspondence of Charles Arbuthnot*, ed. A. Aspinall (Camden 3rd ser., lxv, 1941), viii–ix; *The Parliamentary Papers of John Robinson*, ed. W. T. Laprade (Camden 3rd ser., xxxiii, 1922); Todd, *Parliamentary Government*, ii, 324, 333, 366, 368, 451–4.
[2] T 38/438 flyleaf. For a memorandum of 1710 recommending the creation of a second secretaryship, see BM Loan 29/45B ff. 12/253–4.
[3] Lowndes' statement of 24 April 1695 (*CTB*, x, 1369) implying that the office was in the King's gift is in conflict with other evidence including his own remarks to the Commissioners of Public Accounts in Nov. 1702 (T 64/126 p. 248). Members of the House of Commons who were appointed Secretaries were not obliged to submit themselves for re-election as would have been necessary had the appointment been a royal one.
[4] For dates of appointment before 1695, see Baxter, *Treasury*, 167–203. The only appointment apart from Lowndes' recorded in the minutes before 1730 was that of H. Walpole in 1715. From 1711 the evidence in the fee books enables the date of entry into office to be established with reasonable precision.
[5] The practice first received explicit endorsement in TM 29 May 1762 (T 29/34 p. 295).
[6] In 1850 Wood described himself as having occupied the position of 'Parliamentary Secretary' in 1832–4 (*Rept. of Select Committee on Official Salaries 1850* (HC 1850, xv), 206).

Originally the Secretary was dependent on fees for his remuneration.[7] From the time of the funding of the fees he enjoyed two thirds of the product. Gwyn received in 1685–6 two thirds of the fees arising from Irish business and from the payment of the arrears to the servants of Charles II.[8] After 1711 each Secretary received a third of the fees.[9] In 1782 they were accorded fixed salaries of £3000. These salaries were raised to £4000 in 1800. In 1821 they were reduced, for future holders of the offices, to £3500. They were further reduced to £2500 in 1831 and to £2000 in 1851.[10]

LISTS OF APPOINTMENTS

Senior (Parliamentary) Secretary

1660	June	Warwick, Sir P.	1804	21 May	Sturges Bourne, W.
1667	May	Downing, Sir G.	1806	10 Feb.	Vansittart, N.
1671	Oct.	Howard, Hon. Sir R.	1807	1 April	Wellesley, Hon. H.
1673	July	Bertie, Hon. C.	1809	5 April	Arbuthnot, C.
1679	March	Guy, H.	1823	7 Feb.	Lushington, S. R.
1689	April	Jephson, W.	1827	19 April	Planta, J.
1691	June	Guy, H.	1830	26 Nov.	Ellice, E.
1695	March	Lowndes, W.	1832	10 Aug.	Wood, C.
1724	Jan.	Scrope, J.	1834	19 Dec.	Clerk, Sir G.
1752	9 April	West, J.	1835	21 April	Stanley, E. J.
1756	18 Nov.	Hardinge, N.	1841	19 June	Le Marchant, D.[11]
1758	9 April	West, J.	1841	8 Sept.	Fremantle, Sir T. F.
1762	29 May	Martin, S.	1844	21 May	Young, J.
1763	18 April	Dyson, J.	1846	7 July	Tufnell, H.
1763	24 Aug.	Jenkinson, C.	1850	9 July	Hayter, W. G.
1765	15 July	Mellish, W.	1852	2 March	Forbes
1765	30 Sept.	Lowndes, C.			Mackenzie, W.
1767	18 Aug.	Cooper, G.	1853	5 Jan.	Hayter, W. G.
1782	1 April	Strachey, H.	1858	2 March	Jolliffe, Sir W. G. H.
1782	15 July	Orde, T.	1859	24 June	Brand, Hon.
1783	5 April	Burke, R.			H. B. W.
1783	27 Dec.	Rose, G.	1866	14 July	Taylor, T. E.
1801	24 March	Addington, J. H.	1868	11 Nov.	Noel, Hon. G. J.
1802	8 July	Vansittart, N.	1868	21 Dec.	Glyn, G. G.

[7] Between 1671 and 1679, however, Howard and Bertie received a salary of £250 as Secretaries (Baxter, *Treasury*, 177).   [8] T 38/436.   [9] T 38/438 flyleaf.
[10] TM 30 Nov. 1782 (T 29/52 p. 518), 3 April 1800 (T 29/76 pp. 89–92), 10 Aug. 1821 (T 29/200 p. 241), 15 April 1831 (T 29/316 pp. 259–61), 20 May 1851 (T 29/543 pp. 389–91).
[11] It is uncertain which of the two secretaryships Le Marchant occupied.

JUNIOR (FINANCIAL) SECRETARY

1711	11 June	Harley, T.	1806	10 Feb.	King, J.
1714	Nov.	Taylor, J.	1806	2 Sept.	Fremantle, W. H.
1715	12 Oct.	Walpole, H.	1807	1 April	Huskisson, W.
1717	April	Stanhope, C.	1809	8 Dec.	Wharton, R.
1721	April	Walpole, H.	1814	7 Jan.	Lushington, S. R.
1730	24 June	Walpole, E.	1823	7 Feb.	Herries, J. C.
1739	1 June	Fox, S.	1827	4 Sept.	Lewis, T. F.
1741	30 April	Legge, Hon. H.	1828	28 Jan.	Dawson, G. R.
1742	15 July	Furnese, H.	1830	26 Nov.	Spring Rice, T.
1742	30 Nov.	Jeffreys, J.	1834	6 June	Baring, F. T.
1746	1 May	West, J.	1834	20 Dec.	Fremantle, Sir T. F.
1752	22 April	Hardinge, N.	1835	21 April	Baring, F. T.
1756	18 Nov.	Martin, S.	1839	6 Sept.	Gordon, R.
1757	5 July	West, J.	1841	9 June	More O'Ferrall, R.[12]
1758	31 May	Martin, S.	1841	8 Sept.	Clerk, Sir G.
1762	29 May	Dyson, J.	1845	4 Feb.	Cardwell, E.
1763	18 April	Jenkinson, C.	1846	7 July	Parker, J.
1763	24 Aug.	Whately, T.	1849	22 May	Hayter, W. G.
1765	15 July	Lowndes, C.	1850	9 July	Lewis, G. C.
1765	30 Sept.	Cooper, G.	1852	2 March	Hamilton, G. A.
1767	18 Aug.	Bradshaw, T.	1853	5 Jan.	Wilson, J.
1770	16 Oct.	Robinson, J.	1858	2 March	Hamilton, G. A.
1782	6 April	Burke, R.	1859	21 Jan.	Northcote, Sir S. H.
1782	15 July	Rose, G.	1859	24 June	Laing, S.
1783	5 April	Sheridan, R. B.	1860	2 Nov.	Peel, F.
1783	27 Dec.	Steele, T.	1865	19 Aug.	Childers, H. C. E.
1791	26 Feb.	Long, C.	1866	14 July	Hunt, G. W.
1801	9 April	Vansittart, N.	1868	4 March	Sclater Booth, G.
1802	8 July	Sargent, J.	1868	21 Dec.	Ayrton, A. S.
1804	21 May	Huskisson, W.	1869	Nov.	Stansfeld, J.

[12] It is uncertain which of the two secretaryships More O'Ferrall occupied.

Assistant and Permanent Secretary 1805–70

This office was created in 1805. The Assistant Secretary was thereafter the senior permanent official of the Treasury, ranking immediately after the Joint Secretaries. Until 1816 he was also Law Clerk in which capacity his function was to assist in the preparation of bills for parliament and to report on certain questions of law.[1] In 1856 the Assistant Secretary was, in addition to his other duties, given specific responsibility for one of the divisions of business.[2] He was relieved of this in 1859.[3] In 1867 the duties of the office received a new definition and its title was changed to 'Permanent Secretary'.[4]

The salary scale attached to the office in 1805 was £2000 rising after three years to £2500.[5] In fact Harrison, the first holder of the office, received an increase to £2500 in 1807 and further increases to £3000 in 1809 and £3500 in 1815.[6] On Hill's appointment the salary was fixed at £2500.[7] In 1834 the original scale of £2000 to £2500 was re-established for future holders of the office.[8]

LIST OF APPOINTMENTS

1805	19 Aug.	Harrison, G.	1836	22 Jan.	Spearman, A. Y.
1826	7 April	Hill, W.	1840	21 Jan.	Trevelyan, C. E.
1828	4 July	Stewart, Hon. J. H. K.	1859	21 Jan.	Hamilton, G. A.
			1870	1 Feb.	Lingen, R. R. W.

[1] TM 19 Aug. 1805 (T 29/85 pp. 347–8).   [2] TM 4 July 1856 (T 29/564 p. 47).
[3] TM 24 Dec. 1859 (T 29/577 pp. 427–33).   [4] TM 10 May 1867 (AB, iv, 272–6).
[5] TM 19 Aug. 1805 (T 29/85 p. 349).
[6] TM 24 March 1807 (T 29/89 p. 396), 19 Nov. 1809 (T 29/103 p. 190), 31 March 1815 (T 29/234 pp. 640–3).
[7] TM 7 April 1826 (T 29/256 p. 126). The figure of £2000 had, however, been proposed in TM 10 Aug. 1821 (T 29/200 p. 241).
[8] TM 17 Oct. 1834 (T 29/358 p. 326), 28 March 1845 (T 29/483 pp. 491–2).

Clerks 1660–c.1689

The state of the evidence is such that it is impossible to discern the principles governing the clerical structure of the Treasury before 1689.[1] The following list notes the
names of those persons who occur as Clerks before that date. Such evidence as there is
suggests that until 1679 it was unusual for Clerks to remain in the service of the Treasury after their patrons, whether they were Treasurers, Commissioners or Secretaries,
had left office. Thereafter they established themselves on a more permanent footing.
A significant number of Clerks whose names occur for the first time during Guy's
first secretaryship (1679–89) remained in office until their deaths.[2]

While there is evidence that salaries were paid to Clerks as early as 1676,[3] it seems
probable that for the most part they were dependent on personal fees for their remuneration at least until the funding of the fees which had occurred by 1685.

LIST OF APPOINTMENTS

By 1665	Charnock, R.		By 1676	Dorney, J.
By 1667	Abbott, L.		By 1680	Shaw, W.
By 1669	Lloyd, P.		By 1681	{ Aldworth, R.
By 1671	{ Wolseley, R.			{ Squibb, R.
	{ Aram, T.		1684	Tilson, C.
1673	Fleetwood, A.		By 1686	Godolphin, C.
c. 1675	Lowndes, W.		By 1687	Powys, R.

[1] See Introduction, pp. 1–2. There are suggestions that some form of clerical organisation may have
existed as early as 1673 but its nature is obscure (*Letters to Sir Joseph Williamson 1673–4*, ed. W. D.
Christie (Camden 2nd ser., viii, ix, 1874), i, 67, 117).

[2] Witness the careers of Langford, Shaw, Squibb, Tilson and Powys.

[3] See the case of Dorney (*CTB*, v, 1348).

Chief Clerks c. 1689–1856

This grade dates from at least 1685. The identity of the Chief Clerks cannot be ascertained until 1689 when they were five in number. In about 1697 they were reduced to four.[1] Until 1805 the Chief Clerks ranked after the Joint Secretaries and in addition to their own particular responsibilities acted in a general advisory capacity to the Board.[2] In 1805 they were displaced from their position as the senior members of the permanent staff by the Assistant Secretary. At the same time they were given specific responsibilities for the divisions of business, one being assigned to each of the first two divisions, one to the third and fourth and one to the fifth and sixth.[3] In 1834 the number of Chief Clerks was raised to five, one to preside over each of the reorganised divisions. At the same time they were placed in rank after the Principal Clerk for Colonial Business.[4] When in 1849 the number of divisions was reduced to three there was a corresponding reduction in the number of Chief Clerks.[5] There was a further reduction to two in 1854 when provision was made for a Principal Clerk to preside over the Finance Division.[6] The grade was abolished in 1856.[7]

Until 1782 the Chief Clerks received their remuneration in the form of equal shares in a third part of the office fees. In that year they were accorded fixed salaries of £800.[8] This sum was raised to £1080 in 1798 and in 1801 a progressive scale was introduced rising after fifteen years to £1200 and after twenty years to £1400.[9] In 1821 a fixed salary of £1200 was established for succeeding holders of the offices. This was reduced to £1000 in 1834.[10]

LIST OF APPOINTMENTS

By 1689	Lowndes, W.	By 1695	Powys, R.
	Langford, S.		Taylor, J.
	Squibb, R.	c. 1697	Tilson, C.
	Glanville, W.	1713 Oct.	Thomas, W.
	Evelyn, J.	1714 Nov.	Glanville, W.
By 1693	Shaw, W.	1714 Nov.	Kelsall, H.
	Aldworth, R.	1718 Jan.	Lowndes, W.

[1] See Introduction, pp. 2–3.

[2] For the distribution of business amongst the Chief Clerks, see TM 18 Nov. 1714 (*CTB*, xxix, 30–2), 31 July 1759 (T 29/33 pp. 218–19). The latter provided that, where necessary, each Chief Clerk should be ready to undertake any of the business of the office.

[3] TM 19 Aug. 1805 (T 29/85 p. 348).   [4] TM 17 Oct. 1834 (T 29/358 p. 333).

[5] TM 27 March 1849 (T 29/531 pp. 505–30), 3 April 1849 (T 29/532 p. 78).

[6] TM 24 March 1854 (T 29/554 p. 642).   [7] TM 4 July 1856 (T 29/564 p. 47).

[8] TM 30 Nov. 1782 (T 29/52 p. 518).

[9] TM 5 July 1798 (T 29/73 p. 209), 12 May 1801 (T 29/77 p. 437). By TM 3 April 1812 the Chief Clerks were accorded additional allowances of £100 (T 29/116 pp. 448–55).

[10] TM 10 Aug. 1821 (T 29/200 p. 241), 17 Oct. 1834 (T 29/358 p. 326).

1724	Feb.	Frecker, M.	1799	3 Jan.	Chinnery, W.
1738	Dec.	Bowen, T.	1807	24 March	Cipriani, P.
1742	26 Aug.	Fane, H.	1808	17 May	Speer, W.
1752	1 Nov.	Leheup, P.	1812	3 April	Nicolay, F.
1755	30 July	Lowndes, C.	1815	14 April	Brooksbank, S.
1757	27 July	Burnaby, E.	1818	31 July	Hoblyn, T.
1759	31 July	Postlethwaite, J.	1820	10 Oct.	Cotton, W.
1759	31 July	Yeates, R.	1834	17 Oct.	Brooksbank, T. C.
1761	17 Dec.	Bradshaw, T.	1834	17 Oct.	Sanford, H.
1761	22 Dec.	Rowe, M.[11]	1834	17 Oct.	van der Spiegel, A.
1762	23 Feb.	Rowe, M.	1834	17 Oct.	Fauquier, W. E.
1762	23 Feb.	Poole, F.	1834	17 Oct.	Martin Leake, S. R.
1767	18 Aug.	Davis, W.	1836	13 Sept.	Unwin, J.
1769	16 Nov.	Pratt, T.	1840	1 Jan.	Drummond, E.
1776	22 Feb.	Reynolds, F.	1841	26 Jan.	Boyd, G.
1782	30 Nov.	Cotton, T.	1843	3 Feb.	Harrison, T. C.
1782	30 Nov.	Martin Leake, J.	1845	21 Jan.	Pearson, H. R.
1783	16 Dec.	Mitford, W.	1850	22 March	Crafer, C. L.
1785	29 July	Ramus, G. E.	1851	25 Feb.	Litchfield, C.
1798	5 July	Alcock, J.	1852	22 Oct.	Baker, J.

[11] Supernumerary.

Under Clerks c. 1689–1782

Although the distinction between Chief and Under Clerks probably existed before 1689 it is not until this year that it is possible to place particular Clerks securely in one or other of these grades.[1] The appointments of Under Clerks began to be recorded in the minutes in 1718. Before that date their periods of service can only be approximately determined. Their number was not fixed. It fluctuated considerably before 1714. From the transfer of the salaries of the Under Clerks to the civil list in that year until the reform of 1776 there was an almost continuous increase. Amongst the factors contributing to this increase were, on the one hand, the fact that the Treasury continued to pay salaries to Clerks who had ceased to take an active part in business and, on the other, the practice, invariable after 1762, of placing the Clerks of the Revenue Department on the establishment as a means of increasing their remuneration. In 1776 the active membership of the establishment was fixed at twenty-one, seven places being reserved for the revenue Clerks and the remainder being allocated to the Under Clerks engaged in the business of expenditure.[2]

From at least 1714 the relative standing of the Under Clerks was governed by the principle of seniority. The only exceptions to this rule occurred when Clerks were accorded positions other than the most junior on their appointment. There were six cases of this kind. In all but two the beneficiaries were Clerks or former Clerks of the Revenue Department whose previous service in the Treasury was probably the reason for their special treatment.[3]

The Under Clerks received part of their remuneration in the form of fixed salaries from at least 1695. From that year to 1714 most of these salaries were paid out of the secret service. In certain cases, however, they were paid out of the fee fund, although they were in each case eventually transferred to the secret service. The amount of the salaries varied before 1714. In so far as there was any general rule it was that they began at £40, rising in due course to £50. By 1714 two Clerks were receiving £100.[4] On the transfer of the salaries to the civil list in that year the amounts were standardised. Until 1733 the three senior Under Clerks were paid £100 and the rest £50. After 1733 it was the rule for all to receive £100.[5] In addition to their salaries those Under Clerks

[1] See Introduction, pp. 2–3.

[2] TM 22 Feb. 1776 (T 29/45 pp. 53–8).

[3] For details, see list of appointments below. The clerks of the Revenue Department were Power (1721), Plaxton (1754), E. Boughton (1767) and J. B. West (1768). The special position of the last two was recognised in TM 6 Aug. 1766 (T 29/38 p. 106). The remaining two clerks were H. Fane (1757) and C. Lloyd (1763).

[4] The following Under Clerks received their salaries in the first instance from the fee fund: Medley (1698), East (1699–1707), Varey (1700–7), Frecker (1708–13) and S. King (1712–13). From 1695 to 1707 Bendish received salaries both from the fee fund and from the secret service. For details of the transfers from the fee fund to the secret service see T 1/104 f. 204 (East) and T 1/111 f. 92 (Bendish and Varey).

[5] The only exceptions to this rule occurred in 1736 when two Supernumerary Clerks, W. Davis and Vandinande, were granted £50 each from the civil list (*CTBP 1735–8*, 169–70) and in 1762 when T. Pratt was allowed £200 in consideration of his long service (T 29/34 p. 232).

who were engaged in the business of expenditure enjoyed personal fees on the instruments which they prepared.

LIST OF APPOINTMENTS

By 1689		Powys, R.	1725	14 June	Fane, H.
By 1690	{	Tilson, C.	1725	29 June	Wyndham, W.
		Taylor, J.	1726	3 May	Gibson, T.
		Southworth, S.	1732	18 Sept.	Pennington, J.
c. 1691		Webster, E.	1733	29 June	Beresford, J.[7]
By 1694		Bendish, T.	1733	31 July	de Grey, T.
By 1695	{	Lowndes, T.	1738		Davis, W.
		Booth, G.	1742	29 April	Tompkins, T.
		Segar, H.	1742		Rowe, M.
1698		Jett, T.	1746	11 Feb.	Mill, J.
1698		Granger, M.	1748	3 May	Fane, J.
1698		Medley, T.	1752	1 Nov.	Poole, F.
1699		East, W.	1753	26 Sept.	Reynolds, F.
1699		Lowndes, J.	1754	13 Feb.	Plaxton, W.[8]
1700–1		Varey, J.	1755	10 Jan.	Kerrick, J.
1702		Pelham, J.	1755	30 July	Cartwright, W.
1703–4		Lowndes, W.	1755	17 Dec.	Royer, J.
1707		Spence, T.	1757	27 July	Watkins, J.
1708–9		Frecker, M.	1757	27 July	Wilkin, T.[9]
1711–12		Bowen, T.	1757	27 July	Speer, W.[10]
1711–12		Lowndes, T.	1757	7 Dec.	Fane, H.[11]
1711–12		Burnbury, R.	1758	8 Feb.	Schutz, C.
1711–12		Farewell, P.	1760	23 May	Beldam, W.
1712		King, S.	1761	2 Feb.	Dancer, F.[12]
1714		Chevallier, C.	1761	17 June	Chowne, T.
1715		Wyatt, W.	1761	22 Dec.	Bishop, E.
1718	23 Jan.	Pitt, W.	1762	23 Feb.	Cotton, T.
1720		Robinson, J.	1762	23 Feb.	Herbert, G.[13]
1721		Power, B.[6]	1762	4 May	Fowler, H.[14]
1721	20 April	Leheup, P.	1762	21 May	Chamberlayne, E.
1721	6 Sept.	Lowe, C.	1763	7 April	Browne, G.
1721	20 Nov.	Martin, S.	1763	7 April	Featherstone, R.[15]
1721–2		Lowndes, C.	1763	7 April	Martin Leake, J.
1722–3		Burgh, L.	1763	29 Aug.	Lloyd, C.[16]
1723	14 April	Fox, W. E.	1765	3 July	Mitford, W.
1723	21 April	Burnaby, E.	1765	3 July	Dyer, T.
1724	4 March	Pratt, T.	1766	29 July	Ramus, G. E.

[6] Placed No. 8; former Revenue Clerk.   [7] Revenue Clerk.
[8] Placed No. 13; former Revenue Clerk.   [9] Revenue Clerk.   [10] Revenue Clerk.
[11] Placed No. 15.   [12] Revenue Clerk.   [13] Revenue Clerk.
[14] Revenue Clerk.   [15] Revenue Clerk.   [16] Placed No. 10.

1766	29 July	Brummell, W.	1772	2 July	Smith, W. E.
1766	11 Nov.	Goodenough, G. T.	1773	18 March	Glyn, R. C.
1767	18 Aug.	Boughton, E.[17]	1773	18 March	Webster, H.
1768	26 Jan.	West, J. B.[18]	1779	6 July	Pembroke, W.[19]
1769	16 Nov.	Broughton, B.	1782	25 March	Brummell, B.
1772	2 July	Poyntz, W. D.	1782	10 June	Tufton, A.

[17] Placed No. 22; Revenue Clerk.   [18] Placed No. 23; Revenue Clerk.   [19] Revenue Clerk.

Keeper of Papers 1726–1851

This office was created in 1726.[1] Between 1727 and 1783 it was held by Treasury Clerks. From at least 1765 until 1806 it was a sinecure so far as the principal was concerned, the duties being executed by deputy.[2] In the latter year the Keeper was required to act in person. In 1835 the office was consolidated with the Registry and, on the resignation of the then holder in 1851, it was discontinued.[3]

The salary attached to the office in 1726 was £200. It was increased to £400 in 1762 and reduced to £200 in 1806. In 1812 a progressive scale was introduced rising after fifteen years to £350. In 1829 the salary was fixed at £300.[4]

In addition to the Keeper a number of other persons were from time to time employed to arrange Treasury papers. These included the deputy, Blake, an Extra Clerk, between 1783 and 1813 and Matthews and Moner who were engaged in the sorting and digesting of books between 1782 and 1802. In 1798 an Assistant Keeper was appointed with a salary of £40. This office lapsed in 1810 but was revived in 1820 with a salary of £100. It was discontinued in 1839.[5]

From 1802 the work of arranging current papers was entrusted to Junior Clerks on the establishment, a development which eventually gave rise to the distinct Registry Department.

LIST OF APPOINTMENTS

1726	2 June	Nelson, H.	1783	5 Jan.	Morin, J.
1727	23 July	Fane, H.	1806	20 May	Stevenson, W.
1757	6 June	Lowndes, C.	1829	3 April	Emmans, T.
1765	17 Sept.	Pratt, T.			

[1] TM 24 June 1726 (T 29/25 p. 196). See also BM Add. MS 34736 f. 105. The office was established by warrant under sign manual (T 52/34 pp. 181–2). Appointments were made by Treasury constitution from 1727 to 1783 and by Treasury minute thereafter.

[2] 2nd Rept. on Fees, 75.

[3] TM 20 May 1806 (T 29/87 pp. 33–4), 3 Feb. 1835 (T 29/362 pp. 55–9), 31 Oct. 1851 (T 29/545 pp. 187–8).

[4] TM 24 June 1726 (T 29/25 p. 196), 23 Feb. 1762 (T 29/34 p. 232), 20 May 1806 (T 29/87 pp. 33–4), 7 Aug. 1812 (T 29/118 p. 665), 3 April 1829 (T 29/292 p. 43).

[5] TM 5 July 1798 (T 29/73 p. 212), 4 April 1820 (T 29/184 p. 99), 19 Feb. 1839 (T 29/410 p. 375). The Assistant Keepers were: Powell 1798–1810; Pettit 1820–4; Greenwood 1824–39.

Supernumerary Clerks 1736–1805

Supernumerary Clerks were those who were appointed with the expectation, whether express or implied, of being placed on the establishment, usually on the basis of seniority as vacancies occurred. At first the Clerks in question were described in the records of the Treasury indifferently as 'Supernumerary' or 'Extraordinary'. The term supernumerary has been used throughout these lists in order to avoid confusion with the distinct class of Extra Clerks which emerged after 1777.

In the accounts of the fees for the late seventeenth and early eighteenth centuries the names of certain Clerks appear before they begin to receive salaries which suggests that they may have started their careers as supernumeraries.[1] However, the first record in the minutes of the appointment of Supernumerary Clerks occurs in 1736.[2] A further appointment was made in 1746 but it was not until after 1756 that they became a regular feature of the office. Between that date and 1805, with the exception of the years 1773 to 1784 when none was appointed, it was usual for there to be one or two Supernumerary Clerks. Occasionally the number was higher. In 1765–6 there were five and between 1802 and 1805 there were six. The grade was abolished in the latter year.[3]

The Supernumerary Clerks appointed in 1736 received salaries of £50 from the civil list. Otherwise such Clerks apparently received no salaries until 1763. The Clerks appointed in that year were granted £50.[4] While this seems to have been the normal salary at this period the details are not clear in every case since the relevant accounts of the Treasury incidents, out of which the payments were apparently made, do not survive. Between 1784 and 1805 Supernumerary Clerks received £90 from the fee fund.

LIST OF APPOINTMENTS

1736	1 June	Davis, W.	1763	7 April	Ramus, G. E.
1736	1 June	Vandinande, C.	1765	3 July	West, J. B.
1746	26 June	Fane, J.	1765	10 July	Brummell, W.
1756	8 Nov.	Watkins, J.	1765	10 July	Broughton, B.
1757	17 Feb.	Schutz, C.	1768	26 Jan.	Poyntz, W. D.
1758	10 Oct.	Beldam, W.	1769	16 Nov.	Smith, W. E.
1760	23 May	Chowne, T.	1772	2 July	Glyn, R. C.
1762	9 March	Browne, G.	1784	18 March	Carthew, J.
1762	21 May	Mitford, W.	1786	22 Dec.	Dyer, R. S.
1762	21 May	Dyer, T.	1787	30 Nov.	Egerton, W.
1762	21 July	Featherstone, R.	1789	27 May	Nicolay, F.
1763	7 April	Boughton, E.	1790	16 Aug.	Yorke, J.

[1] East, Frecker, Granger.
[2] TM 1 June 1736 (*CTBP 1735–8*, 169–70).
[3] TM 19 Aug. 1805 (T 29/85 p. 348).
[4] TM 12 April 1763 (T 29/35 p. 67).

1791	1 Feb.	West, T.	1801	20 March	van der Spiegel, A.
1791	9 Nov.	Wyndham, W. W.	1801	24 March	Dean, J.
1792		Brooksbank, S.	1802	19 Jan.	Fauquier, W. E.
1794	25 Nov.	Brawne, J.	1802	13 July	Earle, P. H.
1795	1 April	Wood, E.	1802	16 July	Crafer, T.
1799	23 May	Gibbons, G.	1802	4 Dec.	Vernon, J.
1799	20 Nov.	Unwin, J.	1803	20 May	Martin Leake, S. R.
1800	14 Nov.	Bates, E.	1803		Sargent, W.
1800	21 Nov.	Bradshaw, W.	1804	13 July	Gibbons, E.

Extra and Supplementary Clerks 1777–1870

Extraordinary or Extra Clerks appear to have been introduced into the Treasury in 1777.[1] They differed from Supernumerary Clerks in that they were employed on a temporary basis and had no claim to be placed on the establishment. However, while their tenure was formally precarious they seem soon to have acquired a position comparable to that of other Clerks. From 1783 they were appointed by Treasury minute and were in several cases subsequently placed on the establishment. In 1794 they were being paid at the rate of 5s a day. In 1801 this amount was raised to 6s a day.[2] From time to time they were given particular responsibilities, especially in connection with bills of exchange, for which they received additional allowances.

In 1805 the status of the Extra Clerks was redefined. It was provided that they should be employed on a strictly temporary basis and they were denied the prospect of being placed on the establishment.[3] Between 1805 and 1832 it is impossible always to be certain of their identity or periods of service since their appointments were not recorded in the minutes and they were paid out of the incidents for which the accounts are incomplete. Between 1820 and 1830 there appear to have been about a dozen Extra Clerks, the majority of whom were paid at the rate of 7s a day.[4] In 1829 a progressive scale was introduced beginning at 6s a day and rising after ten years to 10s a day.[5] Some Extra Clerks were given fixed annual salaries and attached permanently to particular departments such as those of the Registry, the Parliamentary Accounts, the Revenue and, later, the Law Clerk.

From about 1830 a distinction can be discerned between 'temporary' and 'permanent' Extra Clerks. The former, who were employed only when the requirements of business made it necessary, never formed part of the staff of the office and are excluded from these lists. The latter, however, were appointed by Treasury minute from 1832 and enjoyed security of tenure.[6] In 1847 the scale of daily payments for these Clerks was extended to provide sixteen shillings a day after fifty years' service.[7] By 1855 the permanent Extra Clerks were generally known as 'Supplementary Clerks'. In the same year it was provided that the previous system whereby some Clerks were paid at a daily rate and some by means of fixed annual salaries should be discontinued and a uniform progressive scale introduced for future appointments. This began at £120 rising by annual increments of £5 to £180. In cases of good conduct it was to be extended from £180 to £300 by annual increments of £10.[8]

In 1861 a reorganisation took place. The Supplementary Clerks were consolidated into a unified structure, divided into three classes. The first class, numbering four,

---

[1] *2nd Rept. on Fees*, 52; see also ibid. 71 where Extra Clerks are confused with Supernumerary Clerks.

[2] T 41/2; TM 13 March 1801 (T 29/77 p. 335).

[3] TM 19 Aug. 1805 (T 29/85 p. 348).　　　　[4] T 38/552.

[5] TM 22 Sept. 1829 (T 29/297 pp. 265–70).

[6] For the recruitment of permanent Extra and Supplementary Clerks, see TM 24 March 1840 (T 29/423 pp. 507–8), 13 July 1855 (T 29/560 pp. 78–80), 3 Aug. 1857 (AB, iii, 353–4), 30 March 1859 (T 29/574 p. 541), 25 Aug. 1861 (AB, iv, 120–3).　　　[7] TM 29 June 1847 (T 29/510 pp. 529–34).

[8] TM 30 Jan. 1855 (T 29/558 p. 303).

consisted of the Assistant Clerk of Parliamentary Accounts, the Assistant Accountant and the Assistant Superintendents of the Registry and Copying Departments. These were accorded a salary scale beginning at £400 rising by annual increments of £15 to £500. The second class, numbering five, began at £250 rising by annual increments of £10 to £350. Provision was made for the number of Clerks in the third class to vary in accordance with the weight of business. In the first instance it consisted of seven. Their salary scale began at £100 rising by annual increments of £10 to £200.[9] In 1868 two Supplementary Audit Clerks were appointed and attached to the Finance Division with salaries beginning at £220 rising by annual increments of £10 to £400.[10]

In 1869 the Supplementary Clerks were again reorganised and divided into two branches. The first, which was concerned with accounts, consisted of two Staff Officers (the Assistant Accountant and the Senior Clerk of the Civil List), one First Class, three Second Class and a varying number of Third Class Clerks. The second branch, which was attached to the Registry and Copying Departments, consisted of three First Class, four Second Class and a varying number of Third Class Clerks.[11]

LISTS OF APPOINTMENTS

Extra Clerks

1777	Dec.	Winter, M.	1822		Algar, W.
c. 1782		Wolfe, L.	1823	2 Dec.	Macrae, K.
c. 1782		Mackintosh, J.	1824	23 Feb.	Stephenson, J.
1783	16 Dec.	Kingsman, T.	1824	28 Feb.	Crafer, E. T.
1785	19 Aug.	Blake, R.	1824	1 April	White, H. A.
1789	18 Feb.	Bullock, E. C.	1832	6 July	Maclean, H. C.
1791	5 April	Stuckey, V.	1834	3 Oct.	Clifford, J.
1794	20 Aug.	Crafer, T.	1836	13 Dec.	Wickens, T. E.
1795	1 April	Rosenhagen, A.	1840	3 April	Rushworth, H.
1796	28 July	Mitford, R.	1840	3 April	Cotton, H. P.
1796	28 July	Brooksbank, T. C.	1841	20 Aug.	Levett, J. W.
1806	14 May	Winkley, W.	1842	7 Oct.	Nash, E.
1807		Metcalfe, J.	1844	10 May	Atchley, W. H.
1807	29 July	Adrian, T.	1845	2 Sept.	Chance, G.
1809		Dwight, W. M.	1849	3 April	Walker, A. H.
1812		Crafer, C. L.	1849	3 April	Nicol, H.
1812		Batchelour, G.	1850	1 Feb.	Lyle, W.
1812		Davis J.	1850	22 Feb.	Roberts, W. B.
By 1815		Adrian, W. O.	1851	7 Feb.	Scrivenor, G. H.
		Nicolay, F. G.	1852	24 Dec.	Geddes, G. T.
		Delattre, J. L.	1855	27 Nov.	Mills, R.
By 1820		Smith, W. B.	1855	18 Dec.	Begent, T. J.
		Pinney, J.	1856	26 Aug.	Cleave, J.
		Makins, G.	1856	26 Aug.	Gunn, A.
1820		Dwight, H. T.	1856	26 Aug.	Gay, E.

[9] TM 24 May 1861 (AB, iv, 113).
[10] TM 27 March 1868 (AB, iv, 301).
[11] TM 19 Nov. 1869 (AB, v, 11).

1856	26 Aug.	Campbell, J. D.	1858	23 April	Jones, W. P.
1856	28 Nov.	Simpson, J.	1858	8 Oct.	Wheeler, F. G.
1856	15 Dec.	Morgan, A. H. V.	1858	8 Oct.	John, E. W.
1857	4 April	Woods, W. W.	1859	27 Jan.	Miller, J. T.
1857	1 May	Craggs, G. W.	1859	13 April	Elliott, T.
1857	24 Aug.	Sidebotham, H.	1859	13 April	Davies, J.
1857	24 Aug.	Durrant, T.	1859	13 April	Philp, E.
1857	1 Oct.	Mills, E.			

First Class Supplementary Clerks

1861	24 May	Batchelour, G.	1864	10 May	Atchley, W. H.
1861	24 May	Wickens, T. E.	1867	7 Feb.	Begent, T. J.
1861	24 May	Cotton, H. P.	1869	21 Feb.	Geddes, G. T.
1861	24 May	Miller, J. T.	1869	19 Nov.	Simpson, J.
1861	24 May	Dwight, H. T.[12]			

Second Class Supplementary Clerks

1861	24 May	Nash, E.	1867	7 Feb.	Simpson, J.
1861	24 May	Atchley, W. H.	1868	15 Aug.	Durrant, T.
1861	24 May	Geddes, G. T.	1869	21 Feb.	Davies, J.
1861	24 May	Begent, T. J.	1869	19 Nov.	Philp, E.
1861	24 May	Craggs, G. W.	1869	19 Nov.	Skinner, G. E.
1861	9 Aug.	Robinson, F. J.	1869	19 Nov.	Follett, F. T.
1864	10 May	Gunn, A.			

Third Class Supplementary Clerks

1861	24 May	Gunn, A.	1863	5 March	Jackson, J.
1861	24 May	Gay, E.	1864	7 Dec.	Stephenson, F. C.
1861	24 May	Simpson, J.	1867	4 Nov.	Luff, W. W.
1861	24 May	Sidebotham, H.	1868	7 July	Ray, W. S.
1861	24 May	Durrant, T.	1869	28 April	Arnold, G. M. B.
1861	24 May	Davies, J.	1869	24 May	Aldridge, E. G.
1861	24 May	Philp, E.	1869	19 Nov.	Hereford, G.
1862	24 Jan.	Skinner, G. E.	1869	19 Nov.	Waters, C.
1862	5 Feb.	Fox, J. B.	1869	19 Nov.	Fraser, A. S.

Supplementary Audit Clerks

1868	23 April	Skinner, G. E.	1868	23 April	Follett, F. T.

[12] Supernumerary.

Clerks of the Minutes 1782–1818

The establishment of a distinct clerkship of the minutes appears to have taken place in 1782.[1] The office grew rapidly in importance and in 1802 the Clerk was ordered to attend all meetings of the Board.[2] An assistant clerkship was instituted in 1793 and at the same time Clerks were debarred from serving in the divisions while holding the two offices in question.[3] Until 1805 the Clerks of the Minutes received annual allowances as such in addition to their basic remuneration. That of the Principal Clerk was fixed at £50 in 1784, at £100 in 1785, at £200 in 1793, at £300 in 1798 and at £400 in 1803.[4] That of the Assistant Clerk was fixed at £130 in 1793 and at £250 in 1798.[5]

In 1805 provision was made for a minute department consisting of a principal, ranking as a Senior Clerk, and two other Clerks.[6] Thereafter the junior positions were filled by rotation from amongst the Assistant and Junior Clerks. In 1808 the department was enlarged to consist of a Senior, two Assistant and two Junior Clerks.[7] In 1818 the post of Senior Minute Clerk was abolished.[8] The department itself was abolished in 1821.[9]

LISTS OF APPOINTMENTS
CLERK OF THE MINUTES

| 1782 | April | Winter, M. | 1799 | 3 Jan. | Stuckey, V. |
| 1798 | 28 Feb. | Nicolay, F. | | | |

ASSISTANT CLERK OF THE MINUTES

| 1795 | 3 Jan. | Nicolay, F. | 1799 | 3 Jan. | Wood, F. |
| 1798 | 5 July | Stuckey, V. | 1800 | 6 March | Hoblyn, T. |

SENIOR CLERK OF THE MINUTES

| 1805 | 19 Aug. | Stuckey, V. | 1812 | 3 April | Brooksbank, S. |
| 1808 | 13 July | Nicolay, F. | 1815 | 14 April | Brawne, J. |

[1] TM 10 Jan. 1784 (T 29/54 p. 538).   [2] TM 15 July 1802 (T 29/79 p. 255).
[3] TM 16 Aug. 1793 (T 29/66 p. 146) brought into operation by TM 3 Jan. 1795 (T 29/67 p. 371).
[4] TM 15 July 1783 (T 29/54 p. 202), 10 Jan. 1784 (ibid. p. 538), 29 July 1785 (T 29/56 p. 517), 16 Aug. 1793 (T 29/66 p. 146), 5 July 1798 (T 29/73 p. 209), 13 May 1803 (T 29/81 p. 64).
[5] TM 16 Aug. 1793 (T 29/66 p. 146), 5 July 1798 (T 29/73 p. 209).
[6] TM 19 Aug. 1805 (T 29/85 pp. 348–9).
[7] TM 13 July 1808 (T 29/95 p. 384); at the same time £200 was added to the salary of the Senior Clerk.
[8] TM 31 July 1818 (T 29/163 p. 681).   [9] TM 13 April 1821 (T 29/196 p. 361).

Senior Clerks 1782–1856

This grade was created in 1782.[1] The number of Senior Clerks was then fixed at six and remained unaltered, as did that of the divisions in which they served, until 1834. Between 1805 and 1818 the Clerk of the Minutes ranked as a Senior Clerk.[2] When in 1834 the number of divisions was reduced to five there was a corresponding reduction in the number of Senior Clerks.[3] In 1850 the number was reduced to four, one for each of the divisions established in the previous year and one to superintend the reorganised Registry Department.[4] The grade was abolished in 1856.[5]

Between 1782 and 1805 the Senior Clerks all received a basic salary of £100 as Clerks on the establishment. In addition they enjoyed allowances which varied in amount according to the divisions in which they were serving. In 1782 these allowances were fixed at £400, £350, £500, £380, £360 and £280 for those serving in the first to sixth divisions respectively.[6] In 1798 they were fixed at £525, £485, £565, £500, £335 and £380 respectively.[7] In certain divisions the amounts were subject to variation according to whether conditions of peace or war prevailed.[8] In 1805 a uniform progressive scale was introduced for the grade, beginning at £600 and rising after fifteen years to £700 and after twenty years to £800.[9] In 1813 the scale was improved and the maximum salary was raised to £1000 after twenty years. In 1821 it was fixed at £600 rising by annual increments of £20 to £800.[10]

LIST OF APPOINTMENTS

1782	30 Nov.	Royer, J.	1785	29 July	Alcock, J.
1782	30 Nov.	Beldam, W.	1787	15 Aug.	Cipriani, P.
1782	30 Nov.	Mitford, W.	1789	1 Nov.	Starck, H. S.
1782	30 Nov.	Dyer, T.	1798	5 July	Chinnery, W.
1782	30 Nov.	Ramus, G. E.	1798	5 July	Speer, W.
1782	30 Nov.	Broughton, B.	1799	3 Jan.	Nicolay, F.
1783	16 Dec.	Poyntz, W. D.	1800	14 Nov.	Yorke, J.
1783	16 Dec.	Brummell, B.	1806	7 Jan.	West, T.

[1] TM 30 Nov. 1782 (T 29/52 pp. 520–1).

[2] TM 19 Aug. 1805 (T 29/85 p. 348).

[3] TM 17 Oct. 1834 (T 29/358 p. 321); a temporary increase to six was authorised by TM 26 Jan. 1841 (T 29/433 p. 453).

[4] TM 22 Feb. 1850 (T 29/538 p. 397); temporary increases were authorised by TM 24 March 1854 (T 29/554 p. 642) and 18 March 1856 (AB, iii, 309).

[5] TM 4 July 1856 (T 29/564 p. 47).   [6] TM 30 Nov. 1782 (T 29/52 pp. 520–1).

[7] TM 5 July 1798 (T 29/73 p. 209).

[8] For examples, see TM 25 Feb. 1783 (T 29/53 p. 183), 29 July 1785 (T 29/56 p. 516), 25 July 1793 (T 29/66 p. 98); see also TM 15 May 1804 (T 29/83 p. 62).

[9] TM 19 Aug. 1805 (T 29/85 p. 350).

[10] TM 23 Feb. 1813 (T 29/121 pp. 711–15), 10 Aug. 1821 (T 29/200 p. 242).

1807	24 March	Brooksbank, S.	1835	30 April	Pearson, H. R.
1808	17 May	Brawne, J.	1836	13 Sept.	Harrison, T. C.
1808	13 July	Hoblyn, T.	1840	1 Jan.	Baker, J.
1809	18 April	Cotton, W.	1841	26 Jan.	Crafer, C. L.
1812	3 April	Mitford, R.	1841	26 Jan.	Litchfield, C.
1815	14 April	West, G.	1843	3 Feb.	Harrison, M.
1816	27 Feb.	Grange, J.	1843	3 Feb.	Speer, E.
1816	27 Oct.	Sanford, H.	1845	21 Jan.	Brummell, W. C.
1817	21 Feb.	Unwin, J.	1850	22 March	Arbuthnot, G.[11]
1818	31 July	Bates, E.	1851	25 Feb.	Stephenson, W. H.
1820	10 Oct.	van der Spiegel, A.	1852	20 Feb.	Courtenay, T. P.
1823	11 March	Fauquier, W. E.	1852	22 Oct.	Drummond, S.
1834	17 Oct.	Walpole, E.	1854	24 March	Gordon, Sir A. C. D.
1834	17 Oct.	Gibbons, E.	1854	24 March	Shelley, S.
1834	17 Oct.	Drummond, E.	1854	8 Dec.	Dwight, W. M.[11]
1834	17 Oct.	Boyd, G.	1856	18 March	Byron, F.

[11] Supernumerary.

Junior (Assistant) Clerks 1782–1805

In 1782 provision was made for one junior Clerk on the establishment to be associated with each of the six Senior Clerks in the conduct of the business of the new divisions.[1] These Clerks were designated 'Junior Clerks' on this occasion. Later they were sometimes called 'Deputies' or 'Assistant Clerks'. For the purpose of these lists they have been described as 'Junior (Assistant) Clerks' in order to distinguish them from the undifferentiated group of junior Clerks on the establishment. In 1805 the Clerks in question were absorbed into the new grade of Assistant Clerks.

The Junior (Assistant) Clerks all received a basic salary of £100 as Clerks on the establishment. In addition they enjoyed allowances which varied in amount according to the divisions in which they were serving. In 1782 these allowances were fixed at £120 for the Clerk serving in the first division, £100 for those serving in the second and third divisions and £80, £60 and £50 for those serving in the fourth, fifth and sixth divisions.[2] In 1798 they were fixed at £200, £200, £150, £100, £100 and £100 respectively.[3]

LIST OF APPOINTMENTS

1782	30 Nov.	Brummell, B.	1789	24 Dec.	Dyer, R. S.
1782	30 Nov.	Tufton, A.	1791	1 Feb.	Egerton, W.
1782	30 Nov.	Alcock, J.	1791	9 Nov.	Nicolay, F.
1782	30 Nov.	Cipriani, P.	1795	3 Jan.	Yorke, J.
1782	30 Nov.	Starck, H. S.	1795	3 Jan.	West, T.
1782	30 Nov.	Ridout, J. C.	1795	3 Jan.	Brooksbank, S.
1783	25 Feb.	Smith, J.	1795	3 Jan.	Brawne, J.
1783	16 Dec.	Chinnery, W.	1798	5 July	Carthew, J.
1785	29 July	Speer, W.	1798	5 July	Cooke, E.
1787	15 Aug.	Trollope, J.	1799	3 Jan.	Hoblyn, T.
1787	15 Aug.	Winter, M.	1800	6 March	Cotton, W.
1787	15 Aug.	Harward, J.	1800	14 Nov.	Mitford, R.
1789	27 May	Carthew, J.			

[1] TM 30 Nov. 1782 (T 29/52 pp. 520–1).   [2] Ibid.   [3] TM 5 July 1798 (T 29/73 p. 209).

Junior Clerks 1782–1856

Between 1782 and 1805 there were a varying number of Clerks on the establishment in addition to the twelve directly involved in the work of the divisions. These Clerks lacked any specific designation. For the purpose of these lists they have been described as 'Junior Clerks'. They must, however, be distinguished from the six Junior (Assistant) Clerks serving in the divisions for whom provision was made in 1782. Beginning at two in 1782 the number of Clerks in question was increased to three in 1783, to five in 1795 and to ten in 1797.[1] They all received a basic salary of £100 as Clerks on the establishment. Certain of them enjoyed additional allowances in consideration of their responsibilities as Copying Clerks,[2] Clerks of the Minutes,[3] Bills of Exchange,[4] or Papers,[5] or as Private Secretaries to the First Lord.[6]

In 1805 a new grade, specifically designated that of Junior Clerk, was instituted. Provision was made for nine such Clerks.[7] The number was increased to eleven in 1808, to twelve in 1811 and to sixteen in 1813.[8] It was reduced to eleven in 1821[9] and increased to thirteen in 1834.[10] The grade was abolished in 1856.[11]

The salary scale attached to the grade in 1805 was £120, rising after three years to £150 and after seven years to £200.[12] In 1813 the scale was improved and the maximum salary was raised to £520 after twenty years.[13] In 1821 it was fixed at £100 rising, after three years, by annual increments of £10 to £200.[14] In 1831 the starting level was reduced to £90.[15]

LIST OF APPOINTMENTS

1782	30 Nov.	Poyntz, W. D.	1783	16 Dec.	Winter, M.
1782	30 Nov.	Smith, J.	1785	29 July	Harward, J.
1783	25 Feb.	Chinnery, W.	1787	15 Aug.	Carthew, J.
1783	23 Aug.	Speer, W.	1787	15 Aug.	Dyer, R. S.
1783	16 Dec.	Trollope, J.	1789	27 May	Egerton, W.

[1] TM 23 Aug. 1783 (T 29/54 p. 332), 3 Jan. 1795 (T 29/67 p. 372), 7 Jan. 1797 (T 29/70 pp. 81–2).
[2] In 1782 provision was made for one of the Junior Clerks to act as Copying Clerk (T 29/52 p. 524). By 1798 the term was in general use to describe the established Clerks who were not serving in the divisions (T 29/73 p. 212).
[3] Hoblyn, F. Nicolay, Stuckey, F. Wood, Winter.
[4] Rosenhagen, Stuckey.   [5] Grange.   [6] J. Smith.
[7] TM 19 Aug. 1805 (T 29/85 p. 348) fully effective from 5 Jan. 1806 (T 41/3).
[8] TM 13 July 1808 (T 29/95 p. 386), 25 June 1811 (T 29/111 pp. 752–3), 23 Feb. 1813 (T 29/121 pp. 704–5).
[9] TM 10 Aug. 1821 (T 29/200 p. 240); by TM 19 March 1822 the three most recently appointed Junior Clerks were declared supernumeraries to be replaced on the establishment as vacancies occurred (T 29/207 p. 542).
[10] TM 17 Oct. 1834 (T 29/358 p. 317).   [11] TM 4 July 1856 (T 29/564 p. 47).
[12] TM 19 Aug. 1805 (T 29/85 p. 350).   [13] TM 23 Feb. 1813 (T 29/121 pp. 711–15).
[14] TM 10 Aug. 1821 (T 29/200 pp. 241–2).   [15] TM 12 April 1831 (T 29/316 pp. 173–7).

1789	24 Dec.	Nicolay, F.		1813	23 Feb.	Vincent, H. W.
1791	1 Feb.	Yorke, J.		1813	23 Feb.	Salwey, A.
1791	9 Nov.	West, T.		1815	14 April	Duke, W.
1794	25 Nov.	Brooksbank, S.		1815	14 April	Litchfield, C.
1795	3 Jan.	Stuckey, V.		1815	19 May	Speer, E.
1795	3 Jan.	Cooke, E.		1816	27 Feb.	Brummell, W. C.
1797	7 Jan.	Wood, E.		1817	4 Nov.	Stapleton, Hon. T.
1797	7 Jan.	Hoblyn, T.		1817	4 Nov.	Sargent, F.
1797	7 Jan.	Cotton, W.		1818	1 Sept.	Pococke, A. F.
1797	7 Jan.	Mitford, R.		1818	10 Nov.	Rodney, Hon. W.
1797	7 Jan.	Brooksbank, T. C.		1819	22 Jan.	Luttrell, F. W.
1798	5 July	West, G.		1820	18 July	Arbuthnot, G.[16]
1798	5 July	Rosenhagen, A.		1820	21 July	Cotterell, H.[17]
1798	5 July	Grange, J.		1821	12 Jan.	Pemberton, C. R.[17]
1798	5 July	Herries, J. C.		1824	13 Feb.	Drummond, S.
1799	23 May	Sanford, H.		1824	13 April	Vandiest, F. G.
1799	23 May	Courtenay, T. P.		1825	18 Aug.	Vesey, E. A.
1800	6 March	Wood, F.		1826	24 Feb.	Courtenay, T. P.
1800	14 Nov.	Gibbons, G.		1826	21 April	Ricketts, E. W.
1801	20 March	Unwin, J.		1826	2 June	Baker, E.
1802	13 July	Bates, E.		1826	15 Aug.	Cole, J. G.
1803	20 May	Bradshaw, W.		1827	23 March	Stephenson, W. H.
1803		van der Spiegel, A.		1827	4 Dec.	Gordon, Sir A. C. D.
1804	13 July	Fauquier, W. E.		1829	3 March	St. John, C. W.
1805	19 Aug.	Earle, P. H.		1830	29 Oct.	Shelley, S.
1805	19 Aug.	Crafer, T.		1832	21 Aug.	Bulteel, T.
1805	19 Aug.	Vernon, J.		1832	12 Oct.	Crafer, E. T.
1805	19 Aug.	Martin Leake, S. R.		1833	17 Sept.	Grey, C. S.
1805	19 Aug.	Sargent, W.		1833	29 Nov.	Waller, A.
1805	19 Aug.	Gibbons, E.		1833	20 Dec.	Stronge, C. W.
1807	24 March	Cocks, W.		1834	4 Nov.	Gore, C. A.
1808	17 May	Hill, W.		1834	2 Dec.	Seton, W.
1808	13 July	Reynolds, J. S.		1834	2 Dec.	Anson, G. E.
1808	25 Aug.	Carpenter, J. D.		1834	19 Dec.	Jones, L. A.
1808	25 Aug.	Walpole, E.		1835	4 Sept.	Napier, R.
1808	25 Aug.	Compton, P. A.		1836	23 Sept.	Ponsonby, R. W.
1809	21 July	Boyd, G.		1838	22 May	Wilbraham, R. W.
1810	23 March	Pearson, H. R.		1838	12 Oct.	Law, W.
1811	21 June	Drummond, E.		1839	20 June	Calder, W. H. W.
1811	25 June	Harrison, T. C.		1839	26 Dec.	Fitzgerald, F.
1812	3 April	Chinnery, G. R.		1840	17 Nov.	Livingstone,
1812	10 April	Baker, J.				H. C. F.
1813	23 Feb.	Freeling, J. C.		1841	10 March	Parratt, G. F.
1813	23 Feb.	Harrison, M.		1841	10 Dec.	Rushworth, H.

[16] Declared supernumerary 19 March 1822 (T 29/207 p. 543); replaced on establishment 13 Feb. 1823 (T 29/218 p. 189).

[17] Declared supernumerary 19 March 1822 (T 29/207 p. 543); replaced on establishment 11 March 1823 (T 29/219 p. 151).

1842	4 Feb.	Dawson, F.		1852	24 Feb.	Ponsonby,
1843	17 Jan.	Cole, J. H.				Hon. G. H. B.
1843	28 Feb.	Drummond, M.		1852	24 Feb.	Ryan, C. L.
1843	17 March	Clerke, W. H.		1852	24 Feb.	Blackwood, S. A.
1845	11 April	Buckland, E. C.		1852	3 Dec.	Murray, H. H.
1845	17 June	Clerk, A.		1852	24 Dec.	Wynne, W.
1846	16 Oct.	Martin Leake, J.		1853	22 April	Fremantle, C. W.
1848	14 April	Barrington, C. G.		1854	28 March	Somerset, R. G. H.
1850	17 Dec.	Plunkett, Hon. E. L.		1854	29 Dec.	Buchan, T.
1851	25 Feb.	Spearman, A. Y.		1856	26 Feb.	Wilson, C. R.
1851	2 Dec.	Russell, G.		1856	26 Feb.	Broughton, V. D.
				1856	2 May	Mowatt, F.

Clerks of the Bills 1782–1854

Originally no special arrangements were made for dealing with the business arising from the Treasury bills of exchange.[1] Between 1782 and 1805, however, it was entrusted to particular Clerks who received on this account allowances in addition to their ordinary remuneration. During this period the number of these Clerks, who were usually Extra Clerks, was two except for the years 1796 to 1798 when it rose to three. In 1783 the allowances were fixed at £30 and £20 a year.[2] In 1794 they were raised to £60 and £40.[3] In 1796, on the appointment of a third Clerk, they were fixed at £100, £60 and £40.[4] In 1798 the clerkship to which the £60 allowance was attached was discontinued.

In 1805 the bill department was recognised as a distinct subdivision of the Treasury. Provision was made for a Senior and an Assistant Clerk of the Bills who were specifically denied the right of promotion to higher posts in the Treasury.[5] In 1835 the responsibilities were extended to include the functions formerly carried out by the Receiver of Fees.[6] In 1854 the department was transferred to the office of the Paymaster General.[7]

In 1805 the salaries of the Senior and Assistant Clerks were fixed at £250 and £120.[8] In 1808 progressive scales were introduced, the Senior Clerk beginning at £300 and rising after fifteen years to £400 and the Junior beginning at £150 and rising after ten years to £200.[9] In 1812 the salaries were linked to those applicable to the grades of Assistant and Junior Clerk on the establishment.[10] Following the transfer of the duties of the Receiver of Fees in 1835 Rumsey was granted an additional allowance of £200 on that account.[11]

LISTS OF APPOINTMENTS

CLERKS

1782	30 Nov.	Wolfe, L.	1794	8 Feb.	Stuckey, V.
1782	30 Nov.	Mackintosh, J.	1796	28 July	Crafer, T.
1785	29 July	Kingsman, T.	1797	7 Jan.	Rosenhagen, A.
1789	24 Dec.	Bullock, E. C.			

---

[1] For Treasury bills of exchange, see D. M. Clark, 'The Office of Secretary to the Treasury in the eighteenth century', *American Hist. Rev.*, xlii (1936–7), 36 and TM 22 Dec. 1854 (T 29/557 p. 484).
[2] TM 25 Feb. 1783 (T 29/53 pp. 183–4).   [3] TM 20 Aug. 1794 (T 29/67 p. 183).
[4] TM 28 July 1796 (T 29/69 p. 341).
[5] TM 19 Aug. 1805 (T 29/85 pp. 350–1), 7 Aug. 1812 (T 29/118 p. 666).
[6] TM 10 Aug. 1821 (T 29/200 p. 242), 17 Oct. 1834 (T 29/358 pp. 322–3), 9 Dec. 1834 (T 29/360 p. 145).
[7] TM 22 Dec. 1854 (effective 6 Jan. 1855) (T 29/557 p. 484).
[8] TM 19 Aug. 1805 (T 29/85 pp. 350–1).   [9] TM 13 July 1808 (T 29/95 p. 389).
[10] TM of 7 Aug. 1812 (T 29/118 pp. 665–6).   [11] TM 17 Oct. 1834 (T 29/358 p. 323).

Senior Clerk

1806	7 Jan.	Herbert, G.	1836	1 Nov.	Rumsey, L.

Assistant Clerk

1806	7 Jan.	Breton, T. G.	1836	1 Nov.	Dwight, W. M.
1808	2 Dec.	Rumsey, L.			

Receiver of Fees 1782–1835

This office was created in 1782.[1] It was abolished in 1835 when its duties were transferred to the bill department.[2] The salary attached to it in 1782 was £100. This was raised to £150 in 1794 and to £300 in 1805.[3] In 1808 a progressive scale was introduced, rising after fifteen years to £450.[4]

LIST OF APPOINTMENTS

1782	30 Nov.	Dugdale, W.	1791	1 Feb.	Macalpine, J.
1789	24 Dec.	Kingsman, T.	1794	20 Aug.	Vernon, J.

[1] TM 30 Nov. 1782 (T 29/52 p. 521).
[2] TM 10 Aug. 1821 (T 29/200 p. 242), 17 Oct. 1834 (T 29/358 pp. 322–3), 9 Dec. 1834 (T 29/360 p. 145).
[3] TM 30 Nov. 1782 (T 29/52 p. 524), 20 Aug. 1794 (T 29/67 p. 183), 19 Aug. 1805 (T 29/85 pp. 350–1).
[4] TM 21 July 1808 (T 29/95 pp. 487–8).

Assistant Clerks 1805–56

Although the term 'Assistant Clerk' was occasionally used before 1805 to describe those junior Clerks who were associated with the Senior Clerks in the business of the divisions, it was not until the general reorganisation of that year that it was adopted specifically as the title of a grade in the clerical structure. Provision was then made for nine Assistant Clerks.[1] The number was raised to eleven in 1808 and to thirteen in 1834.[2] Apart from certain temporary variations it remained fixed at this level until 1856 when the grade was abolished.[3]

The salary scale attached to the grade in 1805 began at £300, rising after seven years to £350, after ten years to £400 and after fifteen years to £500.[4] In 1813 the scale was improved and the maximum salary was raised to £700 after twenty years. In 1821 it was fixed at £300 rising by annual increments of £20 to £500.[5]

LIST OF APPOINTMENTS

1805	19 Aug.	West, T.	1817	21 Feb.	Compton, P. A.
1805	19 Aug.	Brooksbank, S.	1818	31 July	Boyd, G.
1805	19 Aug.	Brawne, J.	1818	31 July	Pearson, H. R.
1805	19 Aug.	Cooke, E.	1820	10 Oct.	Harrison, T. C.
1805	19 Aug.	Hoblyn, T.	1823	11 March	Baker, J.
1805	19 Aug.	Cotton, W.	1823	11 March	Harrison, M.
1805	19 Aug.	Mitford, R.	1823	11 March	Vincent, H. W.
1805	19 Aug.	West, G.	1823	29 Oct.	Salwey, A.
1805	19 Aug.	Rosenhagen, A.	1824	12 Oct.	Duke, W.
1806	7 Jan.	Grange, J.	1826	6 Jan.	Speer, E.
1806	7 Jan.	Sanford, H.	1826	7 April	Brummell, W. C.
1807	24 March	Unwin, J.	1832	21 Aug.	Sargent, F.
1808	17 May	Bates, E.	1832	12 Oct.	Arbuthnot, G.
1808	13 July	van der Spiegel, A.	1834	17 Oct.	Litchfield, C.
1808	13 July	Fauquier, W. E.	1834	17 Oct.	Crafer, C. L.
1808	13 July	Earle, P. H.	1834	17 Oct.	Pemberton, C. R.
1809	18 April	Crafer, T.	1834	17 Oct.	Drummond, S.
1812	3 April	Martin Leake, S. R.	1834	17 Oct.	Courtenay, T. P.
1815	14 April	Sargent, W.	1835	30 April	Ricketts, E. W.
1815	19 May	Gibbons, E.	1836	13 Sept.	Cole, J. G.
1816	27 Feb.	Reynolds, J. S.	1838	22 May	Stephenson, W. H.
1816	27 Oct.	Hislop, J. R.	1840	1 Jan.	Gordon, Sir A. C. D.

[1] TM 19 Aug. 1805 (T 29/85 p. 348).
[2] TM 13 July 1808 (T 29/95 p. 385), 17 Oct. 1834 (T 29/358 p. 321).
[3] TM 4 July 1856 (T 29/564 p. 47). [4] TM 19 Aug. 1805 (T 29/85 p. 350).
[5] TM 23 Feb. 1813 (T 29/121 pp. 711–15), 10 Aug. 1821 (T 29/200 p. 242).

1841	26 Jan.	Shelley, S.	1850	8 Nov.	Parratt, G. F.
1841	27 Aug.	Crafer, E. T.	1851	25 Feb.	Dawson, F.
1841	27 Aug.	Grey, C. S.	1852	20 Feb.	Cole, J. H.
1843	3 Feb.	Waller, A.	1852	22 Oct.	Drummond, M.
1845	21 Jan.	Stronge, C. W.	1854	24 March	Clerke, W. H.
1848	18 Feb.	Seton, W.	1854	24 March	Buckland, E. C.
1849	24 April	Jones, L. A.	1854	6 Oct.	Martin Leake, J.
1850	22 March	Wilbraham, R. W.	1854	5 Dec.	Collier, J. P.
1850	22 March	Law, W.	1856	18 March	Blackwood, S. A.
1850	22 March	Fitzgerald, F.			

Auditors 1807–50

The Treasury auditorships, which were two in number, were created in 1807. In the first instance it was provided that they should be held by the Assistant Secretary and the senior Chief Clerk for the time being.[1] After the resignation of Harrison in 1826, however, the connection with the assistant secretaryship was severed.[2] Thereafter, except in the case of Freeling, the offices were always held by Chief Clerks. In 1849 it was provided that they should be discontinued when vacancies occurred, the duties being transferred to the Auditor of the Civil List.[3] Consequently on the retirement of Fauquier in 1849 and the death of T. C. Brooksbank in 1850 the auditorships ceased to exist.

The Auditors received allowances as such in addition to their ordinary salaries. These allowances were fixed at £300 in 1810.[4] In 1821 they were reduced, for future holders of the offices, to £250.[5] In 1834 there was a further reduction to £150.[6]

LIST OF APPOINTMENTS

1807	29 May	Harrison, G.	1826	14 Sept.	Brooksbank, S.
1807	29 May	Cotton, W.	1834	17 Oct.	Brooksbank, T. C.
1815	14 April	Alcock, J.	1834	17 Oct.	Sanford, H.
1821	2 Jan.	Speer, W.	1836	13 Sept.	van der Spiegel, A.
1826	7 April	Freeling, J. C.	1845	21 Jan.	Fauquier, W. E.

[1] TM 29 May 1807 (T 29/90 p. 317).   [2] TM 7 April 1826 (T 29/256 p. 126).
[3] TM 27 March 1849 (T 29/531 pp. 505–30).
[4] TM 12 Jan. 1810 (T 29/104 p. 87) effective from 1807.
[5] TM 10 Aug. 1821 (T 29/200 p. 242).   [6] TM 17 Oct. 1834 (T 29/358 p. 322).

Superintendent of Parliamentary Returns and Clerk of Parliamentary Accounts 1812–70

Before 1812 the responsibility for the accounts and returns submitted to parliament by the Treasury rested with one of the Chief Clerks. In that year it was entrusted to one of the Assistant Clerks in the Revenue Department with the title of Superintendent of Parliamentary Returns and an allowance of £400 in addition to his salary.[1] The post lapsed in 1821, the work being carried on by the Assistant Superintendent, W. O. Adrian, an Extra Clerk. In 1823 another Extra Clerk, C. L. Crafer, was appointed Clerk of Superannuation Returns with a salary of £300.[2]

In 1824, in view of the increasing complexity of the returns, a new post of Clerk of Parliamentary Accounts was created and conferred upon Spearman, who was at the same time appointed an Assistant Clerk in the Revenue Department and given an additional allowance of £400.[3] In 1825 the office of Clerk of Superannuation Returns was abolished and Crafer was also appointed an Assistant Clerk in the Revenue Department with an additional allowance of £50.[4] Spearman, who was appointed Auditor of the Civil List in 1831, retained responsibility for parliamentary accounts until 1834 when he was succeeded by Crafer with an additional allowance of £100 which was raised to £150 in 1836.[5] In 1854 the work of the office was divided between two Clerks one of whom was responsible for the annual estimates and the other for the rest of the business. Both received additional allowances of £100.[6] In 1856 the allowances were discontinued and it was provided that the office of Clerk of Parliamentary Accounts should be held by a First Class Clerk.[7]

LISTS OF APPOINTMENTS

SUPERINTENDENT OF PARLIAMENTARY RETURNS

1812	3 April	Hill, W.	1815	21 April	Alcock, J.

CLERK OF PARLIAMENTARY ACCOUNTS

1824	13 Feb.	Spearman, A. Y.	1854	24 March	Stronge, C. W.
1834	17 Oct.	Crafer, C. L.	1860	24 Dec.	Wilbraham, R. W.
1850	22 March	Stephenson, W. H.	1869	31 Dec.	Barrington, C. G.
1850	15 Nov.	Shelley, S.			

[1] TM 3 April 1812 (T 29/116 p. 453).   [2] TM 11 March 1823 (T 29/219 p 153).
[3] TM 13 Feb. 1824 (T 29/230 p. 224).
[4] TM 5 Aug. 1825 (T 29/248 p. 115); the allowance was raised to £80 by TM 22 Feb. 1831 (T 29/314 pp. 439–42).
[5] TM 17 Oct. 1834 (T 29/358 p. 326), 13 Sept. 1836 (T 29/381 pp. 227–8); while Crafer was a Senior Clerk 1841–50 the allowance was reduced to £100 (TM 26 Jan. 1841 (T 29/433 p. 454)).
[6] TM 24 March 1854 (T 29/554 p. 642). Shelley was appointed Clerk of the Estimates.
[7] TM 4 July 1856 (T 29/564 p. 47).

Principal Clerk Assistant 1815–56

This office was created in 1815. The holder was given the rank of a Chief Clerk and the function of relieving the Secretaries of part of the burden of their work.[1] In 1834 the Principal Clerk Assistant was placed in rank after the Auditor of the Civil List.[2] The office was abolished in 1856.[3]

The salary attached to the office in 1815 was £1400.[4] In 1821 it was reduced, for future holders, to £1100.[5] In 1841 a progressive salary was introduced, beginning at £1100 and rising after three years to £1150 and after five years to £1200.[6]

LIST OF APPOINTMENTS

1815	17 Feb.	Hill, W.	1841	26 Jan.	Martin Leake, S. R.
1816	22 Oct.	Mitford, R.	1852	20 Feb.	Stephenson, W. H.
1823	11 March	Crafer, T.			

Clerks of the Irish Revenue 1817–40

Following the consolidation of the English and Irish revenues in 1817 two Clerks were transferred from the Irish Treasury and attached to the Revenue Department. It was provided that they should not be confined to Irish business but should also assist in the general work of the office. The salary scale attached to the senior clerkship was £800 rising after five years to £900 and after ten years to £1000; that attached to the junior was £300 rising after every five years by £100 until it reached £1000.[7] On the resignation of the Clerks in question in 1830 and 1840 their offices were discontinued.[8]

LIST OF APPOINTMENTS

1817	28 March	Smith, J.	1817	28 March	Tomlins, A.

[1] TM 17 Feb. 1815 (T 29/133 pp. 745–6). [2] TM 17 Oct. 1834 (T 29/358 p. 333).
[3] TM 4 July 1856 (T 29/564 p. 47). [4] TM 17 Feb. 1815 (T 29/133 p. 745).
[5] TM 10 Aug. 1821 (T 29/200 pp. 241–2). [6] TM 26 Jan. 1841 (T 29/433 p. 452).
[7] TM 28 March 1817 (T 29/147 pp. 629–32).
[8] TM 30 Nov. 1830 (T 29/311 p. 444), 10 March 1840 (T 29/423 p. 219).

Auditor of the Civil List 1831–70

This office was created by statute in 1816.[1] In 1831 it was incorporated in the establishment of the Treasury with the rank of Principal Clerk Assistant. At the same time it was provided that the Auditor, when not concerned with the special duties of auditing the civil list, should assist in the general running of the office.[2] In 1834 he was placed in rank after the Assistant Secretary.[3] In 1856 the Auditor was given responsibility for one of the divisions of business.[4] He was relieved of this in 1867. At the same time the duties were redefined and the Auditor was given the additional title of 'Assistant to the Secretaries'.[5]

The salary attached to the office in 1831 was £1200. It was raised to £1500 in 1855.[6]

LIST OF APPOINTMENTS

1831	22 Feb.	Spearman, A. Y.	1865	28 Aug.	Anderson, W. G.
1836	22 Jan.	Pennington, G. J.	1867	10 May	Law, W.
1850	12 Nov.	Arbuthnot, G.			

[1] 56 Geo. III, c 46, s 8; the first holders of the office were John Charles Herries 1816–23 and Robert Plumer Ward 1823–31.
[2] TM 22 Feb. 1831 (T 29/314 pp. 439–42).   [3] TM 17 Oct. 1834 (T 29/358 p. 333).
[4] TM 4 July 1856 (T 29/564 p. 47).   [5] TM 10 May 1867 (AB, iv, 272–6).
[6] TM 22 Feb. 1831 (T 29/314 pp. 439–42), 27 Nov. 1855 (T 29/561 p. 467).

Clerks of the Civil List 1831–70

When in 1831 the office of Auditor of the Civil List was absorbed into the Treasury, two Clerks of the Civil List were transferred to the establishment. At first both Clerks received a salary of £200.[1] In 1837 a distinction was made between the salaries paid to the Senior and Junior Clerks. The scale provided for the former was £250 rising by annual increments of £10 to £350. In 1851 the upper limit was raised to £400. In 1856 a new scale was established beginning at £350 and rising by annual increments of £15 to £500. At the same time it was laid down that future vacancies should be filled by the best qualified Supplementary Clerk. In 1861 the starting level was increased to £400 and in 1869 the Senior Clerk was given the rank of Staff Officer.[2]

The salary scale accorded to the Junior Clerk in 1837 was £90 rising by annual increments of £10 to £150. In 1861 he was given the rank and salary of a Second Class Supplementary Clerk.[3]

LISTS OF APPOINTMENTS

SENIOR CLERK OF CIVIL LIST

1831	22 Feb.	Saunders, E.	1861	25 June	Nash, E.
1837	5 May	Sawyer, E.			

JUNIOR CLERK OF CIVIL LIST

1831	22 Feb.	Sawyer, E.	1840	10 Aug.	Windsor, H. M.
1837	20 Oct.	Hicks, J.	1851	20 Aug.	Robinson, F. J.
1840	6 July	McCulloch, J. R.			

[1] TM 22 Feb. 1831 (T 29/314 pp. 439–42).
[2] TM 5 May 1837 (AB, ii, 217–18), 28 Aug. 1851 (T 29/544 pp. 465–6), 3 Dec. 1856 (T 29/565 p. 529), 9 Aug. 1861 (AB, iv, 119–20), 19 Nov. 1869 (ibid. v, 11).
[3] TM 5 May 1837 (AB, ii, 217–18), 9 Aug. 1861 (ibid. iv, 119–20).

Clerk for Colonial Business 1832–56

This office was created in 1832 following the dissolution of the Board of Colonial Audit whose former secretary was its first holder. It was then provided that the Clerk for Colonial Business should rank as a Senior Clerk and not be confined wholly to colonial matters.[1] In 1834 he was designated a Principal Clerk and placed in rank after the Principal Clerk Assistant.[2] The office was abolished in 1856.[3]

The salary attached to the office in 1832 was £800. It was raised to £1000 in 1834 and to £1100 in 1836.[4] In 1840 there was a further increase to £1200 and it was provided that future holders of the office should begin at £1100 and rise after five years to £1200.[5]

LIST OF APPOINTMENTS

1832	20 Jan.	Brande, G. W.	1851	25 Feb.	Crafer, C. L.

[1] TM 20 Jan. 1832 (T 29/325 pp. 403–4).
[2] TM 17 Oct. 1834 (T 29/358 p. 333).
[3] TM 4 July 1856 (T 29/564 p. 47).
[4] TM 20 Jan. 1832 (T 29/325 pp. 403–4), 17 Oct. 1834 (T 29/358 p. 326), 22 Jan. 1836 (T 29/373 p. 392).
[5] TM 25 June 1840 (T 29/426 p. 459).

Chief Clerk of the Revenue c. 1688–1834

Regular payments to the Treasury office for keeping accounts of the revenue are traceable to the year 1680. It is only from 1688, however, that such payments were made to specified individuals. In the light of subsequent evidence it seems reasonable to equate the recipients with the later Chief Clerks of the Revenue Department.[1] The duties were at first undertaken by persons who were Treasury Clerks in the strict sense. From 1725 to 1834, however, with the exception of the years 1799 to 1821, the office of Chief Clerk was filled by Clerks promoted from within the department itself. In 1834 the separate existence of the Revenue Department was brought to an end and the then Chief Clerk became the head of a new division of the Treasury to which its functions were transferred.[2]

From 1688 to 1714 an annual allowance of £150 was paid out of the customs to the Chief Clerk. In addition provision was made out of the secret service for clerkship and other incidents. This amounted to £50 from about 1697 and was raised to £150 a year in 1709. In 1714 these separate payments were replaced by a single sum of £260 from the customs to cover the salaries of all the Clerks in the Revenue Department.[3] It is not possible to isolate the actual amount received by the Chief Clerk for his own use until 1776 when his salary was fixed at £800. It was reduced to £700 in 1783 but increased again to £800 in 1793.[4] Between 1733 and 1783 it was usual for the Chief Clerk to receive £100 a year from the civil list establishment as part of his remuneration.[5] In 1798 it was fixed at £1000. In 1801 the Chief Clerk of the Revenue was accorded the same scale as the Chief Clerks on the ordinary establishment rising after fifteen years to £1200 and after twenty years to £1400. In 1821 a fixed salary of £1200 was established for future holders of the office.[6]

LIST OF APPOINTMENTS

By 1688		Taylor, J.	1758	5 Jan.	Speer, W.
1695		Tilson, C.	1799	3 Jan.	Alcock, J.
1714		Frecker, M.	1821	2 Jan.	Bullock, E. C.
1725		Beresford, J.	1829	2 Jan.	Brooksbank, T. C.
1752	11 Oct.	Wilkin, T.			

[1] See Introduction, p. 8.   [2] TM 27 Oct. 1834 (T 29/358 pp. 318–19).
[3] *CTB*, ix, 19; ibid. xxviii, 466–7; ibid. xxix, 107, 628.
[4] TM 22 Feb. 1776 (T 29/45 p. 57), 23 Aug. 1783 (T 29/54 p. 332); *15th Rept. on Finance*, 289.
[5] Beresford was placed on the establishment in 1733 and continued to receive the £100 annuity after his retirement as Chief Clerk until his death in 1760. Wilkin and Speer were placed on the establishment in 1757. The latter resigned his place in 1783.
[6] TM 5 July 1798 (T 29/73 p. 209), 12 May 1801 (T 29/77 p. 437), 10 Aug. 1821 (T 29/200 p. 241). An additional allowance of £100 was granted by TM 3 April 1812 (T 29/116 pp. 448–55).

Under Clerks of the Revenue c. 1715–1805

The nature of the evidence is such that it is impossible to establish with precision the number and identity of the Under Clerks working in the Revenue Department until the latter part of the eighteenth century. In 1712 they were two in number.[1] In the establishment list of 1715, when they were named for the first time, they were three.[2] The number had fallen to two by 1725.[3] For the next twenty years the position is obscure. It is possible that, following a direction of the Board in 1726, the work of the department was undertaken by Under Clerks on the establishment.[4] In 1745, however, there were three distinct Under Clerks of the Revenue.[5] The number was reduced to two in 1752 and to one in 1757 when a further arrangement was made for Under Clerks on the establishment to work in the department.[6]

After 1758 there was a rapid increase in the number of distinct Under Clerks of the Revenue. It reached six in 1767 at which level it remained fixed until 1805 when the then Under Clerks were divided into Senior and Assistant Clerks and linked in point of rank and salary with the corresponding grades of the ordinary establishment.[7]

In 1715 one of the three Under Clerks of the Revenue received a salary of £60 and the other two salaries of £50.[8] In 1725 the two remaining Under Clerks received £50.[9] The details of remuneration are obscure between that date and 1776. In the latter year the salaries of the six Under Clerks were fixed in order of seniority at £450, £400, £350, £300, £250 and £200. In 1798 they were fixed at £600, £500, £400, £350, £300 and £200.[10] The bulk of these salaries was provided out of the customs but between 1762 and 1793 it was the rule for each Under Clerk to receive £100 a year from the civil list.

LIST OF APPOINTMENTS

By 1715	Dent, M.		1749	20 April	Plaxton, W.
	Power, B.		1754	13 Feb.	Kerrick, J.
	Beresford, J.		1758	5 Jan.	Herbert, G.
1718	23 May	Stanhope, E.	1758	5 Jan.	Fowler, H.
By 1722		Webb, I.	1761	2 Feb.	Dancer, F.
1722	18 Aug.	Weaver, R.	1762	21 May	Royer, J.
By 1742	Wilkin, T.		1763	7 April	Featherstone, R.[11]
	Hughes, J.		1767	18 Aug.	Boughton, E. [12]
1742	Aug.	Speer, W.	1768	26 Jan.	West, J. B.[12]

[1] CTB, xxviii, 491.   [2] TM 17 Oct. 1715 (ibid. xxix, 297).   [3] BM Add. MS 34736 f. 105.
[4] TM 3 May 1726 (T 29/25 p. 173).   [5] Chamberlayne, Present State (1745), pt. ii, 61.
[6] TM 11 Oct. 1753 (T 29/32 p. 71), 27 July 1757 (ibid. p. 475).
[7] TM 19 Aug. 1805 (T 29/85 p. 351).   [8] TM 17 Oct. 1715 (CTB, xxix, 297).
[9] BM Add. MS 34736 f. 105.
[10] TM 22 Feb. 1776 (T 29/45 p. 57), 5 July 1798 (T 29/73 p. 209).
[11] Appointed supernumerary 21 July 1762 (T 29/34 p. 328).
[12] Appointed supernumerary 3 July 1765 (T 29/37 p. 51).

1776	22 Feb.	Smith, W. E.	1794	8 Feb.	Bullock, E. C.
1779	6 July	Pembroke, W.	1797	19 Dec.	Brooksbank, T. C.
1791	9 Nov.	Egerton, W.	1799	3 Jan.	Herries, J. C.
1792		Wyndham, W. W.	1799	14 Feb.	Woodford, C.

Senior Clerks of the Revenue 1805–34

This grade was created in 1805 and linked in point of rank and salary to that of Senior Clerk on the ordinary establishment. The number of Senior Clerks of the Revenue was fixed at two. The grade was abolished in 1834.[1]

LIST OF APPOINTMENTS

1805	19 Aug.	Pembroke, W.	1810	23 Feb.	Brooksbank, T. C.
1805	19 Aug.	Wyndham, W. W.	1821	2 Jan.	Woodford, C.
1808	1 March	Bullock, E. C.	1829	2 Jan.	Walpole, E.

Assistant Clerks of the Revenue 1805–34

This grade was created in 1805 and linked in point of rank and salary to that of Assistant Clerk on the ordinary establishment. The number of Assistant Clerks of the Revenue was then fixed at four. It was increased to five in 1824, to six in 1825 and reduced again to five in 1831.[2] From 1828 it was the practice for one of the Junior Clerks on the ordinary establishment to serve as a supernumerary Assistant Clerk of the Revenue.[3] The grade was abolished in 1834.[4]

LIST OF APPOINTMENTS

1805	19 Aug.	Bullock, E. C.	1817	14 Nov.	Drummond, E.
1805	19 Aug.	Brooksbank, T. C.	1821	2 Jan.	Chinnery, G. R.
1805	19 Aug.	Herries, J. C.	1821	23 Nov.	Freeling, J. C.
1805	19 Aug.	Woodford, C.	1824	13 Feb.	Litchfield, C.
1808	1 March	Alcock, J.	1824	13 Feb.	Spearman, A. Y.
1810	23 Feb.	Hill, W.	1825	5 Aug.	Crafer, C. L.
1811	21 June	Carpenter, J. D.	1826	11 Aug.	Pemberton, C. R.
1815	17 Feb.	Walpole, E.	1829	2 Jan.	Vandiest, F. G.

[1] TM 19 Aug. 1805 (T 29/85 p. 351), 17 Oct. 1834 (T 29/358 pp. 318–19).
[2] TM 19 Aug. 1805 (T 29/85 p. 351), 13 Feb. 1824 (T 29/230 p. 224), 5 Aug. 1825 (T 29/248 p. 115), 22 Feb. 1831 (T 29/314 pp. 439–42).
[3] TM 8 Feb. 1828 (Vandiest) (T 29/278 p. 148), 23 Jan. 1829 (Courtenay) (T 29/289 p. 377).
[4] TM 17 Oct. 1834 (T 29/358 pp. 318–19).

Law Clerk 1835–56

Between 1805 and 1816 the designation 'Law Clerk' formed part of the title of the Assistant Secretary.[1] In 1835 it was given to a distinct official with different duties.[2] The appointment was made necessary by the introduction in that year of the practice whereby the crown relieved the county rates of half the expense of criminal prosecutions at assizes and sessions. The principal function of the Law Clerk was the supervision of the business arising in this connection and, after 1846, in connection with the county courts.[3] The office was not filled after the dismissal of its holder in 1856. In the same year its functions were transferred to one of the Principal Clerks and in 1860 to a new County Court Department.[4]

The salary attached to the office in 1835 was £500.[5] In 1841 a progressive scale was introduced rising to £700 after fifteen years.[6] In the event it was increased to £700 in 1846 and there was a further increase to £1000 in 1847.[7]

APPOINTMENT

1835   9 Jan.   Hankins, R.

[1] TM 19 Aug. 1805 (T 29/85 p. 347).   [2] TM 9 Jan. 1835 (T 29/361 p. 98).
[3] For an account of the office, see *Rept. on Misc. Expenditure*, pt. i, 504–25.
[4] TM 4 July 1856 (T 29/564 p. 47), 6 Jan. 1860 (AB, iv, 88–90).
[5] TM 9 Jan. 1835 (T 29/361 p. 98).   [6] TM 15 March 1841 (T 29/435 p. 313).
[7] TM 26 June 1846 (T 29/498 p. 471), 30 March 1847 (T 29/507 p. 525).

Superintendent of the Registry 1835–70

The functions later assumed by the Registry Department appear originally to have been undertaken by the Keeper of Papers. Probably as a result of the lack of an effective principal in that office in the latter part of the eighteenth century the arrangements for dealing with the increasing volume of papers proved inadequate. To remedy this situation provision was made for a register book, containing details of the current business of the office, to be compiled by a Junior Clerk. In 1804 a room was set aside for use as a Registry. In 1805 two Assistant Clerks were assigned to it.[1] In 1830 the department was placed under the supervision of the junior Chief Clerk. In 1831 it was given additional responsibilities in connection with the minutes and its establishment was fixed at one Assistant, one Junior and two Extra Clerks.[2]

In 1835 the Registry was consolidated with the office of Keeper of Papers and placed under a Superintendent selected from amongst the Assistant Clerks with an additional allowance of £100. Under his authority were placed the Keeper of Papers, three Extra Clerks and a Messenger.[3] Further modifications in the establishment and functions of the department were made in 1840, 1841 and 1849.[4] In 1856 it was placed under a First Class Clerk as Superintendent, and its responsibilities were extended to include copying.[5] In 1868 the post of Superintendent was made a distinct office with a salary scale of £700 rising by annual increments of £25 to £1000.[6]

LIST OF APPOINTMENTS

1835	3 Feb.	Speer, E.	1852	24 Aug.	Speer, E.
1843	3 Feb.	Ricketts, E. W.	1856		Waller, A.
1849	25 May	Baker, J.	1857	5 Sept.	Jones, L. A.

[1] TM 21 Dec. 1802 (T 29/80 pp. 112–13), 13 Feb. 1803 (ibid. 271–2), 8 May 1804 (T 29/81 pp. 33–6), 19 Aug. 1805 (T 29/85 p. 348).
[2] TM 26 Feb. 1830 (T 29/302 p. 433), 29 April 1831 (T 29/316 pp. 496–9).
[3] TM 3 Feb. 1835 (T 29/362 pp. 55–9).
[4] TM 17 March 1840 (T 29/423 pp. 359–61), 26 Jan. 1841 (T 29/433 p. 452), 25 May 1849 (AB, iii, 103–4).
[5] TM 4 July 1856 (T 29/564 p. 47).   [6] TM 4 Feb. 1868 (AB, iv, 297–8).

Principal Clerks 1854–70

Although it was employed for the first time to describe a specific grade only in 1856 the term 'Principal Clerk' had been in use in the Treasury long before this date. In the eighteenth century the term was virtually interchangeable with that of Chief Clerk. In the nineteenth century, on the other hand, it was usually employed to describe the new offices of Clerk Assistant (1815), Auditor of the Civil List (1831) and Clerk for Colonial Business (1832). None of these officers was directly involved in the work of the divisions. In 1854, however, a Principal Clerk of Finance was appointed who, while ranking with these Clerks, had specific responsibility for a division.[1] This development, therefore, to some extent foreshadowed the creation in 1856 of a new grade of Principal Clerks. Provision was then made for four such Clerks, each of whom was given responsibility for a division.[2]

The salary attached to the grade in 1856 was £1000 rising by annual increments of £50 to £1200.[3] In view of their special circumstances, however, two successive Principal Clerks of the Finance Division were appointed at fixed salaries of £1500.[4]

LIST OF APPOINTMENTS

1854	24 March	Anderson, W. G.[5]	1860	18 Dec.	Law, W.
1856	4 July	Crafer, C. L.	1862	9 Dec.	Stronge, C. W.
1856	4 July	Stephenson, W. H.	1865	17 Aug.	Cole, J. H.
1856	4 July	Anderson, W. G.	1867	6 March	Foster, M. H.
1856	4 July	Seton, W.	1867	21 June	Clerke, Sir W. H.
1859	24 Dec.	Shelley, S.			

[1] TM 24 March 1854 (T 29/554 p. 642).   [2] TM 4 July 1856 (T 29/564 p. 47).
[3] Ibid.
[4] TM 24 March 1854 (T 29/554 p. 642), 6 March 1867 (AB, iv, 260–1).
[5] Principal Clerk of Finance.

Accountant and Assistant Accountant 1855–70

The offices of Accountant and Assistant Accountant were created in 1855.[1] The salary of the Accountant was then fixed at £600 rising by annual increments of £60 to £800. In 1858 the scale was assimilated to that of the First Class Clerks: £700 rising by annual increments of £25 to £900. In 1859 a new scale was established beginning at £500 and rising by annual increments of £20 to £800. In 1868 this was raised to £600 rising by annual increments of £20 to £850.[2] The salary of the Assistant Accountant was fixed in 1855 at £350 rising by annual increments of £15 to £450. In 1859 the maximum was increased to £500. In 1869 a fixed salary of £550 was substituted.[3]

LISTS OF APPOINTMENTS

ACCOUNTANT

| 1855 | 27 Feb. | Foster, M. H. | 1859 | 15 Aug. | Mills, R. |

ASSISTANT ACCOUNTANT

| 1855 | 27 Feb. | Wickens, T. E. | 1869 | 19 Nov. | Turner, C. G. |

[1] TM 27 Feb. 1855 (T 29/558 p. 758).
[2] TM 10 April 1858 (T 29/571 p. 10), 28 Nov. 1859 (T 29/577 p. 377), 6 April 1868 (AB, iv, 307–11).
[3] TM 27 Feb. 1855 (T 29/558 p. 758), 28 Nov. 1859 (T 29/577 p. 377), 19 Nov. 1869 (AB, v, 11).

First Class Clerks 1856–70

This grade was created in 1856. The number of First Class Clerks was then fixed at ten. It was reduced to nine in 1857, to eight in 1859 and to seven in 1861. A supernumerary First Class Clerk was appointed in 1866, the number returning to seven in 1868.[1] The salary scale attached to the grade in 1856 was £700 rising by annual increments of £25 to £900.[2]

LIST OF APPOINTMENTS

1856	4 July	Drummond, S.	1857	5 Sept.	Jones, L. A.
1856	4 July	Gordon, Sir A. C. D.	1859	24 Dec.	Fitzgerald, F.
1856	4 July	Shelley, S.	1860	18 Dec.	Buckland, E. C.
1856	4 July	Byron, F.	1862	9 Dec.	Dawson, F.
1856	4 July	Waller, A.	1865	17 Aug.	Clerke, Sir W. H.
1856	4 July	Stronge, C. W.	1866	3 July	Barrington, C. G.[3]
1856	4 July	Wilbraham, R. W.	1867	21 June	Plunkett, Hon. E. L.
1856	4 July	Law, W.	1867	21 June	Blackwood, S. A.
1856	4 July	Cole, J. H.	1869	30 Dec.	Murray, H. H.
1856	4 July	Collier, J. P.			

[1] TM 4 July 1856 (T 29/564 p. 47), 20 Aug. 1857 (AB, iii, 347), 24 Dec. 1859 (T 29/577 pp. 427–33), 31 Dec. 1861 (AB, iv, 127), 3 July 1866 (ibid. 224–5), 4 Feb. 1868 (ibid. 297–8).
[2] TM 4 July 1856 (T 29/564 p. 47).   [3] Supernumerary.

Second Class Clerks 1856–70

This grade was created in 1856. The number of Second Class Clerks was then fixed at sixteen. It was reduced to fifteen in 1859, to fourteen in 1860, to thirteen in 1862 and to twelve in 1866.[1] The salary scale attached to the grade in 1856 was £350 rising by annual increments of £20 to £600.[2]

LIST OF APPOINTMENTS

1856	4 July	Jones, L. A.	1856	4 July	Nicol, H.
1856	4 July	Fitzgerald, F.	1856	4 July	Fremantle, C. W.
1856	4 July	Parratt, G. F.	1857	30 June	Wilson, C. R.
1856	4 July	Dawson, F.	1857	5 Sept.	Broughton, V. D.
1856	4 July	Drummond, M.	1860	29 June	Mowatt, F.
1856	4 July	Clerke, W. H.	1860	18 Dec.	Welby, R. E.
1856	4 July	Buckland, E. C.	1865	10 May	Clement, R.
1856	4 July	Martin Leake, J.	1865	17 Aug.	Clay, F. E.
1856	4 July	Barrington, C. G.	1867	21 June	Ryder, G. L.
1856	4 July	Plunkett, Hon. E. L.	1867	21 June	Macaulay, H. G.
1856	4 July	Ponsonby, Hon. G. H. B.	1867	21 June	Bergne, F. A.
			1868	7 Dec.	Gurdon, W. B.
1856	4 July	Ryan, C. L.	1869	12 May	Puller, C. C.
1856	4 July	Blackwood, S. A.	1869	30 Dec.	Hervey, G. W.
1856	4 July	Murray, H. H.			

[1] TM 4 July 1856 (T 29/564 p. 47), 24 Dec. 1859 (T 29/577 pp. 427–33), 6 Jan. 1860 (AB, iv, 88–90), 9 Dec. 1862 (ibid. 134–5), 3 July 1866 (ibid. 224–5).
[2] TM 4 July 1856 (T 29/564 p. 47).

Third Class Clerks 1856–70

This grade was created in 1856. The number of Third Class Clerks was fixed at ten. The salary scale was £100 rising by annual increments of £15 to £250.[1]

LIST OF APPOINTMENTS

1856	4 July	Somerset, R. G. H.	1863	18 April	Gurdon, W. B.
1856	4 July	Wilson, C. R.	1865	12 June	Puller, C. C.
1856	4 July	Broughton, V. D.	1865	20 Oct.	Hervey, G. W.
1856	4 July	Mowatt, F.	1866	24 April	Christie, W. H.
1856	26 Aug.	Welby, R. E.	1867	12 Aug.	Kempe, J. A.
1856	26 Aug.	Clement, R.	1867	31 Aug.	Turnor, A.
1856	29 Aug.	Twiss, Q . W. F.	1867	28 Sept.	Ferguson, R. R. N.
1857	1 Sept.	Stephenson, B. C.	1867	16 Oct.	Seymour, H. A. D.
1857	1 Sept.	Clay, F. E.	1868	21 Dec.	Baillie
1857	1 Sept.	Ryder, G. L.			Hamilton, C. R.
1860	26 June	Macaulay, H. G.	1869	13 Oct.	Primrose, H. W.
1861	22 Jan.	Bergne, F. A.			

[1] TM 4 July 1856 (T 29/564 p. 47).

Private Secretaries to First Lord 1743–1870

Before 1806 very little information exists in the Treasury records concerning the Private Secretaries to the First Lord. They received, as such, no salaries from public funds and their recruitment and remuneration were questions which were entirely within the discretion of successive First Lords to decide. The emergence of the position of Private Secretary as distinct from that of Secretary to the Treasury itself was a gradual process the details of which are likely to remain obscure. However, from the time of Pelham's period of office (1743–54) a regular series of Private Secretaries can be identified with reasonable certainty. During the eighteenth century First Lords usually appointed their Private Secretaries from outside the Treasury. In some cases these individuals were rewarded with favourable positions in the clerical organisation[1] or with sinecure offices within the structure of the department.[2] Occasionally Clerks already on the establishment were selected for this function.[3]

In 1806 provision was made for a salary of £300 for one Private Secretary to the First Lord, payable out of the fee fund.[4] From 1812 a salary of the same amount was made available for a second Private Secretary.[5] Thereafter the First Lord usually selected one of his Private Secretaries from amongst the Treasury Clerks and the other from outside the office.[6] For the former the salaries were additional to their ordinary remuneration. No salary was paid to Private Secretaries who were members of the House of Commons.

LIST OF APPOINTMENTS

Pelham	1743–54	1743	Aug.	Roberts, J.
Newcastle	1754–6	1754	March	Roberts, J.
Devonshire	1756–7	*No appointment traced*		
Newcastle	1757–62	1757	July	Jones, H. V.
Bute	1762–3	1762	May	Jenkinson, C.
Grenville	1763–5	1763	June	Lloyd, C.
Rockingham	1765–6	1765	July	Burke, E.
Grafton	1766–70	1766	Aug.	Stonehewer, R.

[1] Thomas, Private Secretary to Treasurer Oxford, was appointed a Chief Clerk in 1713. C. Lloyd, Private Secretary to Grenville, was placed specially in tenth position as an Under Clerk in 1763.

[2] Morin, Private Secretary to Shelburne, was appointed Keeper of Papers in 1783. H. V. Jones, Private Secretary to Newcastle, had been appointed Solicitor in 1744, before his patron came to the Treasury.

[3] W. Brummell was selected by North; B. Broughton by Shelburne; J. Smith by Pitt. By TM 15 Aug. 1787 Smith was released from departmental work and allowed to retain his salary and seniority as a Clerk while serving as Private Secretary (T 29/58 p. 499).

[4] TM 20 Dec. 1806 (T 29/88 pp. 504–5).

[5] TM 23 July 1813 (T 29/124 p. 359); this salary, originally paid out of the special service fund, was transferred to the estimates by TM 24 March 1835 (T 29/363 pp. 461–2).

[6] Russell had three Private Secretaries for part of his term of office (1846–52).

North	1770–82	1770	Jan.	Brummell, W.
Rockingham	1782	1782	April	King, Rev. W.
Shelburne	1782–3	1782	July	Broughton, B.
		1782	Oct.	Morin, J.
Portland	1783	1783	April	O'Beirne, Rev. T. L.
Pitt	1783–1801	1783	Dec.	Pretyman, Rev. G.
		1787	March	Smith, J.
Addington	1801–4	1801	March	Barton, N.
Pitt	1804–6	1804	May	Adams, W. D.
Grenville	1806–7	1806	10 Feb.	Fisher, J.
Portland	1807–9	1807	1 April	Adams, W. D.
Perceval	1809–12	1809	31 Oct.	Herries, J. C.
		1811	5 July	Brooksbank, T. C.
Liverpool	1812–27	1812	16 June	Willimot, R.
		1812	13 Aug.	Brooksbank, T. C.
Canning	1827	1827	30 April	Stapleton, A. G.
		1827	April	Drummond, E.
Goderich	1827–8	1827	13 Sept.	Balfour, B. T.
		1827	13 Sept.	Drummond, E.
Wellington	1828–30	1828	28 Jan.	Greville, A. F.
		1828	28 Jan.	Drummond, E.
Grey	1830–4	1830	31 Dec.	Wood, C.
		1830	31 Dec.	Martin Leake, S. R.
		1832		Grey, Hon. C.
Melbourne	1834	1834	2 Sept.	Young, T.
		1834	2 Sept.	Martin Leake, S. R.
Wellington	1834	*No appointment traced*		
Peel	1834–5	1834	Dec.	Venables, T.
		1834	Dec.	Drummond, E.
Melbourne	1835–41	1835	April	Cowper, Hon. W. F.
		1835	8 May	Anson, G. E.
		1839	15 Oct.	Howard, Hon. C. W. G.
		1840	24 June	Fortescue, Hon. H.
Peel	1841–6	1841	8 Sept.	Drummond, E.
		1841	8 Sept.	Stephenson, W. H.
		1843	3 Feb.	Arbuthnot, G.
Russell	1846–52	1846	7 July	Howard, Lord E. G.
		1846	7 July	Grey, C. S.
		1846	12 July	Keppel, Hon. G. T.
		1847	23 Nov.	Law, W.
		By 1848		Grey, R. W. (*additional*)
		1850	13 Dec.	Russell, A. J. E.
Derby	1852	1852	5 March	Bootle Wilbraham, Hon. E.
		1852	5 March	Stronge, C. W.
		1852	13 March	Talbot, Hon. W. P. M. C.
Aberdeen	1852–5	1853	18 Jan.	Hamilton Gordon, Hon. A.
		1853	18 Jan.	Cole, J. H.
		1853	8 April	Dawkins, C. G. A.

Palmerston	1855–8	1855	13 Feb.	Clifford, C. C.
		1855	13 Feb.	Law, W.
		1856	25 Oct.	Barrington, C. G.
		1857	13 Nov.	Ponsonby, Hon. G. H. B.
		1858	11 Feb.	Ashley, Hon. A. E. M.
Derby	1858–9	1858	8 March	Bootle Wilbraham, Hon. E.
		1858	8 March	Drummond, M.
		1858	22 March	Talbot, Hon. W. P. M. C.
Palmerston	1859–65	1859	24 June	Ashley, Hon. A. E. M.
		1859	24 June	Barrington, C. G.
Russell	1865–6	1865	27 Dec.	Elliott, Hon. G. F. S.
		1865	27 Dec.	Barrington, C. G.
Derby	1866–8	1866	14 July	Barrington, Hon. G. W.
		1866	14 July	Murray, H. H.
		1867	25 June	Abbot, Hon. R. C. E.
		1867	20 Nov.	Cathcart, A.
Disraeli	1868	1868	5 March	Lowry Corry, M. W.
		1868	5 March	Fremantle, C. W.
Gladstone	1868	1868	24 Dec.	West, A. E.
		1868	24 Dec.	Gurdon, W. B.

Private Secretaries to
Chancellor of the Exchequer 1806–70

As an officer of the court of Exchequer the Chancellor had the services of a Principal and an Under Secretary. The office of the former was abolished in 1830; that of the latter in 1849.[1] Neither of these secretaries formed part of the Treasury office and they have therefore been excluded from these lists.

Before 1806 it is uncertain to what extent Chancellors employed Private Secretaries in their capacity as officers of the Treasury. The situation is complicated by the fact that for most of the eighteenth century the offices of First Lord and Chancellor were combined and that there was in consequence little opportunity for a settled convention to become established.[2] In 1806, however, provision was made for a regular salary of £300 for the Private Secretary to the Chancellor when the two offices were held by separate individuals.[3] Until 1852, with the exception of the years 1830 to 1839, it was the practice for Chancellors to select their Private Secretaries from amongst the Clerks of the Treasury. In 1852 the appointment of a second Private Secretary was authorised on account of the additional work falling upon Disraeli in his capacity as Leader of the House of Commons.[4] Thereafter both Disraeli and Gladstone, when holding the office of Chancellor, usually had two Private Secretaries, one being drawn from outside the Treasury. Until 1858 the second Private Secretary received no salary. In that year £150 was provided.[5] For Treasury Clerks the salaries were additional to their ordinary remuneration. Private Secretaries who were members of the House of Commons received no salary.

LIST OF APPOINTMENTS

Petty	1806–7	*No appointment traced*		
Perceval	1807–12	1811	21 June	Rosenhagen, A.
Vansittart	1812–23	1812	June	Rosenhagen, A.
		1815	19 May	Sargent, W.
		1818	31 July	Freeling, J. C.
Robinson	1823–7	1823	Feb.	Freeling, J. C.
		1826	Aug.	Drummond, E.

[1] *2nd Rept. of Treasury Committee of Enquiry into Fees 1837* (HC 1837 xliv), 357; M. S. Giuseppi, *Guide to the Contents of the Public Record Office*, 2nd ed. (London 1963), i, 65.
[2] Legge, who was Principal Secretary to Walpole as Chancellor of the Exchequer, also assisted him with Treasury business.
[3] TM 20 Dec. 1806 (T 29/88 pp. 504–5); this salary, originally paid out of the special service fund, was transferred to the estimates by TM 24 March 1835 (T 29/363 pp. 461–2).
[4] TM 18 Sept. 1852 (AB, iii, 194).
[5] TM 22 March 1858 (T 29/270 p. 602). By TM 20 May 1865 each of Gladstone's Private Secretaries was given a salary of £150 (AB, iv, 184–5).

Canning	1827	*See* Private Secretaries to First Lord		
Herries	1827–8	1827	13 Sept.	Spearman, A. Y.
Goulburn	1828–30	1828	8 Feb.	Walpole, E.
Althorp	1830–4	1830	31 Dec.	Wickham, H. L.
		1833	28 June	Drummond, T.
Peel	1834–5	*See* Private Secretaries to First Lord		
Spring Rice	1835–9	1835	April	Spring Rice, S. E.
		1838	30 Aug.	Bourke, R.
Baring	1839–41	1839	30 Aug.	Grey, C. S.
Goulburn	1841–6	1841	8 Sept.	Pemberton, C. R.
Wood	1846–52	1846	7 July	Arbuthnot, G.
		1850	15 Nov.	Stephenson, W. H.
		1851	12 Aug.	Cole, J. H.
Disraeli	1852	1852	2 March	Courtenay, T. P.
		1852	18 Sept.	Spearman, A. Y.
Gladstone	1852–5	1853	18 Jan.	Lawley, Hon. F. C.
		1853	18 Jan.	Wilbraham, R. W.
Lewis	1855–8	1855	16 March	Gordon, Sir A. C. D.
		1857	9 Jan.	Drummond, M.
Disraeli	1858–9	1858	22 March	Earle, R. A.
		1858	22 March	Ryan, C. L.
		1859	14 March	Clay, F. E.
Gladstone	1859–66	1859	24 June	Ryan, C. L.
		1860	Jan.	Stuart Wortley, Hon. J. F.
		1865	20 May	Gladstone, W. H.
		1865	20 May	Gurdon, W. B.
		1865	13 July	Gladstone, S. E.
Disraeli	1866–8	1866	14 July	Lowry Corry, M. W.
		1866	14 July	Fremantle, C. W.
Hunt	1868	1868	5 March	Murray, H. H.
Lowe	1868	1868	24 Dec.	Wilson, C. R.

Private Secretary to Third Lord 1868–9

During the period of its existence from 1868 to 1869 the office of Third Lord had attached to it a Private Secretary, drawn from amongst the Treasury Clerks, who received an additional allowance of £150 as such.[1]

APPOINTMENT

Stansfeld	1868–9	1868	24 Dec.	Welby, R. E.

[1] TM 28 Dec. 1868 (AB, iv, 336).

Private Secretaries to Secretaries c. 1812–1870

In the early nineteenth century, and probably from a much earlier period, it was the established practice for the Secretaries to select Treasury Clerks as their Private Secretaries. Before 1812 the Clerks in question appear to have received no salaries or allowances as such. From that year additional salaries of £150 were made available for those serving as Private Secretaries to the two Joint Secretaries and the Assistant Secretary.[1] The office of Private Secretary to the Assistant Secretary was abolished in 1856 but revived in 1859.[2] From 1857 the Parliamentary Secretary also had the services of an Assistant Private Secretary.[3]

LISTS OF APPOINTMENTS

PRIVATE SECRETARIES TO SENIOR (PARLIAMENTARY) SECRETARY

Arbuthnot	1809–23	By 1812	Bates, E.
Lushington	1823–7	1823 4 March	Arbuthnot, G.
Planta	1827–30	1827 April	Arbuthnot, G.
Ellice	1830–2	1830 31 Dec.	Arbuthnot, G.
Wood	1832–4	1832 14 Aug.	Arbuthnot, G.
Clerk	1834–5	1834 Dec.	Arbuthnot, G.
Stanley	1835–41	1835 8 May	Arbuthnot, G.
		1838 16 Feb.	Crafer, E. T.
Le Marchant	1841	*No appointment traced*	
Fremantle	1841–4	1841 8 Sept.	Crafer, E. T.
Young	1844–6	1844 21 May	Crafer, E. T.
Tufnell	1846–50	1846 7 July	Crafer, E. T.
Hayter	1850–2	1850 9 July	Crafer, E. T.
Forbes Mackenzie	1852–3	1852 5 March	Crafer, E. T.
Hayter	1853–8	1853 18 Jan.	Crafer, E. T.
		1854 8 Dec.	Fremantle, C. W.
		1857 26 Sept.	Stephenson, B. C. (*Assistant*)
Jolliffe	1858–9	1858 8 March	Fremantle, C. W.
		1858 March	Stephenson, B. C. (*Assistant*)
Brand	1859–66	1859 24 June	Fremantle, C. W.
		1859 24 June	Twiss, Q. W. F. (*Assistant*)
		1860 9 Jan.	Clay, F. E. (*Assistant*)

[1] TM 19 May 1812 (T 29/117 p. 293), 8 June 1813 (T 29/123 p. 354). The salaries, originally paid out of the special service fund, were transferred to the estimates by TM 24 March 1835 (T 29/363 pp. 461–2). Apart from Collier, a Clerk in the Commissariat and Private Secretary to the Assistant Secretary 1846–56, the Private Secretaries were invariably selected from amongst Clerks on the ordinary Treasury establishment.

[2] TM 4 July 1856 (T 29/564 p. 47), 12 May 1859 (T 29/475 pp. 250–1).

[3] TM 26 Sept. 1857 (AB, iii, 352); no additional allowance was attached to this post.

Taylor	1866–8	1866	14 July	Clement, R.
		1866	14 July	Hervey, G. W. (*Assistant*)
Noel	1868	1868	Nov.	Clement, R.
		1868	Nov.	Hervey, G. W. (*Assistant*)
Glyn	1868	1868	24 Dec.	Clay, F. E.
		1868	24 Dec.	Seymour, H. A. D. (*Assistant*)

PRIVATE SECRETARY TO JUNIOR (FINANCIAL) SECRETARY

Wharton	1809–14	By 1812		Woodford, C.
Lushington	1814–23	By 1817		Chinnery, G. R.
		By 1820		Reynolds, J. S.
Herries	1823–7	1823	11 March	Vincent, W. H.
		1824	24 Aug.	Pemberton, C. R.
Lewis	1827–8	1827	13 Sept.	Walpole, E.
Dawson	1828–30	1828	8 Feb.	Pemberton, C. R.
Spring Rice	1830–4	1830	31 Dec.	Speer, E.
Baring	1834	1834	10 June	Crafer, E. T.
Fremantle	1834–5	1835	13 Jan.	Courtenay, T. P.
Baring	1835–9	1835	8 May	Grey, C. S.
Gordon	1839–41	1839	18 Sept.	Shelley, S.
More O'Ferrall	1841	1841	9 June	Fitzgerald, F.
Clerk	1841–5	1841	8 Sept.	Courtenay, T. P.
Cardwell	1845–6	1845	4 Feb.	Rushworth, H.
		1845	23 May	Cole, J. H.
Parker	1846–9	1846	7 July	Wilbraham, R. W.
Hayter	1849–50	1849	22 May	Wilbraham, R. W.
Lewis	1850–2	1850	9 July	Wilbraham, R. W.
Hamilton	1852–3	1852	5 March	Law, W.
Wilson	1853–8	1853	18 Jan.	Fitzgerald, F.
		1853	20 Dec.	Law, W.
		1855	13 Feb.	Russell, G.
		1856	30 May	Wilson, C. R.
Hamilton	1858–9	1858	8 March	Wilson, C. R.
Northcote	1859	1859	14 March	Ryan, C. L.
Laing	1859–60	1859	24 June	Welby, R. E.
Peel	1860–5	1860	3 Nov.	Welby, R. E.
Childers	1865–6	1865	19 Aug.	Welby, R. E.
Hunt	1866–8	1866	14 July	Welby, R. E.
Sclater Booth	1868	1868	5 March	Welby, R. E.
Ayrton	1868–9	1868	24 Dec.	Ryder, G. L.
Stansfeld	1869	1869	10 Nov.	Welby, R. E.

PRIVATE SECRETARY TO ASSISTANT (PERMANENT) SECRETARY

Harrison	1805–26	By 1812		Compton, P. A.
		By 1817		Harrison, T. C.
		1825	5 Dec.	Harrison, M.

Hill	1826–8	1826	April	Harrison, M.
Stewart	1828–36	1828	4 July	Cole, J. G.
Spearman	1836–40	1836	11 Feb.	Cole, J. G.
		1838	16 Feb.	Arbuthnot, G.
Trevelyan	1840–59	1840	24 Jan.	Arbuthnot, G.
		1843	3 Feb.	Grey, C. S.
		1846	7 July	Collier, J. P.
Hamilton	1859–70	1859	12 May	Wilson, C. R.
		1868	24 Dec.	Broughton, V. D.
Lingen	1870	1870	1 Feb.	Broughton, V. D.

Office Keeper c. 1667–1870

The position of Office or Chamber Keeper first makes its appearance in September 1667.[1] Its holder was the senior of the subordinate officers of the Treasury and was responsible for the general custody of the building and the provision of the usual necessaries. In 1835, at the time of the reorganisation of the Treasury Messengers, the Office Keeper was made their Superintendent.[2] In 1852 the office was united to that of Housekeeper.[3]

In 1668 the salary attached to the office was fixed at £40.[4] In 1694 an allowance of £300 was substituted out of which the usual incidents had to be found.[5] In 1712 this was increased to £400 out of which fixed annual charges of £40 and £12 were payable to the 'Under Chamber Keeper' (Doorkeeper) and 'Cleaner' (Housekeeper).[6] In 1739 there was a further increase to £480.[7] In 1786 the then Office Keeper stated that his net income after deductions was £175.[8] In 1793 a salary of £200, clear of all deductions, was substituted. This was reduced to £150 in 1798.[9] It was fixed at £180 in 1822, at £220 in 1829 and at £180 in 1835.[10] Finally in 1855 a salary of £200 rising by annual increments of £5 to £250 was established for the combined offices of Office Keeper and Housekeeper.[11]

LIST OF APPOINTMENTS

By 1667		Segar, A.	1801	20 March	MacFarlane, J.
1694	27 Feb.	Wekett, W.	1802	13 Nov.	Mann, C.
1715	17 Oct.	Mann, T.	1812	24 April	Ready, W.
1717	29 July	King, C.	1822	8 Oct.	Emmans, T.
1721	4 April	Mann, T.	1829	3 April	Haines, J.
1752	5 March	Palmer, C.	1855	2 Feb.	Newman, J.
1769	14 Nov.	Schaller, B.	1859	2 June	Halligan, T.
1798	10 Jan.	Bullock, J.			

[1] *CTB*, ii, 84. Between 1694 and 1769 appointment was by Treasury constitution; thereafter it was by Treasury minute. For much of the eighteenth century the duties appear to have been executed by deputy. [2] TM 21 Aug. 1835 (T 29/368 pp. 481–7).

[3] TM 20 June 1851 (T 29/543 p. 639), 24 Feb. 1852 (T 29/546 pp. 553–4).

[4] TM 15 July 1668 (*CTB*, ii, 386). [5] Ibid. x, 514. [6] TM 27 Nov. 1712 (ibid. xxvi, 87).

[7] T 53/39 p. 204. [8] *2nd Rept. on Fees*, 76–7.

[9] Order in council 21 June 1793 (*15th Rept. on Finance*, 288); TM 22 June 1793 (T 29/66 p. 22), 10 Jan. 1798 (T 29/71 p. 537).

[10] TM 8 Oct. 1822 (T 29/214 p. 144), 3 April 1829 (T 29/292 p. 44), 7 April 1835 (T 29/364 pp. 148–9). [11] TM 2 Feb. 1855 (T 29/558 p. 458).

Housekeeper (Necessary Woman) c. 1712–1851

The office of Housekeeper, which was invariably held by a woman, had its origin in the position of Cleaner which is first mentioned in 1712. It appears in the establishment list of 1715 under the designation Sweeper.[1] The right of appointment probably rested originally with the Office Keeper. In 1728 the Board was concerning itself with the succession to the office which was then known as that of Necessary Woman.[2] Although the term Housekeeper was in general use in the latter part of the eighteenth century to describe holders of the office it was not until 1805 that it was employed in the minutes.[3] The office was united to that of Office Keeper in 1852.[4]

The salary attached to the office in 1712 was £12 payable by the Office Keeper.[5] In 1786 the Housekeeper had the use of apartments in the Treasury and an income from various sources of £131 8s out of which she paid two servants and other expenses.[6] In 1793 a salary of £130 clear of all deductions was substituted. This was reduced to £100 in 1799.[7] It was fixed at £130 in 1805, at £180 in 1810 and at £100 in 1835.[8]

LIST OF APPOINTMENTS

By 1712	Williams, E.	1774	18 Nov.	Appleby, J.
By 1726	Barnsley, —	1788	17 Jan.	Creswell, A. M.
By 1742	Shepherd, M.	1799	18 July	Thorpe, M.
1768	25 Aug.	Foye, E. M.	1835	7 April	Haines, M.

[1] TM 27 Nov. 1712 (*CTB*, xxvi, 87), 17 Oct. 1715 (ibid. xxix, 297).
[2] TM 27 Aug. 1728 (T 29/26 p. 140); appointments were made by Treasury minute from 1768.
[3] TM 19 Aug. 1805 (T 29/85 p. 351).
[4] TM 20 June 1851 (T 29/543 p. 639), 24 Feb. 1852 (T 29/546 pp. 553–4).
[5] TM 27 Nov. 1712 (*CTB*, xxvi, 87).
[6] *2nd Rept. on Fees*, 80.
[7] Order in council 21 June 1793 (*15th Rept. on Finance*, 288); TM 22 June 1793 (T 29/66 p. 22), 18 July 1799 (T 29/74 p. 491).
[8] TM 19 Aug. 1805 (T 29/85 p. 351), 7 April 1835 (T 29/364 pp. 148–9). For servants, see also TM 7 July 1818 (T 29/163 p. 122).

Housekeeper of Levée Rooms 1762–1814

The apartments known as the Levée Rooms, which had been occupied by the office of the Secretary of State for the Northern Department, were transferred to the Treasury about 1762. In that year the then Bag Carrier was appointed their Housekeeper. From 1765 until its discontinuance in 1814 the office was held by women.[1]

The salary attached to the office in 1762 was £40. By 1794 it had been increased to £50.[2]

LIST OF APPOINTMENTS

1762	21 May	Shaw, E.	1787	15 Nov.	Sparry, E.
1765	10 July	Shaw, E.	1793	25 July	Arden, E.

[1] TM 21 May 1762 (T 29/34 p. 286); T 41/4.   [2] TM 21 May 1762 (T 29/34 p. 286); T 41/2.

Doorkeeper c. 1712–1870 and Chief Doorkeeper 1804–14

The term Doorkeeper was first applied to a member of the Treasury staff in 1715. The office itself was, however, probably of earlier origin since its holder at that date had been employed in the Treasury from at least 1690, being described in 1712 as Under Chamber Keeper.[1] From at least 1763 the office was a sinecure so far as the principal was concerned, the duties being executed by deputy.[2] In 1798 the Board insisted that the functions were performed in person.[3] In 1804 the then Doorkeeper was promoted to the position of Chief Doorkeeper but this office was discontinued on his death in 1814.[4] At the time of the reorganisation of the Messengers in 1835 the Doorkeeper was placed in the first class, ranking after the Messenger of the Chamber.[5]

The salary attached to the office of Doorkeeper in 1712 was £40 payable by the Office Keeper.[6] It was fixed at £70 in 1798 and at £90 in 1802.[7] From 1835 the Doorkeeper received the salary of a First Class Messenger.[8] The salary of the Chief Doorkeeper was fixed at £100 in 1804.[9]

LISTS OF APPOINTMENTS

DOORKEEPER

By 1712		Bailey, W.	1804	8 May	Hatfield, G.
1727	10 May	Jones, J.	1814	22 Nov.	Davis, R.
By 1736		Barnsley, S.	1835	21 Aug.	Morten, L.
1736	27 Jan.	Bryant, E.	1856	27 May	Worsfold, W.
1742	4 Feb.	Kitchin, J.	1861	10 Jan.	Maddams, G.
1763	12 April	Potter, H.	1862	21 Jan.	Bawcutt, J.
1798	10 Jan.	Archilarius, P.	1865	11 April	Foster, T.

CHIEF DOORKEEPER

1804   8 May   Archilarius, P.

[1] TM 27 Nov. 1712 (*CTB*, xxvi, 87), 17 Oct. 1715 (ibid. xxix, 297).   [2] *2nd Rept. on Fees*, 80.
[3] TM 10 Jan. 1798 (T 29/71 p. 265).
[4] TM 8 May 1804 (T 29/83 pp. 36–7), 6 Sept. 1814 (T 29/131 pp. 104–5).
[5] TM 21 Aug. 1835 (T 29/368 pp. 481–7).   [6] TM 27 Nov. 1712 (*CTB*, xxvi, 87).
[7] TM 10 Jan. 1798 (T 29/71 p. 265), 16 July 1802 (T 29/79 p. 265).
[8] TM 21 Aug. 1835 (T 29/368 pp. 481–7).   [9] TM 8 May 1804 (T 29/83 pp. 36–7).

Bag Carrier c. 1714–70

The term Bag Carrier denoted one of the Treasury Messengers whose particular function was to attend the Secretaries at the House of Commons. It was first used in 1715.[1] However, the individual holding the office at this date had entered the employment of the Treasury in the previous year and it is likely that he had predecessors with similar duties.[2] The office ceased to have a separate existence in 1770 when it was conferred upon the then Bookranger. The two posts remained united thereafter.

The salary attached to the office in 1714 was £20. It was raised to £30 in 1725 and to £40 in 1737.[3]

LIST OF APPOINTMENTS

1714		Empsom, W.	1747	1 Oct.	Shaw, E.
1737	29 Dec.	Kemmeter, C.	1770	12 Jan.	Watson, W.

[1] TM 17 Oct. 1715 (*CTB*, xxix, 297), 21 Oct. 1725 (T 29/25 p. 122).

[2] It is possible that the salary which Empsom received from the civil list after 1714 was in continuation of that paid from the secret service to Cohoon (1689–98), R. Green (1698–1702) and E. Williams (1703–14).

[3] *CTB*, xxix, 628; TM 21 Oct. 1725 (T 29/25 p. 122), 29 Dec. 1737 (*CTBP 1735–8*, 354).

Bookranger c. 1717–1870

The office of Bookranger, known at first more generally as that of Assistant to the Chamber Keeper and Messengers, appears to have been created about 1717.[1] In 1770 the then holder of the office was also appointed Bag Carrier and the two posts remained united thereafter.[2] At the time of the reorganisation of the Messengers in 1835 they were discontinued. Later in the same year provision was made for one of the Second Class Messengers to carry out the functions formerly undertaken by the Bookranger.[3] In 1853 the post was revived as a distinct office and given the rank of a First Class Messenger.[4]

The salary attached to the office in 1717 was £20. It was raised to £40 in 1724 and to £50 in 1780.[5] From 1770 to 1793 the Bookranger also received the Bag Carrier's salary of £40. The salary for both offices was fixed at £140 in 1793 and reduced to £100 in 1801.[6] Between 1822 and 1831 the post was held by one of the Messengers with an additional allowance of £30.[7] From 1853 the Bookranger received the salary of a First Class Messenger.[8]

LIST OF APPOINTMENTS

1716–17		Chetwynd, R.	1820	4 April	Emmans, T.
1724		Shepherd, J.	1822	8 Oct.	Greenwood, C.
1745		Burton, L.	1824	5 March	Cleaver, T.
1747	10 Nov.	Gardiner, E.	1831	18 Feb.	Weller, J.
1766	19 April	Watson, W.			
1801	27 May	Mann, C.	1853	12 Aug.	Foot, G.
1802	13 Nov.	Carter, T.	1859	2 June	Bailey, J.
1811	1 Feb.	Pettit, T.	1868	24 Oct.	Biggs. R.

[1] *CTB*, xxxi, 211.   [2] For the functions of these offices, see *2nd Rept. on Fees*, 79–80.
[3] TM 21 Aug. 1835 (T 29/368 pp. 481–7), 20 Oct. 1835 (T 29/370 p. 286).
[4] TM 12 Aug. 1853 (T 29/552 p. 353).   [5] *CTB*, xxxi, 211; T 53/31 p. 350; T 53/54 p. 130.
[6] Order in council 21 June 1793 (*15th Rept. on Finance*, 288); TM 22 June 1793 (T 29/66 p. 22,) 27 May 1801 (T 29/77 p. 472).   [7] TM 8 Oct. 1822 (T 29/214 p. 144).
[8] TM 12 Aug. 1853 (T 29/552 p. 353).

Messengers of the Receipt and Messengers to First Lord 1660–1870; Office Keeper to First Lord 1836–70

The Messengers of the Receipt were four in number and were appointed by the crown by letters patent under the great seal, for life from 1660 to 1689[1] and during pleasure thereafter. They were authorised by their patents to exercise their functions by deputy. Their offices formed part of the establishment of the Receipt of the Exchequer. As such they were subordinate to the Treasurer and, when the Treasury was in commission, came under the nominal authority of the Board.[2] The Messengers of the Receipt and their deputies were included in the Treasury establishment list of 1715 but they proved of little practical utility and the Board was obliged to make other arrangements to secure an adequate messengerial service.[3] In the eighteenth and early nineteenth centuries such functions as they did perform appear to have been undertaken for the First Lord rather than for the Board as a whole.[4]

In 1831 the right of appointment to these offices passed from the crown to the Treasury and in 1836 the Messengers were reorganised. They were obliged to exercise their duties in person and were placed under a Superintendent who bore the additional title of Office Keeper to the First Lord.[5] Thereafter the designation 'Messenger of the Receipt' passed out of currency being replaced by that of 'Messenger to the First Lord'.

The remuneration received by the Messengers of the Receipt was derived from a variety of sources. As officers of the receipt they received salaries of £60 0s 4½d in 1715[6] and a total income of £232 7s 10d in 1786.[7] During the eighteenth century the allowances which had originally been provided for additional Messengers were attached to their offices.[8] In 1793 these allowances were discontinued.[9] In 1836 salaries of £150 were provided for the Messengers to the First Lord. At the same time £200 was provided for the Superintendent and Office Keeper.[10] This was increased to £220 in 1860.[11]

---

[1] With the exception of the grant to Oneby (1668) which was during pleasure.

[2] For the functions of the Messengers of the Receipt in the later seventeenth century, see Baxter, *Treasury*, 210–11.

[3] For an unsuccessful attempt to place the Messengers on a more satisfactory footing, see TM 8 March and 8 Aug. 1783 (T 29/53 pp. 213–14; T 29/54 pp. 271–2).

[4] Certain of the Messengers were in the personal service of the First Lord; for example, J. Wright (1732) (*Gent. Mag.* (1732), ii, 10) and Betty (1801) (ibid. (1805), lxxv (1), 588).

[5] Treasury warrant 7 April 1831 (T 54/56 p. 84); TM 8 Feb. 1831 (T 29/314 pp. 165–6), 19 Jan. 1836 (T 29/373 pp. 347–51).

[6] TM 17 Oct. 1715 (*CTB*, xxix, 297–8).　　　　　　[7] *2nd Rept. on Fees*, 162–3.

[8] The allowances were in the first instance granted to J. Wright in 1737 (T 53/39 p. 204), Harrison in 1770 (T 53/51 p. 409) and Walker and Ross in 1772 (T 53/52 p. 63).

[9] TM 22 June 1793 (T 29/66 p. 22) following a recommendation of the Commissioners on Fees 1786 (*2nd Rept. on Fees*, 58).

[10] TM 19 Jan. 1836 (T 29/373 pp. 347–51).　　　　[11] TM 23 Feb. 1860 (AB, iv, 95–6).

LISTS OF APPOINTMENTS

MESSENGERS OF RECEIPT AND MESSENGERS TO FIRST LORD

By 1660	{ Benbow, T.		1749	21 Nov.	Walker, J.
	{ Benbow, R.		1762	21 May	Harrison, T.
1660	18 July	Kipps, T.	1765	29 June	Ross, W.
1660	3 Aug.	Sturgeon, J.	1767	25 Feb.	Schaller, B.
1662	13 Nov.	Benbow, T.	1769	27 Nov.	Gibbons, T.
1665	7 Dec.	Seymour, E.	1783	12 Sept.	Bailey, A.
1668	14 Feb.	Vine, G.	1791	14 Dec.	Carter, C.
1668	18 Nov.	Oneby, G.	1798	11 Dec.	Wood, J.
1674	5 Sept.	Wright, N.	1799	9 Nov.	Croft, J.
1674	5 Sept.	Wright, E.	1801	23 May	Andrews, T.
1674	5 Sept.	King, J.	1801	23 May	Betty, R.
1674	5 Sept.	King, B.	1802	11 Nov.	Cotterell, S.
By 1689		Vincent, G.	1805	22 July	Salter, R.
1689	30 July	Barrett, W.	1812	31 Oct.	Barfoot, H.
1689	30 July	Taylor, J.	1825	29 Sept.	Ruffe, W.
1689	30 July	Wekett, W.	1836	20 May	Masser, T. W.
1689	29 Aug.	Richards, J.	1836	1 June	Appleton, T.
1690	5 Nov.	Clerke, S.	1836	25 July	Harvey, R.
1698	22 Jan.	Barrett, J.	1836	12 Aug.	Kelly, T.
1718	14 Feb.	Lowther, T.	c. 1836		Tyler, J.
1723	22 May	Grantham, E.	1838	12 April	Colburn, J.
1732	23 Feb.	Wright, J.	1838	2 Aug.	Samways, J.
1742	11 Feb.	Oswald, G.	1839	12 Feb.	Fitness, J.
1742	12 Feb.	Jones, J.	1847	19 March	Johnson, C.
1742	16 Dec.	Sheen, J.	c. 1855		Doe, G.
1743	4 Aug.	Oldnal, J.	1859	9 May	Hollier, S.
1746	29 March	Dubourg, P.			

SUPERINTENDENT AND OFFICE KEEPER TO FIRST LORD

c. 1836	Foggo, P.	1839	12 Feb.	Appleton, T.

Messenger of the Chamber 1660–1870 and City Messenger 1827–35

The Messenger of the Chamber was in origin one of the corps of such Messengers which formed part of the Royal Household. From the Restoration the Messenger in question was attached to the Treasury on a permanent basis. The right of appointment rested with the Treasury[1] although until 1702 the connection with the Household was maintained to the extent that, on entering office, successive messengers were sworn in by the Lord Chamberlain in pursuance of a Treasury Warrant.[2] During the later seventeenth century the Messenger of the Chamber employed a deputy but for most of the eighteenth century he appears to have been a working official.[3] In 1827 part of the duties of the office were assigned to a distinct City Messenger.[4] At the time of the reorganisation of the Messengers in 1835 the latter office was abolished and the Messenger of the Chamber was placed in the first class, ranking after the Messenger of the Registry.[5] In 1865 he was promoted to first place and in 1868 the office was made distinct from the messengerial structure.[6]

The remuneration originally attached to the office of Messenger of the Chamber amounted to £121 13s 4d a year composed of two separate salaries of 3s 4d a day, one paid out of the customs and the other out of the civil list. From 1721 a further salary was paid from the civil list and carried on the Office Keeper's bill. This was at first £20 but was raised to £30 in 1780.[7] In 1793 the payments from the civil list ceased and a salary of £60 from the fee fund was substituted.[8] In 1827 the payment from the customs was discontinued and the Messenger of the Chamber was accorded a single salary of £100 paid wholly by the Treasury.[9] This was raised to £120 in 1835. In 1865 a progressive scale was established beginning at £120 and rising by annual increments of £5 to £150. In 1868 the starting level was increased to £130.[10] The salary of the City Messenger was fixed at £100 in 1827.[11]

LISTS OF APPOINTMENTS
MESSENGER OF THE CHAMBER

c. 1660	Reeve, J.	1663	5 Dec.	Gregory, R.
By 1663	Greene, T.	1677	21 July	Langwith, J.

[1] Between 1663 and 1807 appointment was by Treasury constitution; thereafter by Treasury minute.

[2] *CTB*, v, 688; ibid. viii, 12; ibid. ix, 166, 1865; ibid. x, 512; ibid. xvii, 21.

[3] *2nd Rept. on Fees*, 79.   [4] TM 2 Oct. 1827 (T 29/274 pp. 41–2).

[5] TM 21 Aug. 1835 (T 29/368 pp. 481–7).

[6] TM 11 April 1865 (AB, iv, 178–80), 27 April 1868 (ibid. 201–5).

[7] T 53/28 p. 369; T 53/54 p. 130; *2nd Rept. on Fees*, 79.

[8] Order in council 21 June 1793 (*15th Rept. on Finance*, 288); TM 22 June 1793 (T 29/66 p. 22).

[9] TM 2 Oct. 1827 (T 29/274 pp. 41–2).

[10] TM 21 Aug. 1835 (T 29/368 pp. 481–7), 11 April 1865 (AB, iv, 178–90), 27 April 1868 (ibid. 201–5).   [11] TM 2 Oct. 1827 (T 29/274 pp. 41–2).

1692	14 Oct.	Wekett, W.	1807	27 July	Woodger, T.
1694	27 Feb.	Thurkettle, J.	1827	2 Oct.	Haines, J.
1720	4 Oct.	Thurkettle, T.	1829	3 April	Child, J.
1735	4 March	Jones, J.	1835	21 Aug.	Harvey, R.
1742	10 Feb.	Bryant, E.	1836	25 July	Halligan, T.
1762	30 April	Barnsley, W. W.	1853	12 Aug.	Grove, J.
1765	14 June	Gibbons, T.	1854	11 Aug.	Boddy, J.
1769	14 Nov.	Barnsley, S. J.	1863	24 April	Long, C.
1795	5 July	Wood, T.	1863	27 May	Ford, B.

CITY MESSENGER

1827	2 Oct.	Bowman, P.	1830	23 April	Halligan, T.

Messengers 1660–1870

At the Restoration the Treasury had nominally at its disposal the four Messengers of the Receipt and the Messenger of the Chamber. These officials appear usually to have exercised their functions by deputy and to have failed to provide an adequate service. As a result the Treasury was obliged to employ additional Messengers. At first these were not fixed in number but from 1689 to 1714 there were two receiving salaries which finally became fixed at £20, one paid out of the civil list and the other out of the secret service. The recipient of the former was usually the deputy Messenger of the Chamber while the post to which the latter was attached appears to have been the same as that known after 1714 as the office of Bag Carrier.

Between 1714 and 1793 the salaries of several of the subordinate staff were carried on the civil list. Apart from those attached to the posts of Office Keeper, Bag Carrier, Bookranger and Messenger of the Chamber, a varying number of such salaries were made available for Letter Carriers or Messengers. Beginning at one in 1729 they were increased to two in 1736, to three in 1758 and to five in 1772.[1] The salaries themselves, originally £20, were raised to £40 in 1736 and to £50 in 1780.[2] While they had at first been intended for working Messengers, the salaries came in the course of time to be attached to the offices of the four Messengers of the Receipt and the deputy Door-keeper who regarded them simply as additional perquisites.[3]

In 1793 these salaries were discontinued and provision was made for the employment of a distinct body of Messengers for deliveries paid at a weekly rate out of the fee fund.[4] These Messengers were at first four in number. They were increased to five in 1809, to six in 1817 and to seven in 1824. They were reduced to five in 1831.[5] The employment of a Messenger by the Revenue Department was authorised in 1809 and from 1822 a former Office Keeper was retained on the establishment as an extra Messenger.[6] The remuneration of these Messengers was originally fixed at £1 1s a week. This was raised to £1 5s in 1799 and to £1 7s in 1803.[7]

From at least 1771 it was also the practice to employ Messengers who were paid weekly out of the incidents. In 1786 there were three such Messengers, two of whom were attached to the Joint Secretaries on a permanent basis.[8] In 1806 the Assistant Secretary was authorised to appoint a Messenger.[9] In 1808 the remuneration of the Messengers to the Secretaries was fixed at £100 a year each.[10]

In 1835 a comprehensive reorganisation of the subordinate staff took place. They

---

[1] TM 30 Sept. 1729 (*CTBP 1729–30*, 145); T 53/38 p. 371; T 53/46 p. 10; T 53/52 p. 63.
[2] TM 30 Sept. 1729 (*CTBP 1729–30*, 145); T 53/38 p. 371; T 53/54 p. 130.
[3] *2nd Rept. on Fees*, 77–80.
[4] Order in council 21 June 1793 (*15th Rept. on Finance*, 288); TM 22 June 1793 (T 29/66 p. 22).
[5] TM 8 Dec. 1809 (T 29/103 p. 411), 28 March 1817 (T 29/147 p. 632); T 41/4–8.
[6] TM 8 Dec. 1809 (T 29/103 p. 411), 8 Oct. 1822 (T 29/214 p. 143).
[7] TM 22 June 1793 (T 29/66 p. 22), 8 Nov. 1799 (T 29/75 p. 186), 10 Aug. 1803 (T 29/81 p. 362).
[8] *2nd Rept. on Fees*, 80–1.　　　　　　　　[9] TM 27 March 1806 (T 29/86 p. 338).
[10] TM 16 Dec. 1808 (T 29/98 pp. 159–60); in 1822 these salaries were transferred from the incidents to the fee fund (T 41/5).

were integrated into a unified structure, placed under the supervision of the Office Keeper and divided into three classes. Provision was made for a first class of three consisting of the Messenger of the Registry, the Messenger of the Chamber and the Doorkeeper with salaries of £120 each; a second class of six Messengers for deliveries with salaries of £100 each from whom were selected the three Messengers to the Secretaries who received additional allowances of £20 while serving as such; and a third class of four Messengers for deliveries with salaries of £85 each.[11] In 1842 a temporary increase of one in each class took place when the three Messengers attached to the office of Paymaster of Civil Services were absorbed into the structure. In 1853 the first class was increased to four to accommodate the Bookranger. In 1856 it was further increased to five on the appointment of a Superintendent of the Messengers on the upper floor of the Treasury.[12]

In 1868 the subordinate staff was again reorganised. The post of Messenger of the Chamber was recognised as an office distinct from the other Messengers. Provision was made for the first class of Messengers to consist of four—the Superintendent of the Upper Floor, the Messenger of the Paper Room (Registry), the Bookranger and the Doorkeeper—with a salary scale of £120 rising by annual increments of £5 to £130; for the second class to consist of five Messengers for deliveries with a scale of £100 rising by annual increments of £2 10s to £110; and for the third class to consist of three Messengers for deliveries with a scale of £85 rising by annual increments of £2 10s to £100. The Messengers to the Secretaries were to be selected from the second or third class and to receive an additional £20 while serving as such.[13]

LIST OF APPOINTMENTS

1660	Smeaton, T.	1771	Clubb, G.
1669	Teare, E.	1777	Carter, J.
1683	Lowndes, W.	1780　Nov.	Williams, J.
1683	Wekett, W.	1788	Johnston, T.
1689	Cohoon, M.	1791　12 Aug.	Hare, R.
By 1690	{ Bailey, W.	1793	Knell, T.
	Peirce, J.	1793	Watford, J.
1692	Hurst, J.	1793	Hatwell, J.
1698	Green, R.	By 1796	Fazan, L.
1700	Farra, J.	By 1802	Cleaver, T.
1703	Williams, E.		{ Fencock, D.
1729　30 Sept.	Richards, W.	By 1809	Smith, S.
c. 1735	Barnsley, S.		Reymann, J. F.
1736	Brooks, J.		Brock, J.
1758	Barnsley, W. W.	1809　12 Dec.	Emmans, T.
c. 1761	Barnsley, S. J.	c. 1810	Muckworthy, J.

[11] TM 21 Aug. 1835 (T 29/368 pp. 481–7). The office of Messenger to the Registry had been created by TM 3 Feb. 1835 (T 29/362 pp. 55–9).
[12] TM 29 March 1842 (T 29/447 pp. 579–84), 12 Aug. 1853 (T 29/552 pp. 353–4), 1 Oct. 1856 (AB, iii, 322–3).
[13] TM 27 April 1868 (AB, iv, 301–5).

1814	5 April	Greenwood, C.	1840	9 March	Scorey, J.
1817	28 March	Halligan, T.	1840	3 Nov.	Long, C.
1820	6 March	Morten, L.	1841	30 June	Bailey, J.
By 1822		Taylor, T.	1842	29 March	Scott, C.
1822	6 March	Rose, E.	1842	29 March	Broster, J.
1822	8 Oct.	Ready, W.	1842	29 March	Long, G.
1822	18 Nov.	Manning, W.	1844	27 Sept.	Ford, B.
1824	5 March	Minet, J. W.	1852	24 Dec.	Biggs, R.
1824	8 March	Richards, J.	1853	16 Sept.	Purvis, R.
1824	10 June	Weller, J.	1854	16 June	Davidson, W.
1824	5 July	Harvey, J.	1854	18 Aug.	Bawcutt, J.
1829	29 Jan.	Mitchell, S.	1856	2 Oct.	Maddams, G.
1829	15 Dec.	Worsfold, W.	1856	15 Dec.	Benn, G.
1831	18 Feb.	Oliver, J.	1859	2 June	Gabbitas, J. R.
1834	22 July	Foot, G.	1860	13 April	Fisher, D.
1835	3 Feb.	Bowman, P.	1861	30 April	Hannam, W.
1835	20 April	Boddy, J.	1862	3 Feb.	Stafford, J.
1835	20 Oct.	Bradley, D.	1863	25 May	Foster, T.
1836	15 March	Kelly, T.	1863	10 June	Dawson, C.
1836	29 July	Tyler, J.	1864	23 April	Forward, G.
1836	12 Aug.	Lowman, J.	1865	15 Feb.	Rossiter, W.
1836	12 Aug.	Grove, J.	1865	26 April	Hughes, T.
1836	22 Aug.	Rose, E.	1865	26 June	Maguire, R. H.
1837	25 May	Burrell, W.	1866	14 Feb.	O'Shaughnessy, J.
1837	13 Oct.	Fitness, J.	1866	4 July	Rogers, G.
1839	12 Feb.	Whiting, W.	1868	25 Aug.	Hambling, H.
1839	12 Feb.	Young, T.			

Messengers to Chancellor of the Exchequer 1836–70

Under an arrangement of considerable antiquity there were two Messengers attending the Chancellor of the Exchequer. Originally they appear to have been attached to him in his capacity as an officer of the Exchequer court rather than of the Treasury. In 1836, however, they were placed on a new footing and thereafter formed part of the Treasury establishment. In 1868 the appointment of a third Messenger was authorised.[1]

In 1836 the salaries were fixed at £150 and £140 for the Senior and Junior Messengers then holding the offices and £140 and £130 for subsequent appointments. It was the practice for the Junior Messenger to be promoted to the senior position when it was vacated. In 1868 the salary for the third Messenger was fixed at £120.[2]

LIST OF APPOINTMENTS

1820	22 Nov.	Grant, J.	1860	2 July	Gabbitas, H.
1825	29 April	Parsons, E.	1864	23 Nov.	Turner, T.
1841	1 Jan.	Winter, J.	1868	18 Feb.	Foot, J.[3]
1845	1 April	Humphreys, J.			

[1] TM 19 Jan. 1836 (T 29/373 pp. 347–51), 13 Jan. 1868 (AB, iv, 296).   [2] Ibid.
[3] Third Messenger.

Serjeant at Arms 1660–1832

The Serjeant at Arms attending the Treasurer or Commissioners of the Treasury was appointed by the crown by letters patent under the great seal.[1] The office was granted for life until 1684 and during pleasure thereafter. While it involved its holders in real duties until 1689, it appears to have become virtually a sinecure soon after this date. After having been temporarily discontinued between 1782 and 1790 it was abolished in 1832.[2]

The remuneration attached to the office was originally 1s a day salary and 1s 3d a day board wages (£41 1s 3d a year). In 1664 these sums were raised to 3s and 2s 6d respectively (£100 7s 6d a year).[3] They continued at this level until the abolition of the office.

LIST OF APPOINTMENTS

1660	13 July	Warner, T.	1702	20 Aug.	Ryley, R.
1663		Stephens, F.	1706	28 Feb.	Ryley, P.
1674	6 Nov.	Ramsey, J.	1733	2 March	Allin, Sir T.
1684	25 March	{ Ramsey, J. / Ball, H.	1765	30 Sept.	Brougham, H.
			1810	10 Aug.	Murray, D. R.
1684	27 Nov.	Ryley, P.			

[1] For the origin of the office, see grant of 10 Nov. 1625 to Edward Dendy (C 66/2360). For its duties, see Baxter, *Treasury*, 207–10; T 90/16 pp. 1729–30.
[2] TM 3 Aug. 1789 (T 29/60 p. 536), 29 Jan. 1790 (T 29/61 pp. 347–8), 27 Jan. 1832 (T 29/325 p. 566).   [3] Letters patent to Stephens of 3 June 1664 (C 66/3061).

Solicitors and Assistant Solicitors 1660–1870

There were formerly two distinct offices of Solicitor of the Treasury.[1] The first, known as that of Solicitor for negotiating and looking after the affairs of the Treasury, dated from the Restoration. The duties of the office were defined in 1661.[2] From the time of the establishment of the second solicitorship in 1696 they were confined to business outside Westminster Hall.[3] Probably from 1716 and certainly from 1744 the office was a sinecure.[4] It was abolished in 1800.[5] From 1675 until the abolition of the office the Solicitor received a salary of £200.[6] From time to time he was assisted by a deputy or assistant but this was not a regular appointment and, except in the case of P. Burton (1685–9), it received only a limited degree of official recognition.

The office of the second Solicitor, known as that of Solicitor for the affairs of the Treasury, was established in 1696. The division of duties between the two Solicitors made in that year assigned to this office the business in Westminster Hall.[7] Probably from 1716 its holder was the sole effective Solicitor and conducted all Treasury business. In 1786 it was his function to undertake work for the Secretaries of State and the Attorney General as well.[8] In the early nineteenth century he began to be employed by other government agencies and in 1842 he was made directly responsible for the work of thirteen departments in addition to the Treasury.[9]

A regular salary was attached to this office from 1700. Beginning at £500, it was increased in 1755 to £1000.[10] In 1794 it was further increased to £2000 and at the same time certain earlier allowances were discontinued and the Solicitor was forbidden to engage in private practice without the consent of the Board.[11] In the early nineteenth century he made charges for work undertaken for departments outside his immediate responsibility. Later he was accorded an annual allowance of £850 for these services in addition to his basic salary.[12] In 1851 the salary was fixed at £2000. In 1866 it was provided that it should rise after five years to £2500.[13]

Although the position of assistant to the second Solicitor was recognised between 1722 and 1730 it was not until 1746 that it was established on a regular basis. It was

---

[1] For the earlier history of the Solicitors, see Baxter, *Treasury*, 241–55.

[2] *CTB*, i, 215–16. Appointments were made by Treasury constitution.

[3] TM 1 Sept. 1696 (ibid. xi, 53).

[4] *2nd Rept. on Fees*, 75. There is no evidence that any of the occupants of the office from Horneck onwards undertook any duties.

[5] On the death of H. V. Jones, in conformity with the Order in council 21 June 1793 (*15th Rept. on Finance*, 288).

[6] *CTB*, iv, 389. The salary was paid from the civil list.

[7] TM 1 Sept. 1696 (ibid. xi, 53). Appointments were made by Treasury constitution from 1761 to 1817; at other times usually by Treasury minute.   [8] *2nd Rept. on Fees*, 75–6.

[9] *Rept. on Misc. Expenditure*, pt. i, 527–31; TM 18 March 1842 (T 29/447 pp. 378–86).

[10] *CTB*, xvi, 285; ibid. xviii, 120; TM 19 Feb. 1755 (T 29/32 p. 277). Until 1775 the salary was paid directly from the civil list; in that year it was transferred to law charges.

[11] TM 14 June 1794 (T 29/66 p. 529).

[12] TM 29 Jan. 1833 (T 29/337 pp. 383–5); *Rept. on Misc. Expenditure*, pt. i, 528.

[13] TM 9 Dec. 1851 (T 29/545 p. 511), 3 July 1866 (AB, iv, 229–31).

discontinued in 1794 but revived in 1811.[14] The salary paid to the Assistant Solicitor from 1722 to 1730 was £200. In 1746 it was fixed at £100. It was increased to £250 in 1766 and to £400 in 1781.[15] In 1811 it was fixed at £1200 rising after five years to £1500. Until 1842 the Assistant Solicitor received an additional allowance of £400 for work undertaken for departments outside the immediate responsibility of the office.[16]

Originally the Solicitor was entirely responsible for the employment of such clerical and other assistance as he required. From 1806 he was served by a permanent establishment of subordinate officials paid out of public funds. These subordinate officials have not been included in the lists.[17]

LISTS OF APPOINTMENTS

SOLICITOR (1)[18]

By 1661		Rushworth, J.	1696	11 Sept.	Baker, H.
By 1673		Turner, Sir. W.	1716	18 Jan.	Horneck, P.
1676	15 July	Ramsey, J.	1728	22 Oct.	Roome, E.
1679	8 April	Lloyd, T.	1729	12 Dec.	Jones, C. V.
1685	2 March	Burton, P.	1737	4 Aug.	Hayward, C.
1689	20 April	Smith, A.	1744	9 Aug.	Jones, H. V.

SOLICITOR (2)

1696	Sept.	Baker, N.	1775	28 March	Chamberlayne, W.
1700	15 Oct.	Borrett, W.	1794	1 July	White, J.
1715	31 May	Cracherode, A.	1806	28 March	Litchfield, H. C.
1730	24 Dec.	Paxton, N.	1818	1 Jan.	Maule, G.
1742	27 July	Sharpe, J.	1851	30 Dec.	Reynolds, H. R.
1756	4 Nov.	Webb, P. C.	1866	5 June	Greenwood, J.
1765	30 July	Nuthall, T.			

ASSISTANT SOLICITOR

1679	8 April	Burton, P.	1811	21 Dec.	Hobhouse, H.
1722	20 Dec.	Paxton, N.	1817	2 July	Maule, G.
			1818	1 Jan.	Bourchier, C.
1746	29 April	Leheup, T.	1842	22 Nov.	Reynolds, H. R.
1747	17 Nov.	Wright, R.	1851	30 Dec.	Greenwood, J.
1750	30 May	Francis, T.	1866	19 June	Stephenson,
1781	1 Aug.	White, J.			A. F. W. K.

[14] T 54/30 p. 396; T 54/34 pp. 396–7; TM 29 Nov. 1811 (T 29/114 pp. 284–5). Appointments were made by Treasury warrant to the Solicitor from 1722 to 1781 and by Treasury constitution from 1811 to 1818. Subsequent appointments were by Treasury minute.

[15] T 54/30 p. 396; T 54/34 pp. 396–7; T 54/40 p. 158; T 54/43 p. 391. The salary was paid by the Solicitor out of law charges.

[16] TM 29 Nov. 1811 (T 29/114 pp. 284–5), 18 March 1842 (T 29/447 pp. 378–86).

[17] The development of the Solicitor's department may be traced in TM 17 Sept. 1806 (T 29/88 pp. 128–9), 29 Nov. 1811 (T 29/114 pp. 284–5), 18 March 1842 (T 29/447 pp. 378–86), 29 Oct. 1867 (AB, iv, 290–2).

[18] The position of Bernard (1679) is uncertain. The proposed appointments of East (1696) and Collyer (1711) never became effective (CTB, xi, 29; ibid. xxv, 17).

Parliamentary Counsel and Agent 1769–1870

The post of Parliamentary Counsel to the Treasury was established in 1769.[1] From that year until 1841 the Treasury employed as Counsel a succession of barristers who were responsible for the drafting and settling of its parliamentary bills. In the course of time the Counsel was entrusted with the task of preparing bills for other departments as well.[2] The salary attached to the office in 1769 was £600. This was later raised to £1000.[3] On the death of the then holder in 1841 the office was discontinued and in 1842 it was provided that the work of drafting bills for the Treasury and a number of other departments should be undertaken by the Parliamentary Counsel to the Home Office.[4] The Home Office Counsel remained the principal government draftsman until 1869 when the office of Parliamentary Counsel to the Treasury was revived. The then Home Office Counsel was appointed to this post with a salary of £2500 rising after two years to £3000.[5]

In 1805 one of the duties assigned to the Assistant Secretary as Law Clerk was to assist in the preparation of parliamentary bills.[6] Between 1817 and 1831 a distinct Assistant Counsel was attached to the Treasury with special responsibility for Irish business and a salary of £400.[7]

From 1769 the office of Parliamentary Agent to the Treasury was held by Clerks of the House of Commons. The salary attached to this office was originally fixed at £100. It was raised to £200 in 1770, to £300 in 1774, to £400 in 1779, to £600 in 1781, to £800 in 1812 and to £1100 in 1817.[8] Between 1808 and 1822 a former Treasury Clerk, Stuckey, acted as Clerk of Expiring Laws and Revenue Bills with a salary of £200.[9]

---

[1] TM 28 Nov. 1769 (T 29/40 pp. 117–18). For the arrangements which preceded the establishment of this office, see O. C. Williams, *The Clerical Organisation of the House of Commons 1661–1850* (Oxford 1954), 159–69. S. Lambert, *Bills and Acts* (Cambridge 1971), 45–7.

[2] *Rept. of Select Committee on House of Commons Offices and Fees 1833* (HC 1833 xii), 341–2; J. R. Torrance, 'Sir George Harrison and the growth of bureaucracy in the early nineteenth century' *Eng. Hist. Rev.*, lxxxiii (1968), 69–71; H. Parris, *Constitutional Bureaucracy* (London 1969), 172–8.

[3] TM 28 Nov. 1769 (T 29/40 pp. 117–18). £1000 was described as 'the usual allowance' in TM 30 July 1813 (T 29/124 p. 211).

[4] TM 18 March 1842 (T 29/447 pp. 378–86); *Rept. on Misc. Expenditure*, pt. i, 283, 371–5. The Home Office Counsel were: John Elliott Drinkwater Bethune 1837–48, Walter Coulson 1848–60, Henry Thring 1861–9.

[5] TM 8 Feb. 1869 (T 29/614 pp. 276–80).   [6] TM 19 Aug. 1805 (T 29/85 p. 347).

[7] Sir T. E. Tomlins.

[8] TM 28 Nov. 1769 (T 29/40 pp. 117–18); Williams, *Clerical Organisation*, 169–79.

[9] TM 13 July 1808 (T 29/95 p. 386), 10 Aug. 1821 (T 29/200 p. 243), 18 Jan. 1822 (T 29/205 p. 580).

LISTS OF APPOINTMENTS
Parliamentary Counsel

1769	28 Nov.	Pickering, D.	1798		Harrison, W.
1781	26 July	Hargrave, F.	1869	8 Feb.	Thring, H.
1789	14 Aug.	Lowndes, W.			

Parliamentary Agent

1769	28 Nov.	Rosier, J.	1825	5 Dec.	Dorington, J.
1797	30 June	Dorington, J.			Dorington, J. E.

Periodic Lists of Officials

LIST OF OFFICIALS AT ACCESSION OF ANNE
8 MARCH 1702

Commissioners
  Carlisle, Earl of
  Fox, Sir S.
  Boyle, Hon. H.
  Hill, R.
  Pelham, T.
Chancellor of the
Exchequer
  Boyle, Hon. H.
Secretary
  Lowndes, W.
Chief Clerks
  Glanville, W.
  Taylor, J.
  Powys, R.
  Tilson, C.

Under Clerks
  Bendish, T.
  Webster, E.
  Segar, H.
  Jett, T.
  Granger, M.
  Medley, T.
  East, W.
  Lowndes, J.
  Varey, J.
Chief Clerk of Revenue
  Tilson, C.
Office Keeper
  Wekett, W.
Messengers
  Bailey, W.

  Green, R.
  Farra, J.
Messengers of the Receipt
  Wekett, W.
  Richards, J.
  Clerke, S.
  Barrett, J.
Messenger of the Chamber
  Thurkettle, J.
Serjeant at Arms
  Ryley, P.

Solicitors
  Baker, H.
  Borrett, W.

LIST OF OFFICIALS AT ACCESSION OF GEORGE I
1 AUGUST 1714

Treasurer
  Shrewsbury, Duke of
Chancellor of the
Exchequer
  Wyndham, Sir W.
Senior Secretary
  Lowndes, W.
Junior Secretary
  Vacant
Chief Clerks
  Taylor, J.
  Powys, R.
  Tilson, C.
  Thomas, W.
Under Clerks
  Webster, E.
  Lowndes, W.
  Frecker, M.

  Bowen, T.
  Lowndes, T.
  Burnbury, R.
  King, S.
Chief Clerk of Revenue
  Tilson, C.
Under Clerks of Revenue
  2 or 3 clerks
  (names unknown)
Office Keeper
  Wekett, W.
Housekeeper
  Williams, E.
Doorkeeper
  Bailey, W.
Bag Carrier
  Empsom, W.

Messenger
  Farra, J.
Messengers of the Receipt
  Wekett, W.
  Richards, J.
  Clerke, S.
  Barrett, J.
Messenger of the Chamber
  Thurkettle, J.
Serjeant at Arms
  Ryley, P.

Solicitors
  Baker, H.
  Borrett, W.

LIST OF OFFICIALS AT ACCESSION OF GEORGE II
11 JUNE 1727

Commissioners
  Walpole, Sir R.
  Turner, Sir C.
  Yonge, Sir W.
  Dodington, G.
  Strickland, Sir W.
Chancellor of the
Exchequer
  Walpole, Sir R.
Senior Secretary
  Scrope, J.
Junior Secretary
  Walpole, H.
Chief Clerks
  Tilson, C.
  Kelsall, H.
  Lowndes, W.
  Frecker, M.
Under Clerks
  Webster, E.
  Bowen, T.
  Burnbury, R.
  Leheup, P.

Lowe, C.
Lowndes, C.
Fox, W. E.
Burnaby, E.
Pratt, T.
Fane, H.
Wyndham, W.
Gibson, T.
Chief Clerk of Revenue
  Beresford, J.
Under Clerks of Revenue
  Number and names
    uncertain
Keeper of Papers
  Nelson, H.
Office Keeper
  Mann, T.
Housekeeper
  Barnsley, —
Doorkeeper
  Jones, J.
Bag Carrier
  Empsom, W.

Bookranger
  Shepherd, J.
Messenger
  Barnsley, S.
Messengers of the Receipt
  Richards, J.
  Clerke, S.
  Lowther, T.
  Grantham, E.
Deputy Messenger of the
Receipt
  Richards, W.
Messenger of the Chamber
  Thurkettle, T.
Serjeant at Arms
  Ryley, P.

Solicitors
  Horneck, P.
  Cracherode, A.
Assistant Solicitor
  Paxton, N.

LIST OF OFFICIALS AT ACCESSION OF GEORGE III
25 OCTOBER 1760

Commissioners
  Newcastle, Duke of
  Bilson Legge, Hon. H.
  Grenville, Hon. J.
  North, Lord
  Oswald, J.
Chancellor of the
Exchequer
  Bilson Legge, Hon. H.
Senior Secretary
  West, J.
Junior Secretary
  Martin, S.
Chief Clerks
  Kelsall, H.
  Lowndes, C.

Postlethwaite, J.
Yeates, R.
Under Clerks
  Pratt, T.
  de Grey, T.
  Davis, W.
  Tompkins, T.
  Rowe, M.
  Mill, J.
  Poole, F.
  Reynolds, F.
  Kerrick, J.
  Cartwright, W.
  Royer, J.
  Watkins, J.
  Fane, H.

Speer, W.
Schutz, C.
Beldam, W.
Supernumerary Clerk
  Chowne, T.
Chief Clerk of Revenue
  Speer, W.
Under Clerks of Revenue
  Herbert, G.
  Fowler, H.
Private Secretary to First
Lord
  Jones, H. V.
Keeper of Papers
  Lowndes, C.

Office Keeper
Palmer, C.
Housekeeper
Shepherd, M.
Doorkeeper
Kitchin, J.
Bag Carrier
Shaw, E.
Bookranger
Gardiner, E.

Messengers
Barnsley, S.
Barnsley, W. W.
Messengers of the Receipt
Jones, J.
Oldnal, J.
Dubourg, P.
Walker, J.
Deputy Messenger of the Receipt
Watkins, J.

Messenger of the Chamber
Bryant, E.
Serjeant at Arms
Allin, Sir T.

Solicitors
Jones, H. V.
Webb, P. C.
Assistant Solicitor
Francis, T.

LIST OF OFFICIALS FOLLOWING REORGANISATION
30 NOVEMBER 1782

Commissioners
Shelburne, Earl of
Pitt, Hon. W.
Grenville, J.
Jackson, R.
Eliot, E. J.
Chancellor of the Exchequer
Pitt, Hon. W.
Senior Secretary
Orde, T.
Junior Secretary
Rose, G.
Chief Clerks
Pratt, T.
Reynolds, F.
Cotton, T.
Martin Leake, J.
Senior Clerks
Royer, J.
Beldam, W.
Mitford, W.
Dyer, T.
Ramus, G. E.
Broughton, B.
Junior (Assistant) Clerks
Brummell, B.
Tufton, A.
Alcock, J.
Cipriani, P.
Starck, H. S.

Ridout, J. C.
Junior Clerks
Poyntz, D.
Smith, J.
Extra Clerks
Winter, M.
Wolfe, L.
Mackintosh, J.
Clerk of Minutes
Winter, M.
Chief Clerk of Revenue
Speer, W.
Under Clerks of Revenue
Herbert, G.
Fowler, H.
Dancer, F.
Boughton, Sir E.
Smith, W. E.
Pembroke, W.
Private Secretary to First Lord
Morin, J.
Keeper of Papers
Pratt, T.
Sorter of Books
Matthews, J.
Receiver of Fees
Dugdale, W.
Office Keeper
Schaller, B.
Housekeeper
Appleby, J.

Housekeeper of Levée Rooms
Shaw, E.
Doorkeeper
Potter, H.
Bookranger
Watson, W.
Messengers
Barnsley, S.
Clubb, G.
Carter, J.
Williams, J.
Messengers of the Receipt
Walker, J.
Harrison, T.
Ross, W.
Gibbons, T.
Messenger of the Chamber
Barnsley, S. J.
Serjeant at Arms
Brougham, H.

Solicitors
Jones, H. V.
Chamberlayne, W.
Assistant Solicitor
White, J.
Parliamentary Counse
Hargrave, F.
Parliamentary Agent
Rosier, J.

LIST OF OFFICIALS FOLLOWING REORGANISATION
19 AUGUST 1805

Commissioners
Pitt, Hon. W.
Lovaine, Lord
Fitzharris, Viscount
Long, C.
Blandford,
  Marquess of
Chancellor of the
Exchequer
Pitt, Hon. W.
Senior Secretary
Sturges Bourne, W.
Junior Secretary
Huskisson, W.
Assistant Secretary
Harrison, G.
Chief Clerks
Cotton, T.
Mitford, W.
Ramus, G. E.
Chinnery, W.
Senior Clerks
Broughton, B.
Brummell, B.
Cipriani, P.
Speer, W.
Nicolay, F.
Yorke, J.
Senior Clerk of the
Minutes
Stuckey, V.
Assistant Clerks
West, T.
Brooksbank, S.
Brawne, J.
Cooke, E.
Hoblyn, T.
Cotton, W.
Mitford, R.
West, G.

Rosenhagen, A.
Junior Clerks[1]
Grange, J.
Sanford, H.
Unwin, J.
Bates, E.
van der Spiegel, A.
Fauquier, W. E.
Earle, P. H.
Crafer, T.
Vernon, J.
Martin Leake, S. R.
Sargent, W.
Gibbons, E.
Extra Clerk
Blake, R.
Clerks of the Bills
Crafer, T.
Rosenhagen, A.
Receiver of Fees
Vernon, J.
Chief Clerk of Revenue
Alcock, J.
Senior Clerks of Revenue
Pembroke, W.
Wyndham, W. W.
Assistant Clerks of
Revenue
Bullock, E. C.
Brooksbank, T. C.
Herries, J. C.
Woodford, C.
Private Secretary to First
Lord
Adams, W. D.
Keeper of Papers
Tirel Morin, J.
Assistant Keeper of
Papers
Powell, T.

Office Keeper
Mann, C.
Housekeeper
Thorpe, M.
Housekeeper of
Levée Rooms
Arden, E.
Chief Doorkeeper
Archilarius, P.
Doorkeeper
Hatfield, G.
Bookranger
Carter, T.
Messengers to Secretaries
Fazan, L.
Cleaver, T.
Messengers for Deliveries
4 (not named)
Messengers of the Receipt
Carter, C.
Andrews, T.
Cotterell, S.
Salter, R.
Messenger of the Chamber
Wood, T.
Serjeant at Arms
Brougham, H.

Solicitor
White, J.
Parliamentary Counsel
Harrison, W.
Parliamentary Agent
Dorington, J. E.

[1] The number of Junior Clerks was not reduced to nine, the number provided for in TM 19 Aug. 1805, until 6 Jan. 1806 (T 29/86 p. 1).

LIST OF OFFICIALS FOLLOWING REORGANISATION
17 OCTOBER 1834

Commissioners
Melbourne, Viscount
Althorp, Viscount
Smith, R. V.
Ponsonby, Hon. G.
Graham, R.
Byng, G. S.
Chancellor of the
Exchequer
Althorp, Viscount
Parliamentary Secretary
Wood, C.
Financial Secretary
Baring, F. T.
Assistant Secretary
Stewart, Hon. J. H. K.
Auditor of the Civil List
Spearman, A. Y.
Principal Clerk Assistant
Crafer, T.
Principal Clerk for
Colonial Business
Brande, G. W.
Chief Clerks
Brooksbank, T. C.
Sanford, H.
van der Spiegel, A.
Fauquier, W. E.
Martin Leake, S. R.
Senior Clerks
Unwin, J.
Walpole, E.
Gibbons, E.
Drummond, E.
Boyd, G.
Assistant Clerks
Pearson, H. R.
Harrison, T. C.
Baker, J.
Harrison, M.
Litchfield, C.
Crafer, C. L.
Speer, E.

Pemberton, C. R.
Brummell, W. C.
Sargent, F.
Arbuthnot, G.
Drummond, S.
Courtenay, T. P.
Junior Clerks
Ricketts, E. W.
Cole, J. G.
Stephenson, W. H.
Gordon, Sir A. C. D.
Shelley, S.
Crafer, E. T.
Grey, C. S.
Waller, A.
Stronge, C. W.
Clerk of Parliamentary
Accounts
Crafer, C. L.
Auditors
Brooksbank, T. C.
Sanford, H.
Clerk of Irish Revenue
Tomlins, A.
Clerks of the Bills
Herbert, G.
Rumsey, L.
Clerks to Auditor
of the Civil List
Saunders, E.
Sawyer, E.
Extra Clerks
Winkley, W.
Adrian, T.
Dwight, W. M.
Batchelour, G.
Davis, J.
Smith, W. B.
Metcalfe, J.
Dwight, H. T.
Algar, W.
Stephenson, J.
Macrae, K.

Clifford, J.
Private Secretaries
To First Lord
Young, T.
Martin Leake, S. R.
To Chancellor of
the Exchequer
Drummond, T.
To Parliamentary
Secretary
Arbuthnot, G.
To Financial Secretary
Crafer, E. T.
To Assistant Secretary
Cole, J. G.
Keeper of Papers
Emmans, T.
Assistant Keeper of
Papers
Greenwood, C.
Office Keeper
Haines, J.
Housekeeper
Thorpe, M.
Doorkeeper
Davis, R.
Bookranger
Weller, J.
Messengers to Secretaries
Harvey, R.
Mitchell, S.
Minet, J. W.
Messengers for Deliveries
Morten, L.
Richards, J.
Worsfold, W.
Oliver, J.
Foot, G.
Messengers of the Receipt
Andrews, T.
Salter, R.
Barfoot, H.
Ruffe, W.

Messenger of the
Chamber
  Child, J.
City Messenger
  Halligan, T.

Solicitor
  Maule, G.
Assistant Solicitor
  Bourchier, C.

Parliamentary Counsel
  Harrison, W.
Parliamentary Agent
  Dorington, J. E.

LIST OF OFFICIALS FOLLOWING REORGANISATION
4 JULY 1856

Commissioners
  Palmerston, Viscount
  Lewis, Sir G. C.
  Brand, Hon. H. B. W.
  Duncan, Viscount
  Monck, Viscount
Chancellor of the
Exchequer
  Lewis, Sir G. C.
Parliamentary Secretary
  Hayter, W. G.
Financial Secretary
  Wilson, J.
Assistant Secretary
  Trevelyan, Sir C. E.
Auditor of the Civil List
  Arbuthnot, G.
Principal Clerks
  Crafer, C. L.
  Stephenson, W. H.
  Anderson, W. G.
  Seton, W.
First Class Clerks
  Drummond, S.
  Gordon, Sir A. C. D.
  Shelley, S.
  Byron, F.
  Waller, A.
  Stonge, C. W.
  Wilbraham, R. W.
  Law, W.
  Cole, J. H.
  Collier, J. P.
Second Class Clerks
  Jones, L.
  Fitzgerald, F.
  Parratt, G. F.

  Dawson, F.
  Drummond, M.
  Clerke, W. H.
  Buckland, E. C.
  Martin Leake, J.
  Barrington, C. G.
  Plunkett, Hon. E. L.
  Ponsonby,
    Hon. G. H. B.
  Ryan, C. L.
  Blackwood, S. A.
  Murray, H. H.
  Nicol, H.
  Fremantle, C. W.
Third Class Clerks
  Somerset, R. H. G.
  Wilson, C. R.
  Broughton, V. D.
  Mowatt, F.
  (3 Vacancies)
Clerk of Parliamentary
Accounts
  Stronge, C. W.
Superintendent of
Registry
  Waller, A.
Supernumerary Senior
Clerk
  Dwight, W. M.
Accountant
  Foster, M. H.
Assistant Accountant
  Wickens, T. E.
Clerks to Auditor
of the Civil List
  Sawyer, E.
  Robinson, F. J.

Extra (Supplementary)
Clerks
  Adrian, T.
  Batchelour, G.
  Davis, J.
  Dwight, H. T.
  Wickens, T. E.
  Cotton, H. P.
  Nash, E.
  Atchley, W. H.
  Chance, G.
  Lyle, W.
  Geddes, G. T.
  Mills, R.
  Begent, T. J.
Private Secretaries
To First Lord
  Clifford, C. C.
  Law, W.
To Chancellor
of the Exchequer
  Gordon, Sir A. C. D.
To Parliamentary
Secretary
  Fremantle, C. W.
To Financial Secretary
  Wilson, C. R.
Office Keeper
  Newman, J.
Messengers
  Halligan, T. (*Messenger*
    of the Registry)
  Boddy, J. (*Messenger of*
    the Chamber)
  Worsfold, W. (*Door-*
    keeper)
  Foot, G. (*Bookranger*)

Young, T. (*Messenger to Secretary*)
Long, C. (*Messenger to Secretary*)
Bailey, J.
Long, G. (*Messenger to Secretary*)
Ford, B.
Biggs, R.
Purvis, R.

Davidson, W.
Bawcutt, J.
Office Keeper and Superintendent of Messengers to First Lord
Appleton, T.
Messengers to First Lord
Fitness, J.
Colburn, J.
Johnson, C.

Doe, G.
Messengers to Chancellor of the Exchequer
Winter, J.
Humphreys, G.

Solicitor
Reynolds, H. R.
Assistant Solicitor
Greenwood, J.

LIST OF OFFICIALS ON EVE OF REORGANISATION
25 MAY 1870

Commissioners
Gladstone, W. E.
Lowe, R.
Lansdowne, Marquess of
Adam, W. P.
Vivian, Hon. J. C. W.
Gladstone, W. H.
Chancellor of the Exchequer
Lowe, R.
Parliamentary Secretary
Glyn, Hon. G. G.
Financial Secretary
Stansfeld, J.
Permanent Secretary
Lingen, R. R. W.
Auditor of the Civil List and Assistant to Secretaries
Law, W.
Principal Clerks
Stronge, C. W.
Cole, J. H.
Foster, M. H.
Clerke, Sir W. H.
First Class Clerks
Wilbraham, R. W.
Fitzgerald, F.
Buckland, E. C.
Dawson, F.
Barrington, C. G.

Blackwood, S. A.
Murray, H. H.
Second Class Clerks
Parratt, G. F.
Wilson, C. R.
Broughton, V. D.
Mowatt, F.
Welby, R. E.
Clement, R.
Clay, F. E.
Ryder, G. L.
Bergne, F. A.
Gurdon, W. B.
Puller, C. C.
Hervey, G. W.
Third Class Clerks
Christie, W. H.
Kempe, J. A.
Turnor, A.
Ferguson, R. R. N.
Seymour, H. A. D.
Baillie Hamilton, C. R.
Primrose, H. W.
Clerk of Parliamentary Accounts
Barrington, C. G.
Superintendent and Principal Clerk of Registry
Jones, L. A.
Accountant
Mills, R.

Assistant Accountant
Turner, C. G.
Clerks to Auditor of the Civil List
Nash, E.
Robinson, F. J.
First Class Supplementary Clerk (Accounts)
Simpson, J.
Second Class Supplementary Clerks (Accounts)
Robinson, F. J.
Skinner, G. E.
Follett, F. T.
Third Class Supplementary Clerks (Accounts)
Hereford, G.
Waters, C.
Fraser, A. S.
First Class Supplementary Clerks (Registry)
Cotton, H. P.
Begent, T. J.
Geddes, G. T.
Second Class Supplementary Clerks (Registry)
Craggs, G. W.
Durrant, T.
Davies, J.
Philp, E.

*Third Class Supplementary
Clerks (Registry)*
  Jackson, J.
  Stephenson, F. C.
  Luff, W. W.
  Ray, W. S.
  Arnold, G. M. B.
  Aldridge, E. G.
Private Secretaries
To First Lord
  West, A. E.
  Gurdon, W. B.
*To Chancellor of the
Exchequer*
  Wilson, C. R.
*To Parliamentary
Secretary*
  Clay, F. E.
  Seymour, H. A. D.
  (Assistant)
To Financial Secretary
  Welby, R. E.
To Permanent Secretary
  Broughton, V. D.

Office Keeper
  Halligan, T.
Messenger of the Chamber
  Ford, B.
Messengers
  Bailey, J. (*Superinten-
    dent of Upper Floor*)
  Maddams, G.
    (*Messenger of the
    Registry*)
  Foster, T. (*Doorkeeper*)
  Biggs, R. (*Bookranger*)
  Gabbitas, J. R.
    (*Messenger to
    Secretary*)
  Stafford, J.
    (*Messenger to
    Secretary*)
  Forward, G.
    (*Messenger to
    Secretary*)
  Rossiter, W.
  Hughes, T.
  Maguire, R.
  O'Shaughnessy, J.

  Rogers, G.
  Hambling, H.
*Office Keeper and
Superintendent of
Messengers to First Lord*
  Appleton, T.
Messengers to First Lord
  Fitness, J.
  Johnson, C.
  Doe, G.
  Hollier, S.
*Messengers to Chancellor
of the Exchequer*
  Gabbitas, H.
  Turner, T.
  Foot, J.

Solicitor
  Greenwood, J.
Assistant Solicitor
  Stephenson,
    A. F. W. K.
Parliamentary Counsel
  Thring, H.

Alphabetical List of Officials

Abbot, Hon. Reginald Charles Edward (succ. as 3rd Lord **Colchester** 18 Oct. 1867) *Private Secretary to First Lord* (Derby) 25 June–20 Nov. 1867 (AB, iv, 271, 294).

Abbott, Lawrence *Clerk* occ. from 26 Sept. 1667 to 5 July 1673 (*CTB*, ii, 94; ibid. iv, 188).

Aberdeen, George (Hamilton Gordon) 4th Earl of *First Lord* 28 Dec. 1852–8 Feb. 1855 (*Times*, 29 Dec. 1852).

Adam, William Patrick *Commissioner* 26 April 1865–13 July 1866; 17 Dec. 1868.

Adams, William Dacres *Private Secretary to First Lord* (Pitt) May 1804–Jan. 1806 (*New Companion*, 85); (Portland) 1 April 1807–30 Oct. 1809 (T 41/3).

Addington, Henry *Chancellor of Exchequer* 14 March 1801–10 May 1804 (T 90/144). *First Lord* 21 March 1801–16 May 1804.

Addington, John Hiley *Commissioner* 9 Dec. 1800–21 March 1801. *Senior Secretary* 24 March 1801–5 July 1802 (T 29/77 p. 348). *Commissioner* 5 July 1802–18 Nov. 1803.

Adrian, T. *Extra Clerk* 29 July 1807–24 Sept. 1857 (T 41/9). Ret. 24 Sept. 1857 (AB, iii, 351).

Adrian, William Obadiah *Extra Clerk* first occ. 21 April 1815 (T 29/134 p. 1018). D. 5 Aug. 1825 (T 41/5).

Aislabie, John *Chancellor of Exchequer* 20 March 1718–2 Feb. 1721 (C 66/3524). *Commissioner* 20 March 1718–3 April 1721.

Albemarle, Duke of *see* **Monck,** Sir George, kt.

Alcock, Joseph *Junior (Assistant) Clerk* 30 Nov. 1782–29 July 1785 (T 29/52 pp. 517, 520). *Senior Clerk* 29 July 1785–5 July 1798 (T 29/56 p. 517). *Chief Clerk* 5 July 1798–3 Jan. 1799 (T 29/73 p. 208). *Chief Clerk of Revenue* 3 Jan. 1799–2 Jan. 1821 (T 29/74 p. 64). Res. 2 Jan. 1821 (T 29/193 p. 76).
    Auditor 14 April 1815–2 Jan. 1821 (T 29/134 p. 877).

Alcock, Joseph *Assistant Clerk of Revenue* 1 March 1808–23 Nov. 1821 (T 29/93 p. 422). Res. 23 Nov. 1821 (T 29/203 p. 620).
    Superintendent of Parliamentary Returns 21 April 1815–23 Nov. 1821 (T 29/134 p. 1018).

Aldridge, E. G. *Supplementary Third Class Clerk* 24 May 1869 (AB, v, 4).

Aldworth, Robert *Clerk* occ. 20 Jan. 1681 (*CTB*, vii, 18). *Chief Clerk* occ. 1693 (Miège, *New State* (1693), pt. iii, 404); received dividend of fees from April 1695 to Dec. 1696 (T 1/35 f. 204; T 1/42 f. 129).

Algar, W. *Extra Clerk* 1822–2 Sept. 1845 (T 29/489 p. 3). Ret. 2 Sept. 1845 (ibid.).

Allin, Sir Thomas, 2nd Bart. *Serjeant at Arms* 2 March 1733–4 Aug. 1765 (C 66/3589, 3678). D. 4 Aug. 1765 (T 53/50 p. 84).

Althorp, George John (Spencer) *styled* Viscount *Commissioner* 1 April–13 July 1782.

Althorp, John Charles (Spencer) *styled* Viscount (succ. as 3rd Earl **Spencer** 10 Nov. 1834) *Commissioner* 10 Feb. 1806–31 March 1807.
    Chancellor of Exchequer 22 Nov. 1830–2 Dec. 1834 (E 197/8 p. 287; *Times*, 23 Nov. 1830).
    Commissioner 24 Nov. 1830–22 Nov. 1834.

Anderson, William George *Principal Clerk of Finance* 24 March 1854–4 July 1856 (T 29/554 p. 642). *Principal Clerk* 4 July 1856–28 Aug. 1865 (T 29/564 p. 47). *Auditor of Civil List* 28 Aug. 1865–6 March 1867 (AB, iv, 194–5). Res. 6 March 1867 on app. as Assistant Comptroller and Auditor General (ibid. 260).

Andrews, Thomas *Messenger of Receipt* 23 May 1801–2 May 1836 (C 66/3990; T 54/56 p. 84). Res. 2 May 1836 (T 29/377 pp. 40–1).

Anson, George Edward *Junior Clerk* 2 Dec. 1834–31 March 1840 (T 29/360 p. 37). Left office 31 March 1840 on app. as Private Secretary to Prince Albert (T 41/8; *Gent. Mag.* (1849), cxxv, 540).

    Private Secretary to First Lord (Melbourne) 8 May 1835–31 March 1840 (T 29/365 p. 165).

Appleby, Jane *Housekeeper* 18 Nov. 1774–3 Dec. 1787 (T 29/44 p. 85). D. 3 Dec. 1787 (T 53/59 p. 224).

Appleton, Thomas *Messenger to First Lord* 1 June 1836–12 Feb. 1839 (T 54/56 p. 423; T 29/379 pp. 427–8). *Office Keeper to First Lord* 12 Feb. 1839 (T 29/410 p. 235).

Apsley, Henry (Bathurst) *styled* Lord *Commissioner* 10 Aug. 1789–20 June 1791.

Aram, Thomas *Clerk* occ. from 24 Nov. 1671 to 3 July 1673 (*CTB,* iii, 976; ibid. iv, 186).

Arbuthnot, Charles *Senior Secretary* 5 April 1809–7 Feb. 1823 (T 29/100 p. 166).

Arbuthnot, George *Junior Clerk* 18 July 1820–12 Oct. 1832 (T 29/187 p. 478). *Assistant Clerk* 12 Oct. 1832–22 March 1850 (T 29/334 pp. 178–9). *Senior Clerk* 22 March–12 Nov. 1850 (T 29/538 p. 615). *Auditor of Civil List* 12 Nov. 1850–28 July 1865 (T 29/541 p. 286). D. 28 July 1865 (*Gent. Mag.* (1865), clvii, 394).

    Private Secretary: to Senior (Parliamentary) Secretary (Lushington, Planta, Ellice, Wood, Clerk, Stanley) 4 March 1823–Feb. 1838 (T 38/552 pp. 46, 91; T 29/312 p. 486; T 29/332 p. 307; T 41/8; T 29/365 p. 165); *to Assistant Secretary* (Spearman, Trevelyan) 16 Feb. 1838–Feb. 1843 (T 29/398 p. 349; T 29/421 p. 426); *to First Lord* (Peel) 3 Feb. 1843–July 1846 (T 29/458 p. 44); *to Chancellor of Exchequer* (Wood) 7 July 1846–Nov. 1850 (T 29/499 p. 144).

Archilarius, Philip *Doorkeeper* 10 Jan. 1798–8 May 1804 (T 29/71 p. 537). *Chief Doorkeeper* 8 May 1804–8 Feb. 1814 (T 29/83 p. 36). D. 8 Feb. 1814 (T 41/4).

Arden, Elizabeth *Housekeeper of Levée Rooms* 25 July 1793–April 1814 (T 29/66 p. 107). Left office April 1814 (T 41/4).

Arnold, — App. 'a Clerk of the Treasury' Oct. 1743 (*Gent. Mag.* (1743), xiii, 554). Position uncertain.

Arnold, George Moss Brock *Supplementary Third Class Clerk* 28 April 1869 (AB, v, 1).

Arundel, Hon. Richard *Commissioner* 26 Dec. 1744–27 June 1746.

Ashley, Anthony (Ashley Cooper) 1st Lord (cr. Earl of **Shaftesbury** 23 April 1672) *Chancellor of Exchequer* 13 May 1661–21 Nov. 1672 (C 66/1995); surrendered office 21 Nov. 1672 (C 75/6).

    Commissioner 24 May 1667–2 Dec. 1672.

Ashley, Hon. Anthony Evelyn Melbourne *Private Secretary to First Lord* (Palmerston) 11 Feb.–March 1858 (T 29/570 p. 285); 24 June 1859–Oct. 1865 (T 29/575 p. 482).

Atchley, W. H. *Extra Clerk* 10 May 1844–24 May 1861 (T 29/473 p. 199). *Supplementary Second Class Clerk* 24 May 1861–10 May 1864 (AB, iv, 113). *Supplementary*

First Class Clerk 10 May 1864–21 Feb. 1869 (ibid. 164). Ret. 21 Feb. 1869 (ibid. 350).

Aubrey, John (succ. as 6th Bart. 4 Sept. 1786)   *Commissioner* 26 Dec. 1783–10 Aug. 1789.

Ayrton, Acton Smee   *Financial Secretary* 21 Dec. 1868–Nov. 1869 (AB, iv, 343).

Bagwell, John   *Commissioner* 23 June 1859–26 March 1862.

Bailey, Arthur   *Messenger of Receipt* 12 Sept. 1783–c. 11 Dec. 1798 (C 66/3806). D. by 11 Dec. 1798 (app. of J. Wood).

Bailey, J.   *Messenger* 30 June 1841 (T 29/438 p. 559).
  Messenger to Secretary 1 Oct. 1856–2 June 1859 (AB, iii, 323). *Bookranger* 2 June 1859–24 Oct. 1868 (T 29/575 p. 458). *Superintendent of Upper Floor* 24 Oct. 1868 (AB, iv, 323–4).

Bailey, William   *Messenger* occ. from 4 Feb. 1690 to 22 July 1702 (*CTB*, xvii, 554; ibid. xxviii, 403). *Doorkeeper* first occ. 27 Nov. 1712 (ibid. xxvi, 87). D. by 10 May 1727 (T 29/25 p. 295).

Baillie, George   *Commissioner* 15 Apr. 1717–27 May 1725.

Baillie Hamilton, Charles Robert   *Third Class Clerk* 21 Dec. 1868 (AB, iv, 339).

Baker, Eric   *Junior Clerk* 2 June 1826–18 Oct. 1833 (T 29/258 p. 57). Res. 18 Oct. 1833 (T 29/346 p. 332).

Baker, Henry   *Solicitor* 11 Sept. 1696–16 Jan. 1716 (*CTB*, xi, 265; ibid. xvii, 244; ibid. xxix, 541). D. 16 Jan. 1716 (*Hist. Reg. Chron.* (1716), i, 112).

Baker, Joseph   *Junior Clerk* 10 April 1812–11 March 1823 (T 29/116 p. 584). *Assistant Clerk* 11 March 1823–1 Jan. 1840 (T 29/219 p. 151). *Senior Clerk* 1 Jan. 1840–22 Oct. 1852 (T 29/421 p. 1A). *Chief Clerk* 22 Oct. 1852–4 July 1856 (T 29/549 p. 127). Ret. 4 July 1856 (T 29/564 p. 47).
  Superintendent of Registry 25 May 1849–22 Oct. 1852 (AB, iii, 104).

Baker, Nicholas   *Solicitor* Sept. 1696–June 1700 (*CTB*, xi, 53). Dis. June 1700 (ibid. xv, 100, 109).

Balfour, Blayney Townley   *Private Secretary to First Lord* (Goderich) 13 Sept. 1827–Jan. 1828 (T 29/273 p. 164).

Ball, Henry   *Serjeant at Arms* 25 March–c. 27 Nov. 1684 (*CTB*, viii, 137). Surrendered office by 27 Nov. 1684 (ibid.; app. of P. Ryley).

Bankes, George   *Commissioner* 24 April–24 Nov. 1830.

Barfoot, Henry   *Messenger of Receipt* 31 Oct. 1812–30 June 1836 (C 66/4128; T 54/56 p. 84). Res. 30 June 1836 (T 29/378 pp. 550–1).

Baring, Francis Thornhill   *Commissioner* 24 Nov. 1830–6 June 1834. *Financial Secretary* 6 June–20 Dec. 1834 (T 29/354 p. 100); 21 April 1835–26 Aug. 1839 (T 29/364 p. 337). *Chancellor of Exchequer* 26 Aug. 1839–3 Sept. 1841 (*Times*, 27 Aug. 1839).
  Commissioner 30 Aug. 1839–8 Sept. 1841.

Baring, Henry Bingham   *Commissioner* 8 Sept. 1841–6 July 1846.

Barnard, Lord *see* **Vane**, Hon. Henry

Barne, Snowden   *Commissioner* 6 Dec. 1809–5 Oct. 1812.

Barnsley, —   *Housekeeper* occ. 26 May 1726, 27 Aug. 1728 (T 29/25 p. 304; T 29/26 p. 140).

Barnsley, Samuel   *Messenger* app. c. 1722 (*CTBP 1742–5*, 157); pd. from 25 Dec. 1735 to 5 July 1793 (T 53/38 p. 163; T 53/60 p. 145).
  Doorkeeper left office 27 Jan. 1736 (*CTBP 1735–8*, 159).

Deputy Messenger of Receipt app. 27 Jan. 1736 (ibid.); last occ. 1746 (T 48/63).

Deputy Doorkeeper occ. from 1785 to 1794 (*Royal Kal.* (1785), 181; ibid. (1794), 181; *2nd Rept. on Fees*, 80; T 29/63 p. 419; T 29/71 p. 537).

Deputy Office Keeper occ. from 1785 to 1794 (*Royal Kal.* (1785), 181; ibid. (1794), 181).

D. 31 July 1794 (*Gent. Mag.* (1794), lxiv (2), 768).

Barnsley, Samuel John   *Messenger* pd. from 10 Oct. 1761 to 10 Oct. 1769 (T 53/48 p. 9; T 53/51 p. 92). *Messenger of Chamber* 14 Nov. 1769–9 Sept. 1794 (T 54/41 p. 80). D. 9 Sept. 1794 (T 41/2).

Barnsley, William Weekes   *Messenger* pd. from 5 July 1758 to 30 April 1762 (T 53/46 p. 10; T 53/48 p. 311). *Messenger of Chamber* 30 April 1762–2 Jan. 1765 (T 54/38 p. 355). D. 2 Jan. 1765 (T 53/49 p. 418).

Barrett, John   *Messenger of Receipt* 22 Jan. 1698–c. 22 May 1723 (C 66/3392, 3434, 3502). D. by 22 May 1723 (app. of Grantham).

Barrett, William   *Messenger of Receipt* 30 July 1689–22 Jan. 1698 (C 66/3328). Left office 22 Jan. 1698 (app. of J. Barrett).

Barrington, Charles George   *Junior Clerk* 14 April 1848–4 July 1856 (T 29/520 p. 211). *Second Class Clerk* 4 July 1856–3 July 1866 (T 29/564 p. 47). *First Class Clerk* 3 July 1866 (AB, iv, 224–5).

Private Secretary to First Lord (Palmerston) 25 Oct. 1856–13 Nov. 1857 (T 29/565 p. 29; T 29/569 p. 245); (Palmerston, Russell) 24 June 1859–July 1866 (T 29/575 p. 482; AB, iv, 205).

Clerk of Parliamentary Accounts 31 Dec. 1869 (AB, v, 18–19).

Barrington, Hon. George William   *Private Secretary to First Lord* (Derby) 14 July 1866–June 1867 (AB, iv, 236, 271).

Barrington, William (Barrington) 2nd Viscount   *Chancellor of Exchequer* 19 March 1761–29 May 1762 (C 66/3673).

Commissioner 19 March 1761–28 May 1762.

Barry *see* **Maxwell Barry**

Barton, Newton   *Private Secretary to First Lord* (Addington) March 1801–May 1804 (*New Companion*, 85).

Batchelour, George   *Extra Clerk* 1812–24 May 1861 (T 29/510 p. 529). *Supplementary First Class Clerk* 24 May 1861–7 Feb. 1867 (AB, iv, 113). Ret. 7 Feb. 1867 (ibid. 251).

Bates, Edward   *Supernumerary Clerk* 14 Nov. 1800–13 July 1802 (T 29/77 p. 60). *Junior Clerk* 13 July 1802–17 May 1808 (T 41/2). *Assistant Clerk* 17 May 1808–31 July 1818 (T 29/94 p. 512). *Senior Clerk* 31 July 1818–10 Feb. 1823 (T 29/163 p. 682). Res. 10 Feb. 1823 on app. as Secretary to Board of Taxes (T 29/218 p. 129).

Private Secretary to Senior Secretary (Arbuthnot) first occ. 19 May 1812 (T 29/117 p. 293); remained in office until res. (T 38/552 p. 46).

Bateson, Thomas   *Commissioner* 28 Feb. 1852–4 Jan. 1853.

Bawcutt, J.   *Messenger* 18 Aug. 1854–c. 11 April 1865 (T 29/556 p. 391). D. by 11 April 1865 (AB, iv, 178–80).

Doorkeeper 21 Jan. 1862–c. 11 April 1865 (ibid. 127).

Bayham, John Jeffreys (Pratt) *styled* Viscount (succ. as 2nd Earl **Camden** 18 April 1794)   *Commissioner* 10 Aug. 1789–7 May 1794.

Beauchamp, Francis (Seymour Conway) *styled* Viscount   *Commissioner* 11 March 1774–12 Sept. 1780.

Becket, Sir John, 2nd Bart. *Commissioner* 22 Nov.–31 Dec. 1834.

Begent, Thomas John *Extra Clerk* 18 Dec. 1855–24 May 1861 (T 29/561 p. 693). *Supplementary Second Class Clerk* 24 May 1861–7 Feb. 1867 (AB, iv, 113). *Supplementary First Class Clerk* 7 Feb. 1867 (ibid. 251).

Belasyse, John (Belasyse) 1st Lord *First Lord* 4 Jan. 1687–9 April 1689.

Beldam, William *Supernumerary Clerk* 10 Oct. 1758–23 May 1760 (T 29/33 p. 92). *Under Clerk* 23 May 1760–30 Nov. 1782 (ibid. p. 327). *Senior Clerk* 30 Nov. 1782–21 April 1787 (T 29/52 p. 520). D. 21 April 1787 (*Gent. Mag.* (1787), lvii (1) 366).

Bellew, Richard Montesquiou *Commissioner* 6 Aug. 1847–28 Feb. 1852.

Benbow, Robert *Messenger of Receipt* grant in reversion 28 June 1642 (recited in deed of surrender); in office by 18 July 1660 (app. of Kipps). Surrendered office 29 June 1674 (C 75/6).

Benbow, Thomas *Messenger of Receipt* grant in reversion 1 July 1625 (C 66/2348); in office by 13 May 1635 (grant to Amys; C 66/2701). Surrendered office by 7 Dec. 1665 (app. of E. Seymour).

Benbow, Thomas *Messenger of Receipt* 13 Nov. 1662–29 June 1674 (C 66/3009). Surrendered office 29 June 1674 (C 75/6).

Bendish, Thomas *Clerk* occ. 1 May 1694 (*CTB*, xvii, 728). *Under Clerk* pd. from 25 March 1695 to 24 June 1710 (ibid. 759; ibid. xxviii, 473; T 1/35 f. 208; T 1/111 f. 92). D. c. 22 June 1710 (Luttrell, *Hist. Relation*, vi, 596).

Benn, George *Messenger* 15 Dec. 1856–2 April 1864 (T 29/565 p. 550). Dis. 2 April 1864 (AB, iv, 159–60).

Benson, Robert (cr. Lord **Bingley** 21 July 1713) *Commissioner* 10 Aug. 1710–30 May 1711. *Chancellor of Exchequer* 4 June 1711–21 Aug. 1713 (C 66/3479).

Beresford, John *Under Clerk of Revenue* occ. 17 Oct. 1715, 1725 (*CTB*, xxix, 297; BM Add. MS 34736 f. 105). *Chief Clerk of Revenue* pd. from 25 March 1725 (T 53/32 p. 79). Res. 11 Oct. 1752 (T 29/32 p. 71).

Placed on establishment as *Under Clerk* 29 June 1733 (*CTBP 1731–4*, 390) and continued as such until d. D. by 23 May 1760 (T 29/33 p. 327; T 53/47 p. 85).

Bergne, Frederick A'Court *Third Class Clerk* 22 Jan. 1861–21 June 1867 (AB, iv, 109). *Second Class Clerk* 21 June 1867 (ibid. 277–8).

Bernard, John *Solicitor* occ. 23 March, 4 April 1679 (*CTB*, v, 1307; ibid. vi, 14). Position uncertain.

Bertie, Hon. Charles *Secretary* July 1673–March 1679 (Baxter, *Treasury*, 181–8).

Bessborough, Earl of *see* **Duncannon**, Viscount

Betty, Robert *Messenger of Receipt* 23 May 1801–3 June 1805 (C 66/3990). D. 3 June 1805 (*Gent. Mag.* (1805), lxxv (1), 588).

Biggs, R. *Messenger* 24 Dec. 1852 (T 29/549 p. 697).

Messenger to Secretary 24 April 1863–24 Oct. 1868 (AB, iv, 145). *Bookranger* 24 Oct. 1868 (ibid. 323–4).

Bilson Legge *see* **Legge**

Bingley, Lord *see* **Benson**, Robert

Bishop, Edward *Under Clerk* 22 Dec. 1761–30 Nov. 1782 (T 29/34 p. 206). Res. 30 Nov. 1782 on app. as Commissioner of Salt Duties (T 29/52 p. 517).

Blackburn, Peter *Commissioner* 16 March–23 June 1859.

Blackwood, Stevenson Arthur *Junior Clerk* 24 Feb. 1852–18 March 1856 (T 29/546 p. 553). *Assistant Clerk* 18 March–4 July 1856 (AB, iii, 310). *Second Class Clerk*

4 July 1856–21 June 1867 (T 29/564 p. 47). *First Class Clerk* 21 June 1867 (AB, iv, 277).

Blake, Roebuck *Extra Clerk* 19 Aug. 1785–3 May 1813 (T 29/56 p. 549). D. 3 May 1813 (T 41/4).

Blandford, George (Spencer) *styled* Marquess of *Commissioner* 7 Aug. 1804–10 Feb. 1806.

Boddy, J. *Messenger* 20 April 1835–21 April 1863 (T 29/364 p. 333). Ret. 21 April 1863 (AB, iv, 143).

  Messenger to Secretary 20 April 1835–11 Aug. 1854 (T 29/364 p. 333). *Messenger of Chamber* 11 Aug. 1854–21 April 1863 (T 29/556 p. 321).

Bond, Nathaniel *Commissioner* 21 March 1801–16 May 1804.

Bonham Carter, John *Commissioner* 7 June–13 July 1866.

Booth, George *Under Clerk* pd. from 25 March 1695 to 25 Dec. 1698 (*CTB*, xvii, 759, 844); representative pd. 8 April 1699 for quarter 25 Dec. 1698 to 25 March 1699 (ibid. 855). D. by 1 April 1699 (Prob 8/92).

Booth *see also* **Sclater Booth**

Bootle Wilbraham, Hon. Edward *Private Secretary to First Lord* (Derby) 5–12 March 1852 (T 29/546 p. 637; T 41/9); 8–22 March 1858 (T 29/570 pp. 583, 602).

Borrett, William *Solicitor* 15 Oct. 1700–31 May 1715 (*CTB*, xvi, 285). Left office 31 May 1715 (ibid. xxix, 265).

Boughton, Edward (succ. as 8th Bart. 29 Aug. 1780) *Supernumerary Clerk* 7 April 1763–18 Aug. 1767 (T 29/35 p. 63). *Under Clerk of Revenue* 18 Aug. 1767–4 Feb. 1794 (T 29/38 p. 451). D. 4 Feb. 1794 (*Gent. Mag.* (1794), lxiv (1), 278).

Bourchier, Charles *Assistant Solicitor* 1 Jan. 1818–22 Nov. 1842 (T 54/53 p. 462). Res. 22 Nov. 1842 (T 29/455 p. 413).

Bourke, Richard *Private Secretary to Chancellor of Exchequer* (Spring Rice) 30 Aug. 1838–30 Aug. 1839 (T 29/404 p. 671).

Bourne *see* **Sturges Bourne**

Bowen, Thomas *Under Clerk* pd. from 25 Dec. 1711 to 29 Sept. 1739 (*CTB*, xxviii, 491, 501; ibid. xxix, 628; T 53/39 p. 342). *Chief Clerk* Dec. 1738–16 Oct. 1752 (*Gent. Mag.* (1738), viii, 660). D. 16 Oct. 1752 (ibid. (1752), xxii, 478).

Bowman, Peter *City Messenger* 2 Oct. 1827–23 April 1830 (T 29/274 p. 42). Dis. 23 April 1830 (T 29/304 p. 369). *Messenger of Registry* 3 Feb.–21 Aug. 1835 (T 29/362 p. 57). *Messenger* 21 Aug. 1835–21 Dec. 1852 (T 29/368 pp. 481–7). Dis. 21 Dec. 1852 (T 29/549 p. 689).

Boyd, George *Junior Clerk* 21 July 1809–31 July 1818 (T 29/101 p. 510). *Assistant Clerk* 31 July 1818–17 Oct. 1834 (T 29/163 p. 682). *Senior Clerk* 17 Oct. 1834–26 Jan. 1841 (T 29/358 p. 330). *Chief Clerk* 26 Jan. 1841–22 Oct. 1852 (T 29/433 p. 453). Res. 22 Oct. 1852 (T 29/549 p. 127).

Boyle, Hon. Henry *Commissioner* 1 June 1699–8 May 1702.

  Chancellor of Exchequer 27 March 1701–22 April 1708 (C 66/3420, 3424, 3459).

Bradley, Daniel *Messenger* 20 Oct. 1835–26 July 1836 (T 29/370 p. 286). Dis. 26 July 1836 (T 29/479 pp. 465–6).

Bradshaw, Thomas *Chief Clerk* 17 Dec. 1761–18 Aug. 1767 (T 29/34 p. 206). *Junior Secretary* 18 Aug. 1767–16 Oct. 1770 (T 29/38 p. 451).

Bradshaw, William *Supernumerary Clerk* 21 Nov. 1800–20 May 1803 (T 29/77 p. 84). *Junior Clerk* 20 May–c. 5 July 1803 (T 29/81 p. 89). Pd. to 5 July 1803 (T 41/3).

Brand, Hon. Henry Bouverie William *Commissioner* 17 April 1855–1 March 1858. *Parliamentary Secretary* 24 June 1859–14 July 1866 (T 29/575 p. 482).

Brande, George William *Clerk for Colonial Business* 20 Jan. 1832–25 Feb. 1851 (T 29/325 p. 403). Res. 25 Feb. 1851 (T 29/542 p. 397).

Brawne, John *Supernumerary Clerk* 25 Nov. 1794–3 Jan. 1795 (T 29/67 p. 295). *Junior (Assistant) Clerk* 3 Jan. 1795–19 Aug. 1805 (ibid. p. 372). *Assistant Clerk* 19 Aug. 1805–17 May 1808 (T 29/85 p. 348). *Senior Clerk* 17 May 1808–14 April 1815 (T 29/94 p. 512). *Senior Clerk of Minutes* 14 April 1815–31 July 1818 (T 29/134 p. 875). Ret. 31 July 1818 (T 29/163 p. 683).

Breton, Thomas Goldwin *Assistant Clerk of Bills* 7 Jan. 1806–13 July 1808 (T 29/86 p. 1). Res. 13 July 1808 (T 29/95 p. 389).

Brock, John *Messenger to Secretary* first occ. 1809 (*Royal Kal.* (1809), 255). D. 10 June 1824 (T 41/5).

Brodrick, Hon. William *Commissioner* 18 Nov. 1803–16 May 1804; 2 Dec. 1807–16 June 1812.

Brogden, James *Commissioner* 5 Oct. 1812–20 Dec. 1813.

Brooks, John *Deputy Messenger of Receipt* occ. 8 Jan. 1734, 26 June 1739 (*CTBP 1731–4*, 528; *CTBP 1739–41*, 35).
   Messenger pd. from 24 June 1736 to 25 Dec. 1737 (T 53/38 p. 371; T 53/39 p. 32).

Brooksbank, Stamp *Supernumerary Clerk* April/July 1792–25 Nov. 1794 (T 41/3). *Junior Clerk* 25 Nov. 1794–3 Jan. 1795 (T 29/67 p. 295). *Junior (Assistant) Clerk* 3 Jan. 1795–19 Aug. 1805 (ibid. p. 372). *Assistant Clerk* 19 Aug. 1805–24 March 1807 (T 29/85 p. 348). *Senior Clerk* 24 March 1807–3 April 1812 (T 29/89 p. 397). *Senior Clerk of Minutes* 3 April 1812–14 April 1815 (T 29/116 p. 456). *Chief Clerk* 14 April 1815–14 Dec. 1833 (T 29/134 p. 875). D. 14 Dec. 1833 (T 41/8).
   Auditor 14 Sept. 1826–14 Dec. 1833 (T 29/261 p. 170).

Brooksbank, Thomas Constantine *Extra Clerk* 28 July 1796–7 Jan. 1797 (T 29/69 p. 341). *Junior Clerk* 7 Jan.–19 Dec. 1797 (T 29/70 p. 82). *Under Clerk of Revenue* 19 Dec. 1797–19 Aug. 1805 (T 29/71 p. 110; T 41/2). *Assistant Clerk of Revenue* 19 Aug. 1805–23 Feb. 1810 (T 29/85 p. 351). *Senior Clerk of Revenue* 23 Feb. 1810–2 Jan. 1829 (T 29/104 p. 399). *Chief Clerk of Revenue* 2 Jan. 1829–17 Oct. 1834 (T 29/289 p. 48). *Chief Clerk* 17 Oct. 1834–14 March 1850 (T 29/358 p. 317). D. 14 March 1850 (T 41/9).
   Private Secretary to First Lord (Perceval, Liverpool) 5 July 1811–April 1827 (T 41/3; T 29/124 p. 359; T 38/552 p. 252).
   Auditor 17 Oct. 1834–14 March 1850 (T 29/358 p. 333).

Broster, J. *Messenger* 29 March 1842–31 Oct. 1848 (T 29/447 pp. 579–84). Ret. 31 Oct. 1848 (T 41/9).

Brougham, Henry *Serjeant at Arms* 30 Sept. 1765–19 Feb. 1810 (C 66/3703). D. 19 Feb. 1810 (*Gent. Mag.* (1810), lxxx (1), 385).

Broughton, Bryan *Supernumerary Clerk* 10 July 1765–16 Nov. 1769 (T 29/37 p. 66). *Under Clerk* 16 Nov. 1769–30 Nov. 1782 (T 29/40 p. 102). *Senior Clerk* 30 Nov. 1782–7 Jan. 1806 (T 29/52 p. 521). Res. 7 Jan. 1806 (T 29/86 p. 1).
   Private Secretary to First Lord (Shelburne) July 1782–April 1783 (*Gent. Mag.* (1782), lii, 407–8).

Broughton, Vernon Delves *Junior Clerk* 26 Feb.–4 July 1856 (T 29/562 p. 512). *Third Class Clerk* 4 July 1856–5 Sept. 1857 (T 29/564 p. 47). *Second Class Clerk* 5 Sept. 1857 (T 29/568 p. 446).

Private Secretary to Permanent Secretary (Hamilton, Lingen) 24 Dec. 1868 (AB, iv, 344–5; ibid. v, 22).

Browne, George   *Supernumerary Clerk* 9 March 1762–7 April 1763 (T 29/34 p. 243). *Under Clerk* 7 April 1763–11 Nov. 1766 (T 29/35 p. 63). Res. 11 Nov. 1766 (T 29/38 p. 192).

Brummell, Benjamin   *Under Clerk* 25 March–30 Nov. 1782 (T 29/51 p. 181). *Junior (Assistant) Clerk* 30 Nov. 1782–16 Dec. 1783 (T 29/52 p. 520). *Senior Clerk* 16 Dec. 1783–25 Feb. 1816 (T 29/54 p. 496). D. 25 Feb. 1816 (T 41/4).

Brummell, William   *Supernumerary Clerk* 10 July 1765–29 July 1766 (T 29/37 p. 66). *Under Clerk* 29 July 1766–25 March 1782 (T 29/38 p. 98). Res. 25 March 1782 (T 29/51 p. 181).

Private Secretary to First Lord (North) Jan. 1770–March 1782 (*New Companion*, 85).

Brummell, William Charles   *Junior Clerk* 27 Feb. 1816–7 April 1826 (T 29/139 p. 337). *Assistant Clerk* 7 April 1826–21 Jan. 1845 (T 29/256 p. 128). *Senior Clerk* 21 Jan. 1845–5 Feb. 1850 (T 29/481 p. 424). Ret. 5 Feb. 1850 (T 29/538 p. 277).

Bryant, Edward   *Doorkeeper* 27 Jan. 1736–4 Feb. 1742 (*CTBP 1735–8*, 159). *Messenger of Chamber* 10 Feb. 1742–c. 30 April 1762 (*CTBP 1742–5*, 211). D. by 30 April 1762 (T 54/38 p. 355).

Buchan, Thomas   *Junior Clerk* 29 Dec. 1854–31 March 1856 (T 29/557 p. 565). Res. 31 March 1856 (T 41/9).

Buckland, Edward Coplestone   *Junior Clerk* 11 April 1845–24 March 1854 (T 29/484 p. 285). *Assistant Clerk* 24 March 1854–4 July 1856 (T 29/554 p. 642). *Second Class Clerk* 4 July 1856–18 Dec. 1860 (T 29/564 p. 47). *First Class Clerk* 18 Dec. 1860 (AB, iv, 106).

Buller, John   *Commissioner* 12 Sept. 1780–1 April 1782; 26 Dec. 1783–26 July 1786. D. 26 July 1786 (*Gent. Mag.* (1786), lxvi (2), 622).

Bullock, Edward Cranke   *Extra Clerk* 18 Feb. 1789–8 Feb. 1794 (T 29/60 p. 219). *Under Clerk of Revenue* 8 Feb. 1794–19 Aug. 1805 (T 29/66 p. 308). *Assistant Clerk of Revenue* 19 Aug. 1805–1 March 1808 (T 29/85 p. 351). *Senior Clerk of Revenue* 1 March 1808–2 Jan. 1821 (T 29/93 p. 422). *Chief Clerk of Revenue* 2 Jan. 1821–2 Jan. 1829 (T 29/193 p. 77). Res. 2 Jan. 1829 (T 29/289 p. 48).

Clerk of Bills 24 Dec. 1789–8 Feb. 1794 (T 29/61 p. 293).

Bullock, Joseph   *Office Keeper* 10 Jan. 1798–20 March 1801 (T 29/71 p. 537). Res. 20 March 1801 (T 29/77 p. 335).

Bulteel, Thomas   *Junior Clerk* 21 Aug. 1832–29 Nov. 1833 (T 29/332 p. 474). Res. 29 Nov. 1833 (T 29/347 p. 618).

Burgh, Leonard   *Under Clerk* pd. from 25 Dec. 1722 to 29 Sept. 1725 (T 53/30 p. 146; T 53/32 p. 156). D. by 29 Nov. 1725 (T 29/25 p. 127).

Burke, Edmund   *Private Secretary to First Lord* (Rockingham) July 1765–Aug. 1766 *New Companion*, 85).

Burke, Richard   *Junior Secretary* 6 April–15 July 1782 (T 29/52 p. 6). *Senior Secretary* 5 April–27 Dec. 1783 (T 29/54 p. 1).

Burnaby, Edward   *Under Clerk* 21 Sept. 1723–27 July 1757 (*Hist. Reg. Chron.* (1723), viii, 41). *Chief Clerk* 27 July 1757–31 July 1759 (T 29/32 p. 475). Ret. 31 July 1759 (T 29/33 p. 218).

Burnbury, Robert   *Under Clerk* pd. from 25 Dec. 1711 to 25 March 1736 (*CTB*, xxviii, 491, 501; ibid. xxix, 628; T 53/38 p. 36). D. by 1 June 1736 (*CTBP 1735-8*, 169).

Burrell, W.   *Messenger* 25 May 1837–16 Oct. 1840 (AB, ii, 219). Dis. 16 Oct. 1840 (T 29/430 p. 63).

Burton, Lawrence   *Bookranger* pd. from 24 June 1745 to 29 Sept. 1747 (T 53/42 p. 46). D. by 10 Nov. 1747 (T 29/31 p. 59).

Burton, Philip   *Assistant Solicitor* 8 April 1679–2 March 1685 (*CTB*, vi, 16). *Solicitor* 2 March 1685–c. 20 April 1689 (ibid. viii, 24). Left office by 20 April 1689 (ibid. ix, 88).

Bute, John (Stuart) 3rd Earl of   *First Lord* 28 May 1762–15 April 1763.

Byng, George Stevens   *Commissioner* 23 June–22 Nov. 1834.

Byron, Francis   *Senior Clerk* 18 March–4 July 1856 (AB, iii, 309). *First Class Clerk* 4 July 1856–31 Dec. 1861 (T 29/564 p. 47). Ret. 31 Dec. 1861 (AB, iv, 127).

Calder, William Henry Walsingham   *Junior Clerk* 20 June 1839–12 Nov. 1841 (T 29/414 p. 312). Res. 12 Nov. 1841 (T 29/443 p. 269).

Camden, Earl *see* **Bayham,** Viscount

Campbell, J. D.   *Extra Clerk* 26 Aug. 1856–c. 1858 (T 29/564 p. 441). Last occ. 1858 (*Royal Kal.* (1858), 165).

Campbell, John   *Commissioner* 27 June 1746–6 April 1754.

Campbell, Pryse   *Commissioner* 2 Aug. 1766–14 Dec. 1768. D. 14 Dec. 1768 (*Lond. Mag.* (1768), xxxvii, 705).

Canning, George   *First Lord* 20 April–8 Aug. 1827 (*Times*, 21 April 1827). D. 8 Aug. 1827 (*Gent. Mag.* (1827), xcii (2), 174).
   Chancellor of Exchequer 20 April–8 Aug. 1827 (*Times*, 21 April 1827).

Capel, Hon. Sir Henry, kt.   *Commissioner* 9 April 1689–18 March 1690.

Cardwell, Edward   *Financial Secretary* 4 Feb. 1845–7 July 1846 (T 29/482 p. 47).

Carlisle, Charles (Howard) 3rd Earl of   *First Lord* 30 Dec. 1701–8 May 1702; 23 May–11 Oct. 1715.

Carnegie, Hon. Swynfen Thomas   *Commissioner* 11 March–6 July 1846.

Carpenter, John Delaval (succ. as 4th Earl of **Tyrconnel** 20 Dec. 1812)   *Junior Clerk* 25 Aug. 1808–21 June 1811 (T 29/96 p. 275). *Assistant Clerk of Revenue* 21 June 1811–14 Nov. 1817 (T 29/111 p. 665). Res. 14 Nov. 1817 (T 29/155 p. 263).

Carter, Charles   *Messenger of Receipt* 14 Dec. 1791–c. 29 Sept. 1825 (C 66/3875). D. by 29 Sept. 1825 (app. of Ruffe).

Carter, James   *Messenger* 1777–c. 12 Aug. 1791 (*2nd Rept. on Fees*, 81). Left office by 12 Aug. 1791 (T 29/63 p. 420).

Carter, Thomas   *Bookranger* 13 Nov. 1802–16 Jan. 1811 (T 29/79 p. 523). D. 16 Jan. 1811 (T 41/3).

Carter *see also* **Bonham Carter**

Carthew, John   *Supernumerary Clerk* 18 March 1784–15 Aug. 1787 (T 29/56 p. 123). *Junior Clerk* 15 Aug. 1787–27 May 1789 (T 29/58 p. 499). *Junior (Assistant) Clerk* 27 May 1789–3 Jan. 1795 (T 29/60 p. 384). *Junior Clerk* 3 Jan. 1795–5 July 1798 (T 29/67 pp. 371–2). *Junior (Assistant) Clerk* 5 July 1798–3 Jan. 1799 (T 29/73 p. 209). *Junior Clerk* 3 Jan. 1799–20 March 1801 (T 29/74 p. 65). Res. 20 March 1801 on app. as Collector of Customs, Jamaica (T 29/77 p. 335).

Cartwright, William   *Under Clerk* 30 July 1755–3 July 1765 (T 29/32 p. 333). Res. 3 July 1765 (T 29/37 p. 51).

Cathcart, Andrew   *Private Secretary to First Lord* (Derby) 20 Nov. 1867–Feb. 1868 (AB, iv, 294).

Cavendish, Lord John   *Commissioner* 13 July 1765–2 Aug. 1766. *Chancellor of Exchequer* 27 March–10 July 1782 (T 90/142); 2 April–19 Dec. 1783 (ibid.). *Commissioner* 1 April–13 July 1782; 4 April–26 Dec. 1783.

Chamberlayne, Edward   *Under Clerk* 21 May 1762–6 April 1782 (T 29 34 p. 286). D. 6 April 1782 (*Gent. Mag.* (1782), lii, 206).

Chamberlayne, William   *Solicitor* 28 March 1775–14 June 1794 (T 54/42 p. 86). Res. 14 June 1794 on app. as Commissioner of Audit (T 29/66 p. 528).

Chance, George   *Extra Clerk* 2 Sept. 1845–1 April 1857 (T 29/489 p. 3). Res. 1 April 1857 on app. as Accountant, Treasury Solicitor's Office (AB, iii, 341).

Chandos, Richard Plantagenet (Temple Nugent Brydges Chandos Grenville) *styled* Marquess of   *Commissioner* 28 Feb. 1852–4 Jan. 1853.

Charnock, Roger   *Clerk* occ. from 10 July 1665 to 24 Jan. 1672 (*Diary of Samuel Pepys*, ed. H. B. Wheatley (London 1897–9), v, 11; *CTB*, ii, 137; ibid. iii, 1020).

Charteris Wemyss Douglas, Hon. Francis Richard (*styled* Lord **Elcho** 28 Jan. 1853) *Commissioner* 4 Jan. 1853–8 March 1855.

Chetwynd, Richard   *Bookranger* pd. from 25 Dec. 1716 to 29 Sept. 1724 (*CTB*, xxxi, 211; T 53/31 p. 14). D. by 25 Dec. 1724 (T 53/31 p. 350).

Chevallier, Charles   *Under Clerk* pd. from 29 Sept. 1714 to 25 March 1725 (*CTB*, xxix, 628; T 53/31 p. 75). D. by 5 July 1725 (T 53/32 p. 79).

Child, James   *Messenger of Chamber* 3 April 1829–21 Aug. 1835 (T 29/292 p. 44). *Messenger of Registry* 21 Aug. 1835–9 Aug. 1853 (T 29/368 pp. 481–7). Res. 9 Aug. 1853 (T 29/552 p. 327).

Childers, Hugh Culling Eardley   *Financial Secretary* 19 Aug. 1865–14 July 1866 (AB, iv, 194).

Chinnery, George Robert   *Junior Clerk* 3 April 1812–2 Jan. 1821 (T 29/116 p. 455). *Assistant Clerk of Revenue* 2 Jan. 1821–26 Nov. 1823 (T 29/193 p. 77). Res. 26 Nov. 1823 (T 29/227 p. 293).
    Private Secretary to Junior Secretary (Lushington) occ. 14 Nov. 1817, 31 July 1818 (T 29/155 p. 264; T 29/163 p. 685).

Chinnery, William   *Junior Clerk* 25 Feb.–16 Dec. 1783 (T 29/53 p. 183). *Junior (Assistant) Clerk* 16 Dec. 1783–5 July 1798 (T 29/54 p. 496). *Senior Clerk* 5 July 1798–3 Jan. 1799 (T 29/73 p. 209). *Chief Clerk* 3 Jan. 1799–17 March 1812 (T 29/74 p. 64). Dis. 17 March 1812 (T 29/116 pp. 221–2).

Cholmondeley, George (Cholmondeley) 3rd Earl of   *Commissioner* 19 May 1735–20 May 1736.

Chowne, Thomas   *Supernumerary Clerk* 23 May 1760–17 June 1761 (T 29/33 p. 327). *Under Clerk* 17 June 1761–2 July 1772 (T 29/34 p. 116). Dis. 2 July 1772 (T 29/42 p. 133).

Christie, William Henry   *Third Class Clerk* 24 April 1866 (AB, iv, 215).

Cipriani, Philip   *Junior (Assistant) Clerk* 30 Nov. 1782–15 Aug. 1787 (T 29/52 pp. 517, 521). *Senior Clerk* 15 Aug. 1787–24 March 1807 (T 29/58 p. 498). *Chief Clerk* 24 March 1807–17 Sept. 1820 (T 29/89 p. 397). D. 17 Sept. 1820 (T 41/5).

Clay, Frederick Emes   *Third Class Clerk* 1 Sept. 1857–17 Aug. 1865 (T 29/568 p. 429). *Second Class Clerk* 17 Aug. 1865 (AB, iv, 194).
    Private Secretary: to Chancellor of Exchequer (Disraeli) 14 March–June 1859

(ibid. 27); *to Parliamentary Secretary* (Brand) (*Assistant*) 9 Jan. 1860–July 1866 (ibid. 74); (Glyn) 24 Dec. 1868 (ibid. 344–5).

Clayton, William (cr. Lord **Sundon** 2 June 1735) *Commissioner* 20 March 1718–11 June 1720; 28 July 1727–16 Feb. 1742.

Cleave, J. *Extra Clerk* 26 Aug. 1856–26 Aug. 1858 (T 29/564 p. 441). Res. 26 Aug. 1858 on app. to post in British Museum (T 29/572 p. 294).

Cleaver, Thomas *Messenger to Secretary* first occ. 1802 (*Royal Kal.* (1802), 251); remained in office to 5 March 1824 (T 29/231 p. 88). *Messenger and Bookranger* 5 March 1824–18 Feb. 1831 (ibid.). Res. 18 Feb. 1831 (T 29/314 p. 347).

Clement, Richard *Third Class Clerk* 26 Aug. 1856–10 May 1865 (AB, iii, 316). *Second Class Clerk* 10 May 1865 (ibid. iv, 181).
  Private Secretary to Parliamentary Secretary (Taylor, Noel) 14 July 1866–Dec. 1868 (ibid. 237, 340–1).

Clerk, Alexander *Junior Clerk* 17 June 1845–18 March 1853 (T 29/486 p. 316). Res. 18 March 1853 (AB, iii, 224).

Clerk, Sir George, 6th Bart. *Parliamentary Secretary* 19 Dec. 1834–21 April 1835 (T 29/360 p. 359). *Financial Secretary* 8 Sept. 1841–4 Feb. 1845 (T 29/441 p. 77).

Clerke, Samuel *Messenger of Receipt* 5 Nov. 1690–c. 12 Feb. 1742 (C 66/3338, 3434, 3504, 3572). D. by 12 Feb. 1742 (app. of J. Jones).

Clerke, William Henry (succ. as 10th Bart. 16 Feb. 1861) *Junior Clerk* 17 March 1843–24 March 1854 (T 29/459 p. 372). *Assistant Clerk* 24 March 1854–4 July 1856 (T 29/554 p. 642). *Second Class Clerk* 4 July 1856–17 Aug. 1865 (T 29/564 p. 47). *First Class Clerk* 17 Aug. 1865–21 June 1867 (AB, iv, 193). *Principal Clerk* 21 June 1867 (ibid. 277).

Clifford, Charles Cavendish *Private Secretary to First Lord* (Palmerston) 13 Feb. 1855–11 Feb. 1858 (T 29/558 p. 465; T 29/570 p. 285).

Clifford, J. *Extra Clerk* 3 Oct. 1834–7 Oct. 1842 (T 29/358 p. 54). Res. 7 Oct. 1842 on app. to post in Customs (T 29/454 p. 92).

Clifford, Sir Thomas, kt. (cr. Lord **Clifford of Chudleigh** 22 April 1672) *Commissioner* 24 May 1667–2 Dec. 1672. *Treasurer* 2 Dec. 1672–24 June 1673.

Clubb, George *Messenger* 1771–12 April 1793 (*2nd Rept. on Fees*, 80). Res. 12 April 1793 (T 29/65 p. 460).

Clutterbuck, Thomas *Commissioner* 28 April 1741–16 Feb. 1742.

Cocks, William *Junior Clerk* 24 March 1807–10 April 1812 (T 29/89 p. 397). Res. 10 April 1812 (T 29/116 p. 583).

Cohoon, Matthew *Messenger* pd. from 25 Dec. 1689 to 25 Dec. 1698 (*CTB*, xvii, 649, 846). D. 17 Jan./18 Feb. 1699 (ibid. 846, 848).

Colburn, Jonas *Messenger to First Lord* 12 April 1838–6 May 1859 (T 29/400 p. 305). Res. 6 May 1859 (AB, iv, 33).

Colchester, Lord *see* Abbot, Hon. Reginald Charles Edward

Cole, James George *Junior Clerk* 15 Aug. 1826–13 Sept. 1836 (T 29/260 pp. 228–9). *Assistant Clerk* 13 Sept. 1836–1 May 1838 (T 29/381 p. 227). Res. 1 May 1838 (T 29/401 p. 26).
  Private Secretary to Assistant Secretary (Stewart, Spearman) 4 July 1828–Feb. 1838 (T 29/283 p. 88; T 29/374 p. 159).

Cole, James Henry *Junior Clerk* 17 Jan. 1843–20 Feb. 1852 (T 29/457 p. 289). *Assistant Clerk* 20 Feb. 1852–4 July 1856 (T 29/546 p. 529). *First Class Clerk* 4 July 1856–17 Aug. 1865 (T 29/564 p. 47). *Principal Clerk* 17 Aug. 1865 (AB, iv, 193).

Private Secretary: to Financial Secretary (Cardwell) 23 May 1845–July 1846 (T 29/485 p. 404); *to Chancellor of Exchequer* (Wood) 12 Aug. 1851–Feb. 1852 (T 29/544 pp. 340–1); *to First Lord* (Aberdeen) 18 Jan. 1853–Feb. 1855 (T 29/550 p. 136).

Colepepper, John (Colepepper) 1st Lord   *Commissioner* 19 June–8 Sept. 1660.

Collier, John Pyecroft   *Private Secretary to Assistant Secretary* (Trevelyan) 7 July 1846–4 July 1856 (T 29/499 p. 144).
     Assistant Clerk 5 Dec. 1854–4 July 1856 (AB, iii, 251). *First Class Clerk* 4 July 1856–21 March 1867 (T 29/564 p. 47). Res. 21 March 1867 on app. as Assistant Paymaster General (AB, iv, 264).

Collins, —   'A Clerk of the Treasury'; d. c. May 1751 (*Gent. Mag.* (1751), xxi, 237). Position uncertain.

Compton, Hon. George   *Commissioner* 16 Feb. 1742–26 Dec. 1744.

Compton, Peter Alfred   *Junior Clerk* 25 Aug. 1808–21 Feb. 1817 (T 29/96 p. 275). *Assistant Clerk* 21 Feb. 1817–6 Jan. 1826 (T 29/146 p. 451). Res. 6 Jan. 1826 (T 29/253 pp. 153–4).
     Private Secretary to Assistant Secretary (Harrison) occ. 19 May 1812 (T 29/117 p. 293).

Cooke, Edward   *Junior Clerk* 3 Jan. 1795–5 July 1798 (T 29/67 p. 372). *Junior (Assistant) Clerk* 5 July 1798–19 Aug. 1805 (T 29/73 p. 209). *Assistant Clerk* 19 Aug. 1805–7 Jan. 1806 (T 29/85 p. 348). Ret. 7 Jan. 1806 (T 29/86 p. 1).

Cooly, Edward   *Deputy Messenger of Receipt* occ. 17 Oct. 1715 (*CTB*, xxix, 297).

Cooper, Grey (*styled* Bart. from c. 1775)   *Junior Secretary* 30 Sept. 1765–18 Aug. 1767 (T 29/37 p. 151). *Senior Secretary* 18 Aug. 1767–29 March 1782 (T 29/38 p. 451). *Commissioner* 4 April–26 Dec. 1783.

Cornewall, Charles Wolfran   *Commissioner* 11 March 1774–12 Sept. 1780.

Corry *see* **Lowry Corry**

Cotterell, Henry   *Junior Clerk* 21 July 1820–18 July 1825 (T 29/187 p. 549). D. 18 July 1825 (T 41/5).

Cotterell, Stephen   *Messenger of Receipt* 11 Nov. 1802–c. 31 Oct. 1812 (C 66/4012). D. by 31 Oct. 1812 (app. of Barfoot).

Cotton, H. P.   *Extra Clerk* 3 April 1840–24 May 1861 (T 29/424 pp. 76–7). *Supplementary First Class Clerk* 24 May 1861 (AB, iv, 113).

Cotton, Thomas   *Under Clerk* 23 Feb. 1762–30 Nov. 1782 (T 29/34 p. 232). *Chief Clerk* 30 Nov. 1782–4 April 1815 (T 29/52 p. 517). Res. 4 April 1815 (T 29/134 pp. 700–1).
     Auditor 29 May 1807–4 April 1815 (T 29/90 p. 317).

Cotton, William   *Junior Clerk* 7 Jan. 1797–6 March 1800 (T 29/70 p. 82). *Junior (Assistant) Clerk* 6 March 1800–19 Aug. 1805 (T 29/76 p. 18). *Assistant Clerk* 19 Aug. 1805–18 April 1809 (T 29/85 p. 348). *Senior Clerk* 18 April 1809–10 Oct. 1820 (T 29/100 p. 334). *Chief Clerk* 10 Oct. 1820–21 Aug. 1832 (T 29/190 p. 223). Res. 21 Aug. 1832 (T 29/332 p. 469).

Courtenay, John   *Commissioner* 10 Feb. 1806–31 March 1807.

Courtenay, Thomas Peregrine   *Junior Clerk* 23 May 1799–13 July 1802 (T 29/74 p. 400). Res. 13 July 1802 on app. as Cashier, Stationery Office (T 29/79 p. 237).

Courtenay, Thomas Peregrine   *Junior Clerk* 24 Feb. 1826–17 Oct. 1834 (T 29/254 p. 321). *Assistant Clerk* 17 Oct. 1834–20 Feb. 1852 (T 29/358 p. 333). *Senior Clerk* 20 Feb. 1852–4 Dec. 1855 (T 29/546 p. 529). Res. 4 Dec. 1855 (AB, iii, 290).

Private Secretary: to Financial Secretary (Fremantle) 13 Jan.–April 1835 (T 29/361 p. 189); (Clerk) 8 Sept. 1841–Feb. 1845 (T 29/441 p. 77); *to Chancellor of Exchequer* (Disraeli) 2 March–Dec. 1852 (T 29/546 pp. 608–9).

Coventry, Hon. Sir William, kt. *Commissioner* 24 May 1667–8 April 1669.

Cowley, William *Deputy Messenger of Receipt* occ. 1716, 1718 (Chamberlayne, *Present State* (1716), 494; ibid. (1718), pt. ii, 53).

Cowper, Hon. William Francis *Private Secretary to First Lord* (Melbourne) April 1835–c. 1839 (*Times,* 25 April 1835); last occ. 1840 (sic) (*Royal Kal.* (1840), 234); probably left office by 15 Oct. 1839 (app. of C. W. G. Howard). *Commissioner* 25 June–8 Sept. 1841.

Cracherode, Anthony *Solicitor* 31 May 1715–24 Dec. 1730 (*CTB,* xxix, 265). Res. 24 Dec. 1730 (*CTBP 1729–30,* 498).

Crafer, Charles Long *Extra Clerk* 1812–5 Aug. 1825 (T 29/219 p. 153). *Assistant Clerk of Revenue* 5 Aug. 1825–17 Oct. 1834 (T 29/248 p. 115). *Assistant Clerk* 17 Oct. 1834–26 Jan. 1841 (T 29/358 p. 333). *Senior Clerk* 26 Jan. 1841–22 March 1850 (T 29/433 p. 453). *Chief Clerk* 22 March 1850–25 Feb. 1851 (T 29/538 p. 615). *Clerk for Colonial Business* 25 Feb. 1851–4 July 1856 (T 29/542 pp. 397–8). *Principal Clerk* 4 July 1856–24 Dec. 1859 (T 29/564 p. 47). Res. 24 Dec. 1859 (T 29/577 p. 427).
Clerk of Superannuation Returns 11 March 1823–5 Aug. 1825 (T 29/219 p. 153). *Assistant Clerk of Parliamentary Accounts* 5 Aug. 1825–17 Oct. 1834 (T 29/248 p. 115). *Clerk of Parliamentary Accounts* 17 Oct. 1834–22 March 1850 (T 29/358 p. 326).

Crafer, Edwin Turner *Extra Clerk* 28 Feb. 1824–12 Oct. 1832 (T 38/552 p. 54). *Junior Clerk* 12 Oct. 1832–27 Aug. 1841 (T 29/334 p. 179). *Assistant Clerk* 27 Aug. 1841–16 Sept. 1854 (T 29/440 pp. 493–5). D. 16 Sept. 1854 (T 41/9).
Private Secretary: to Financial Secretary (Baring) 10 June–Dec. 1834 (T 29/354 pp. 198–9); *to Parliamentary Secretary* (Stanley) 16 Feb. 1838–June 1841 (T 29/398 p. 349); (Fremantle, Young, Tufnell, Hayter, Forbes Mackenzie, Hayter) 8 Sept. 1841–16 Sept. 1854 (T 29/441 p. 77; T 29/473 p. 389; T 29/499 p. 144; T 29/540 pp. 81–2; T 29/546 p. 637; T 29/550 p. 137).

Crafer, Thomas *Extra Clerk* 20 Aug. 1794–16 July 1802 (T 29/67 p. 183). *Supernumerary Clerk* 16 July 1802–19 Aug. 1805 (T 29/79 p. 265). *Junior Clerk* 19 Aug. 1805–18 April 1809 (T 29/85 p. 348). *Assistant Clerk* 18 April 1809–11 March 1823 (T 29/100 p. 334). *Principal Clerk Assistant* 11 March 1823–15 Jan. 1841 (T 29/219 p. 151). D. 15 Jan. 1841 (T 41/9).
Clerk of Bills 28 July 1796–7 Jan. 1806 (T 29/69 p. 341).

Craggs, G. Wallace *Extra Clerk* 1 May 1857–24 May 1861 (T 29/567 p. 243). *Supplementary Second Class Clerk* 24 May 1861 (AB, iv, 113).

Craig *see* **Gibson Craig**

Cranley, Lord *see* **Onslow,** George

Creswell, Anne Mary *Housekeeper* 17 Jan. 1788–27 June 1799 (T 29/59 p. 81). D. 27 June 1799 (*Gent. Mag.* (1799), lxix (2), 622).

Cripps, William *Commissioner* 9 Aug. 1845–6 July 1846.

Croft, James *Messenger of Receipt* 9 Nov. 1799–c. 11 Nov. 1802 (C 66/3965). D. by 11 Nov. 1802 (app. of S. Cotterell).

Danby, Earl of *see* **Osborne,** Viscount

Dancer, Francis *Under Clerk of Revenue* 2 Feb. 1761–2 Nov. 1791 (T 29/34 p. 30). D. 2 Nov. 1791 (T 53/60 p. 145).

Darlington, Earl of *see* **Vane**, Hon. Henry

Dashwood, Sir Francis, 2nd Bart. *Commissioner* 28 May 1762–15 April 1763. *Chancellor of Exchequer* 29 May 1762–16 April 1763 (C 66/3684).

Davidson, William   *Messenger* 16 June 1854–14 Feb. 1866 (AB, iii, 242). Res. 14 Feb. 1866 (ibid. iv, 212).
   Messenger to Secretary 21 Jan. 1862–14 Feb. 1866 (ibid. 127).

Davies, J.   *Extra Clerk* 13 April 1859–24 May 1861 (T 29/575 p. 49). *Supplementary Third Class Clerk* 24 May 1861–21 Feb. 1869 (AB, iv, 113). *Supplementary Second Class Clerk* 21 Feb. 1869 (ibid. 350).

Davis, James   *Extra Clerk* 1812–c. 1858 (T 29/510 p. 529). Last occ. 1858 (*Royal Kal.* (1858), 166).

Davis, Richard   *Doorkeeper* 22 Nov. 1814–21 Aug. 1835 (T 29/132 p. 371). Ret. 21 Aug. 1835 (T 29/368 p. 487).

Davis, William   *Supernumerary Clerk* 1 June 1736–c. 29 Sept. 1738 (*CTBP 1735–8*, 169). *Under Clerk* c. 29 Sept. 1738–18 Aug. 1767 (T 53/39 p. 342). *Chief Clerk* 18 Aug. 1767–c. 22 Feb. 1776 (T 29/38 p. 451). D. by 22 Feb. 1776 (T 29/45 p. 53).

Dawkins, Clinton George Augustus   *Private Secretary to First Lord* (Aberdeen) 8 April 1853–Feb. 1855 (AB, iii, 225).

Dawson, Charles   *Messenger* 10 June 1863–4 July 1866 (AB, iv, 148). Res. 4 July 1866 (ibid. 232).

Dawson, Frederick   *Junior Clerk* 4 Feb. 1842–25 Feb. 1851 (T 29/446 p. 98). *Assistant Clerk* 25 Feb. 1851–4 July 1856 (T 29/542 p. 399). *Second Class Clerk* 4 July 1856–9 Dec. 1862 (T 29/564 p. 47). *First Class Clerk* 9 Dec. 1862 (AB, iv, 134–5).

Dawson, George Robert   *Junior Secretary* 28 Jan. 1828–26 Nov. 1830 (T 29/277 p. 350).

Dean, John   *Supernumerary Clerk* 24 March 1801–19 Jan. 1802 (T 29/77 p. 352). Res. 19 Jan. 1802 (T 29/78 p. 312).

de Grey, Thomas   *Under Clerk* 31 July 1733–c. 21 May 1762 (*CTBP 1731–4*, 394). Left office by 21 May 1762 (T 29/34 p. 286).

Delamere, Henry (Booth) 2nd Lord   *Chancellor of Exchequer* 9 April 1689–18 March 1690 (C 66/3325).
   Commissioner 9 April 1689–18 March 1690.

Delattre, J. L.   *Extra Clerk* pd. from 10 Oct. 1820 (T 38/552 p. 26). Res. 5 June 1832 (T 29/330 p. 142).

Dent, Matthew   *Under Clerk of Revenue* occ. 17 Oct. 1715 (*CTB*, xxix, 297). D. by 23 May 1718 (ibid. xxxii, 58).

de Ouney, Barton   'Formerly an Assistant Clerk of the Treasury'; d. 13 Feb. 1734 (*Gent. Mag.* (1734), iv, 107). Position uncertain.

Derby, Edward Geoffrey (Stanley) 14th Earl of   *First Lord* 27 Feb.–28 Dec. 1852 (*Times*, 28 Feb. 1852); 26 Feb. 1858–18 June 1859 (ibid. 27 Feb. 1858); 6 July 1866–29 Feb. 1868 (ibid. 7 July 1866).

Dering, Sir Edward, 2nd Bart. *Commissioner* 26 March 1679–24 June 1684. D. 24 June 1684.

Desart, John Otway (Cuffe) 2nd Earl of   *Commissioner* 6 Dec. 1809–26 June 1810.

Devonshire, William (Cavendish) 4th Duke of   *First Lord* 15 Nov. 1756–2 July 1757.

Disraeli, Benjamin   *Chancellor of Exchequer* 27 Feb.–28 Dec. 1852 (*Times*, 28 Feb.

1852); 26 Feb. 1858–18 June 1859 (ibid. 27 Feb. 1858); 6 July 1866–29 Feb. 1868 (ibid. 7 July 1866).

 Commissioner 28 Feb. 1852–4 Jan. 1853; 1 March 1858–23 June 1859; 13 July 1866–29 Feb. 1868. *First Lord* 29 Feb.–9 Dec. 1868 (*Times*, 2 March 1868).

Dodington, George *Commissioner* 2 April 1724–20 Oct. 1740.

Doe, George *Messenger to First Lord* occ. from 1855 (*Royal Kal.* (1855), 165).

Dorington, John *Parliamentary Agent* 30 June 1797–27 June 1827 (T 29/70 p. 434— 'George Dorington'; T 29/252 p. 64). D. 27 June 1827 (MI St Margaret's, Westminster).

Dorington, John Edward *Parliamentary Agent* 5 Dec. 1825 (T 29/252 p. 64).

Dorney, John *Clerk* occ. 10 Jan., 16 Feb. 1676 (*CTB*, v, 4, 130). D. by 23 March 1676 (ibid. 34, 1348).

Douglas, Sylvester (cr. Lord **Glenbervie** 30 Nov. 1800) *Commissioner* 3 Feb. 1797– 9 Dec. 1800.

Dover, Henry (Jermyn) 1st Lord *Commissioner* 4 Jan. 1687–9 April 1689.

Dowdeswell, William *Commissioner* 13 July 1765–2 Aug. 1766.

 Chancellor of Exchequer 16 July 1765–2 Aug. 1766 (C 66/3701).

Downing, Sir George, 1st Bart. *Secretary* May 1667–Sept. 1671 (Baxter, *Treasury*, 177–81).

Drummond, Edward *Junior Clerk* 21 June 1811–14 Nov. 1817 (T 29/111 p. 666). *Assistant Clerk of Revenue* 14 Nov. 1817–17 Oct. 1834 (T 29/155 p. 263). *Senior Clerk* 17 Oct. 1834–1 Jan. 1840 (T 29/358 p. 330). *Chief Clerk* 1 Jan. 1840–25 Jan. 1843 (T 29/421 p. 1A). D. 25 Jan. 1843 (T 41/9).

 Private Secretary: to Chancellor of Exchequer (Robinson) Aug. 1826–April 1827 (T 38/552 p. 82); to First Lord (Canning, Goderich, Wellington) April 1827–Nov. 1830 (T 38/552 p. 94; T 29/273 p. 164; T 29/277 p. 350); (Peel) Dec. 1834–April 1835 (T 41/8); 8 Sept. 1841–25 Jan. 1843 (T 29/441 p. 77).

Drummond, Maurice *Junior Clerk* 28 Feb. 1843–22 Oct. 1852 (T 29/458 p. 535). *Assistant Clerk* 22 Oct. 1852–4 July 1856 (T 29/549 p. 127). *Second Class Clerk* 4 July 1856–1 May 1860 (T 29/564 p. 47). Res. 1 May 1860 (AB, iv, 87).

 Private Secretary: to Chancellor of Exchequer (Lewis) 9 Jan. 1857–March 1858 (T 29/566 p. 8); to First Lord (Derby) 8 March 1858–June 1859 (T 29/570 p. 583).

Drummond, Spencer *Junior Clerk* 13 Feb. 1824–17 Oct. 1834 (T 29/230 p. 224). *Assistant Clerk* 17 Oct. 1834–22 Oct. 1852 (T 29/358 p. 333). *Senior Clerk* 22 Oct. 1852–4 July 1856 (T 29/549 p. 127). *First Class Clerk* 4 July 1856–24 Dec. 1859 (T 29/564 p. 47). Ret. 24 Dec. 1859 (T 29/577 p. 432).

Drummond, Thomas *Private Secretary to Chancellor of Exchequer* (Althorp) 28 June 1833–Dec. 1834 (T 29/342 p. 649).

Dubourg, Peter *Messenger of Receipt* 29 March 1746–10 Feb. 1767 (C 66/3618, 3681). D. 10 Feb. 1767 (*Lond. Mag.* (1767), xxxvi, 147).

Dugdale, William *Receiver of Fees* 30 Nov. 1782–c. 24 Dec. 1789 (T 29/52 p. 524). D. by 24 Dec. 1789 (T 29/61 p. 293).

Duke, William *Junior Clerk* 14 April 1815–12 Oct. 1824 (T 29/134 p. 875). *Assistant Clerk* 12 Oct. 1824–10 Aug. 1832 (T 29/238 p. 155). Dis. 10 Aug. 1832 (T 29/332 pp. 222–3).

Dunbar, Sir William, 7th Bart. *Commissioner* 23 June 1859–26 April 1865.

Duncan, Adam (Duncan Haldane) *styled* Viscount *Commissioner* 8 March 1855– 1 March 1858.

Duncannon, William (Ponsonby) *styled* Viscount (succ. as 2nd Earl of **Bessborough** 4 July 1758) *Commissioner* 15 Nov. 1756–2 June 1759.

Duncombe, Sir John, kt. *Commissioner* 24 May 1667–2 Dec. 1672. *Chancellor of Exchequer* 22 Nov. 1672–2 May 1676 (C 66/3142).

Dupplin, Thomas (Hay) *styled* Viscount *Commissioner* 6 April 1754–22 Dec. 1755.

Durrant, Thomas *Extra Clerk* 24 Aug. 1857–24 May 1861 (T 29/568 p. 253). *Supplementary Third Class Clerk* 24 May 1861–15 Aug. 1868 (AB, iv, 113). *Supplementary Second Class Clerk* 15 Aug. 1868 (ibid. 330–2).

Dwight, Henry Thomas *Extra Clerk* 1820–24 May 1861 (T 29/510 p. 529). *Supernumerary Supplementary First Class Clerk* 24 May 1861–3 April 1866 (AB, iv, 113). Res. 3 April 1866 (ibid. 246–7).

Dwight, William Moss *Extra Clerk* 1809–1 Nov. 1836 (T 29/383 p. 51). *Assistant Clerk of Bills* 1 Nov. 1836–8 Dec. 1854 (ibid.). *Supernumerary Senior Clerk* 8 Dec. 1854–30 Jan. 1858 (T 29/557 p. 401). Res. 30 Jan. 1858 (T 29/570 pp. 22–4).

Dyer, Richard Swinnerton *Supernumerary Clerk* 22 Dec. 1786–15 Aug. 1787 (T 29/58 p. 162). *Junior Clerk* 15 Aug. 1787–24 Dec. 1789 (ibid. p. 499). *Junior (Assistant) Clerk* 24 Dec. 1789–17 Dec. 1794 (T 29/61 pp. 291–2). D. 17 Dec. 1794 (T 41/2).

Dyer, Thomas *Supernumerary Clerk* 21 May 1762–3 July 1765 (T 29/34 p. 286). *Under Clerk* 3 July 1765–30 Nov. 1782 (T 29/37 p. 51). *Senior Clerk* 30 Nov. 1782–9 Aug. 1800 (T 29/52 p. 521). D. 9 Aug. 1800 (T 41/2).

Dyson, Jeremiah *Junior Secretary* 29 May 1762–18 April 1763 (T 29/34 p. 295). *Senior Secretary* 18 April–24 Aug. 1763 (T 29/35 p. 69). *Commissioner* 28 Dec. 1768–11 March 1774.

Earle, Giles *Commissioner* 22 June 1737–16 Feb. 1742.

Earle, Percival Hare *Supernumerary Clerk* 13 July 1802–19 Aug. 1805 (T 41/2). *Junior Clerk* 19 Aug. 1805–13 July 1808 (T 29/85 p. 348). *Assistant Clerk* 13 July 1808–6 Sept. 1831 (T 29/95 p. 387). Res. 6 Sept. 1831 (T 29/321 pp. 128–9).

Earle, Ralph Anstruther *Private Secretary to Chancellor of Exchequer* (Disraeli) 22 March 1858–June 1859 (T 29/570 p. 602).

East, William *Under Clerk* occ. May 1699 (T 1/62 f. 81); pd. from 29 Sept. 1699 to 25 Dec. 1711 (ibid. f. 120; T 1/104 f. 190; *CTB*, xxviii, 449, 479).

Ebrington, Viscount *see* **Fortescue,** Hon. Hugh

Edgcumbe, Richard *Commissioner* 25 June 1716–15 April 1717; 11 June 1720–2 April 1724.

Egerton, William *Supernumerary* Clerk 30 Nov. 1787–27 May 1789 (T 29/59 p. 39). *Junior Clerk* 27 May 1789–1 Feb. 1791 (T 29/60 p. 384). *Junior (Assistant) Clerk* 1 Feb.–9 Nov. 1791 (T 29/62 p. 415). *Under Clerk of Revenue* 9 Nov. 1791–c. 5 April 1792 (T 29/63 p. 549). Pd. to 5 April 1792 (T 53/60 p. 145).

Elcho, Lord *see* **Charteris Wemyss Douglas,** Hon. Francis Richard

Eliot, Edward Granville (Eliot) *styled* Lord *Commissioner* 30 April 1827–24 Nov. 1830.

Eliot, Edward James (*styled* Hon. 30 Jan. 1784) *Commissioner* 13 July 1782–4 April 1783; 26 Dec. 1783–22 June 1793.

Eliot, Hon. William *Commissioner* 31 March 1807–6 Jan. 1812.

Ellenborough, Edward (Law) 2nd Lord *Commissioner* 22 Nov.–31 Dec. 1834.

Ellice, Edward *Parliamentary Secretary* 26 Nov. 1830–10 Aug. 1832 (T 29/311 p. 381).

Elliott, Hon. George Francis Stewart *Private Secretary to First Lord* (Russell) 27 Dec. 1865–July 1866 (AB, iv, 205).

Elliott, Gilbert *Commissioner* 19 March 1761–28 May 1762.

Elliott, T. *Extra Clerk* 13 April 1859–c. 1860 (T 29/475 p. 49). Last occ. 1860 (*Royal Kal.* (1860), 169).

Emmans, Thomas *Messenger* 12 Dec. 1809–4 April 1820 (T 41/3). *Bookranger* 4 April 1820–8 Oct. 1822 (T 29/184 p. 99). *Office Keeper* 8 Oct. 1822–3 April 1829 (T 29/214 p. 144). *Keeper of Papers* 3 April 1829–6 Nov. 1851 (T 29/292 p. 43). Res. 6 Nov. 1851 (T 29/544 p. 281; T 29/545 pp. 187–8).

Empsom, William *Bag Carrier* pd. from 24 June 1714 to 25 Dec. 1737 (*CTB*, xxix, 628; T 53/39 p. 32). D. by 29 Dec. 1737 (*CTBP 1735–8*, 354).

Ernle, Sir John, kt. *Chancellor of Exchequer* 2 May 1676–9 April 1689 (E 403/2464 p. 54; C 66/3262).
 Commissioner 26 March 1679–16 Feb. 1685; 4 Jan. 1687–9 April 1689.

Esmonde, John *Commissioner* 7 June–13 July 1866.

Essex, Arthur (Capel) 1st Earl of *First Lord* 26 March–21 Nov. 1679.

Evelyn, John *Chief Clerk* first occ. July 1689 (LS 13/231 p. 13). Dis. June 1691 (Evelyn MSS, John Evelyn, sen. to Mrs Boscawen, 29 June 1691).

Fane, Henry *Under Clerk* 14 June 1725–26 Aug. 1742 (T 29/25 p. 61). *Chief Clerk* 26 Aug. 1742–1 June 1757 (*CTBP 1742–5*, 71). Res. 1 June 1757 (T 29/32 p. 466).
 Keeper of Papers 23 July 1727–1 June 1757 (T 54/30 p. 380).

Fane, Henry (*styled* Hon. 26 Aug. 1762) *Under Clerk* 7 Dec. 1757–29 Aug. 1763 (T 29/33 p. 2). Res. 29 Aug. 1763 (T 29/35 p. 156).

Fane, John *Supernumerary Clerk* 26 June 1746–3 May 1748 (T 29/30 p. 299). *Under Clerk* 3 May 1748–7 Dec. 1757 (T 29/31 p. 116). Res. 7 Dec. 1757 (T 29/33 p. 2).

Farewell, Phillips *Under Clerk* pd. from 25 Dec. 1711 to 24 June 1712 (*CTB*, xxviii, 491).

Farra, John *Messenger* pd. from 24 June 1700 to 25 Dec. 1720 (*CTB*, xvi, 131; T 53/28 p. 260). Dis. 31 Aug. 1721 (T 29/24, pt. ii, 90).

Fauquier, William Edward *Supernumerary Clerk* 19 Jan. 1802–13 July 1804 (T 29/78 p. 312). *Junior Clerk* 13 July 1804–13 July 1808 (T 29/83 p. 229). *Assistant Clerk* 13 July 1808–11 March 1823 (T 29/95 p. 387). *Senior Clerk* 11 March 1823–17 Oct. 1834 (T 29/219 p. 151). *Chief Clerk* 17 Oct. 1834–3 April 1849 (T 29/358 p. 330). Ret. 3 April 1849 (T 29/531 p. 78).
 Auditor 21 Jan. 1845–3 April 1849 (T 29/481 p. 424).

Fazan, Louis *Messenger to Secretary* occ. from 1796 to 1809 (*Royal Kal.* (1796), 181; ibid. (1809), 255).

Featherstone, Ralph *Supernumerary Clerk* 21 July 1762–7 April 1763 (T 29/34 p. 328). *Under Clerk of Revenue* 7 April 1763–c. 26 Jan. 1768 (T 29/35 p. 63). D. by 26 Jan. 1768 (T 29/39 p. 63).

Fencock, Daniel *Messenger* app. by 12 Dec. 1809 (app. of Emmans); pd. from 5 Jan. 1814 to 8 March 1824 (T 41/4). D. 8 March 1824 (T 41/5).

Ferguson, Ronald Robert Norman *Third Class Clerk* 28 Sept. 1867 (AB, iv, 288).

Finch, Daniel (Finch) *styled* Lord *Commissioner* 11 Oct. 1715–25 June 1716.

Fisher, Daniel *Messenger* 13 April 1860–15 Feb. 1865 (AB, iv, 85–6). Res. 15 Feb. 1865 (ibid. 177).

Fisher, James *Private Secretary to First Lord* (Grenville) 10 Feb. 1806–March 1807 (T 41/3).

Fitness, John *Messenger* 13 Oct. 1837–12 Feb. 1839 (T 29/394 p. 215). *Messenger to First Lord* 12 Feb. 1839 (T 29/410 p. 235).

Fitzgerald, Frederick *Junior Clerk* 26 Dec. 1839–22 March 1850 (T 29/420 p. 387). *Assistant Clerk* 22 March 1850–4 July 1856 (T 29/538 p. 616). *Second Class Clerk* 4 July 1856–24 Dec. 1859 (T 29/564 p. 47). *First Class Clerk* 24 Dec. 1859 (T 29/577 p. 432).
    Private Secretary: to Secretary (More O'Ferrall) 9 June–Sept. 1841 (T 29/438 p. 181); *to Financial Secretary* (Wilson) 18 Jan.–20 Dec. 1853 (T 29/550 p. 137; T 29/553 p. 553).

Fitzgerald, Maurice *Commissioner* 31 July 1827–26 Jan. 1828.

Fitzgerald (from 13 Feb. 1815 **Vesey Fitzgerald**), William *Commissioner* 5 Oct. 1812–7 Jan. 1817.

Fitzharris, James Edward (Harris) *styled* Viscount *Commissioner* 16 May 1804–10 Feb. 1806.

Fleetwood, Arthur *Clerk* app. c. June 1673 (*Letters to Sir Joseph Williamson 1673–4*, ed. W. D. Christie (Camden 2nd ser., viii, ix, 1874), i, 117); occ. from 10 April 1675 to 16 Sept. 1676 (*CTB*, iv, 726; ibid. v, 330). D. by 31 Oct. 1677 (ibid. v, 477).

Foggo, Peter *Office Keeper to First Lord* app. not traced but probably occ. at time of reorganisation 19 Jan. 1836 (T 29/373 pp. 347–51); in office at d. D. 5 Feb. 1839 (T 29/410 p. 235).

Follett, Frederick Tucker *Supplementary Audit Clerk* 23 April 1868–19 Nov. 1869 (AB, iv, 305). *Supplementary Second Class Clerk* 19 Nov. 1869 (ibid. v, 11).

Foot, George *Messenger* 22 July 1834–11 April 1865 (T 29/355 pp. 529–30). Ret. 11 April 1865 (AB, iv, 178–80).
    Bookranger 12 Aug. 1853–2 June 1859 (T 29/552 p. 354). *Messenger of Registry* 2 June 1859–11 April 1865 (T 29/575 p. 458).

Foot, James *Messenger to Chancellor of Exchequer* 18 Feb. 1868 (AB, iv, 299).

Forbes Mackenzie, William *Commissioner* 28 April 1845–11 March 1846. *Parliamentary Secretary* 2 March 1852–5 Jan. 1853 (T 29/546 p. 607).

Ford, Benjamin *Messenger* 27 Sept. 1844–27 April 1868 (T 29/477 p. 416; AB, iv, 301–5).
    Messenger to Secretary 2 June 1859–27 May 1863 (T 29/575 p. 458). *Messenger of Chamber* 27 May 1863 (AB, iv, 149, 301–5).

Fortescue, Chichester Samuel *Commissioner* 8 March 1854–17 April 1855.

Fortescue, Hon. Hugh (*styled* Viscount **Ebrington** 16 June 1841) *Private Secretary to First Lord* (Melbourne) 24 June 1840–Sept. 1841 (T 29/426 p. 438). *Commissioner* 6 July 1846–24 Dec. 1847.

Forward, G. *Messenger* 23 April 1864 (AB, iv, 160).
    Messenger to Secretary 24 Oct. 1868 (ibid. 323–4).

Foster, John *Commissioner* 16 Sept. 1807–6 Jan. 1812.

Foster, Morgan Hugh *Accountant* 27 Feb. 1855–15 Aug. 1859 (T 29/558 p. 578). Res. 15 Aug. 1859 on app. as Assistant Paymaster General (T 29/576 p. 243). *Principal Clerk* 6 March 1867 (AB, iv, 261).

Foster, Thomas *Messenger* 25 May 1863 (AB, iv, 149).
    Doorkeeper 11 April 1865 (ibid. 178–80).

Fowler, Henry *Under Clerk of Revenue* 5 Jan. 1758–3 Jan. 1799 (*2nd Rept. on Fees*, 72). Res. 3 Jan. 1799 (T 29/74 p. 64).

    Placed on establishment 4 May 1762 (T 29/34 p. 272).

Fox, Hon. Charles James *Commissioner* 12 Jan. 1773–11 March 1774.

Fox, Henry *Commissioner* 23 Dec. 1743–27 June 1746.

Fox, John Barrett *Supplementary Third Class Clerk* 5 Feb. 1862–2 Jan. 1863 (AB, iv, 131). Dis. 2 Jan. 1863 (ibid. 142).

Fox, Sir Stephen, kt. *Commissioner* 21 Nov. 1679–16 Feb. 1685; 4 Jan. 1687–9 April 1689; 18 March 1690–31 Oct. 1696. *First Lord* 31 Oct. 1696–1 May 1697. *Commissioner* 1 May 1697–8 May 1702.

Fox, Stephen *Junior Secretary* 1 June 1739–30 April 1741 (*CTBP 1739–41*, 26).

Fox, William Erdman *Under Clerk* 14 April 1723–24 June 1732 (*Hist. Reg. Chron.* (1723), viii, 19). D. 24 June 1732 (*Gent. Mag.* (1732), ii, 827).

Foye, Elizabeth Magdalen *Housekeeper* 25 Aug. 1768–c. 18 Nov. 1774 (T 29/39 p. 216). D. by 18 Nov. 1774 (T 29/44 p. 85).

Francis, Thomas *Assistant Solicitor* 30 May 1750–24 July 1781 (T 54/35 p. 200). D. 24 July 1781 (*Gent. Mag.* (1781), li, 394).

Fraser, A. S. *Supplementary Third Class Clerk* 19 Nov. 1869 (AB, v, 11).

Frecker, Mark *Under Clerk* occ. Aug., Sept. 1703 (T 1/88 f. 323); pd. from 25 Dec. 1708 to 25 Dec. 1723 (T 1/118 f. 112; T 1/171 f. 37; *CTB*, xxviii, 497, 501; ibid. xxix, 628; T 53/31 p. 18). *Chief Clerk* Feb. 1724–Dec. 1738 (T 38/442 p. 95). D. Dec. 1738 (*Hist. Reg. Chron.* (1738), xxiii, 48).

    Chief Clerk of Revenue pd. from 29 Sept. 1714 to 25 March 1725 (*CTB*, xxix, 628; T 53/31 p. 380).

Freeling, John Clayton *Junior Clerk* 23 Feb. 1813–23 Nov. 1821 (T 29/121 p. 705). *Assistant Clerk of Revenue* 23 Nov. 1821–11 Aug. 1826 (T 29/203 p. 620). Res. 11 Aug. 1826 on app. as Secretary to Board of Excise (T 29/260 p. 192).

    Private Secretary to Chancellor of Exchequer (Vansittart, Robinson) 31 July 1818–11 Aug. 1826 (T 29/163 p. 684; T 38/552 pp. 268, 82).

    Auditor 7 April–11 Aug. 1826 (T 29/256 p. 127).

Fremantle, Charles William *Junior Clerk* 22 April 1853–4 July 1856 (T 29/551 p. 199). *Second Class Clerk* 4 July 1856–30 Nov. 1868 (T 29/564 p. 47). Res. 30 Nov. 1868 on app. as Deputy Master and Comptroller of Mint (AB, iv, 327).

    Private Secretary: to Parliamentary Secretary (Hayter, Jolliffe, Brand) 8 Dec. 1854–July 1866 (AB, iii, 255; T 29/570 p. 583; T 29/575 p. 482); *to Chancellor of Exchequer* (Disraeli) 14 July 1866–March 1868 (AB, iv, 236–7); *to First Lord* (Disraeli) 5 March–30 Nov. 1868 (ibid. 300).

Fremantle, Sir Thomas Francis, 1st Bart. *Financial Secretary* 20 Dec. 1834–21 April 1835 (T 29/360 p. 369). *Parliamentary Secretary* 8 Sept. 1841–21 May 1844 (T 29/441 p. 77).

Fremantle, William Henry *Junior Secretary* 2 Sept. 1806–1 April 1807 (T 29/88 p. 1).

Furnese, Henry *Junior Secretary* 15 July–30 Nov. 1742 (*CTBP 1742–5*, 54). *Commissioner* 22 Dec. 1755–28 Aug. 1756. D. 28 Aug. 1756 (T 53/45 p. 469; *Lond. Mag.* (1756), xxv, 452).

Gabbitas, Henry *Messenger to Chancellor of Exchequer* 2 July 1860 (AB, iv, 88).

Gabbitas, John R. *Messenger* 2 June 1859 (T 29/575 p. 458).

    Messenger to Secretary 11 April 1865 (AB, iv, 178–80).

Gale, William or John   *Messenger to Secretary* occ. 12 Aug. 1791, 1801 (T 29/63 p. 421; *Royal Kal.* (1801), 218).

Gardiner, Edward   *Bookranger* 10 Nov. 1747–c. 19 April 1766 (T 29/31 p. 59). D. by 19 April 1766 (T 29/37 p. 421).

Gaskell *see* **Milnes Gaskell**

Gay, Edward   *Extra Clerk* 26 Aug. 1856–24 May 1861 (T 29/564 p. 441). *Supplementary Third Class Clerk* 24 May 1861–29 July 1865 (AB, iv, 113). Res. 29 July 1865 (ibid. 188).

Geddes, George T.   *Extra Clerk* 24 Dec. 1852–24 May 1861 (T 29/549 pp. 689–90). *Supplementary Second Class Clerk* 24 May 1861–21 Feb. 1869 (AB, iv, 113). *Supplementary First Class Clerk* 21 Feb. 1869 (ibid. 350).

Gibbons, Edward   *Supernumerary Clerk* 13 July 1804–19 Aug. 1805 (T 29/83 p. 229). *Junior Clerk* 19 Aug. 1805–19 May 1815 (T 29/85 p. 348). *Assistant Clerk* 19 May 1815–17 Oct. 1834 (T 29/135 p. 311). *Senior Clerk* 17 Oct. 1834–27 April 1835 (T 29/358 p. 330). D. 27 April 1835 (T 29/364 pp. 417–18).

Gibbons, George   *Supernumerary Clerk* 23 May 1799–14 Nov. 1800 (T 29/74 p. 400). *Junior Clerk* 14 Nov. 1800–c. 5 July 1804 (T 29/77 p. 60). Pd. to 5 July 1804 (T 41/3).

Gibbons, T. S.   *Deputy Messenger of Receipt* occ. from 1788 to 1795 (*Royal Kal.* (1788), 181; ibid. (1795), 181).

Gibbons, Thomas   *Messenger of Chamber* 14 June 1765–14 Nov. 1769 (T 54/39 p. 465). *Messenger of Receipt* 27 Nov. 1769–c. 9 Nov. 1799 (C 66/3724). D. by 9 Nov. 1799 (app. of Croft).

Gibson, Thomas   *Under Clerk* 3 May 1726–15 April 1742 (T 29/25 p. 173). D. 15 April 1742 (*Gent. Mag.* (1742), xii, 219).

Gibson Craig, William (succ. as 2nd Bart. 6 March 1850)   *Commissioner* 6 July 1846–28 Feb. 1852.

Gladstone, Stephen Edward   *Private Secretary to Chancellor of Exchequer* (Gladstone) 13 July 1865–July 1866 (AB, iv, 232–3).

Gladstone, William Ewart   *Commissioner* 31 Dec. 1834–19 March 1835. *Chancellor of Exchequer* 28 Dec. 1852–28 Feb. 1855 (*Times,* 29 Dec. 1852); 18 June 1859–6 July 1866 (ibid. 20 June 1859).

    Commissioner 4 Jan. 1853–8 March 1855; 23 June 1859–13 July 1866.

    First Lord 9 Dec. 1868 (*Times,* 10 Dec. 1868).

Gladstone, William Henry   *Private Secretary to Chancellor of Exchequer* (Gladstone) 20 May–July 1865 (AB, iv, 184–5). *Commissioner* 9 Nov. 1869.

Glanville, William   *Chief Clerk* first occ. July 1689 (LS 13/231 p. 13); received dividend of fees from April 1695 to 11 July 1713 (T 1/35 f. 204; T 1/171 f. 4); left office 11 July 1713 (T 1/171 f. 4); reappointed Nov. 1714 (T 38/439 p. 28). D. 23 Jan. 1718 (T 38/440 p. 92).

Glenbervie, Lord *see* **Douglas,** Sylvester

Glyn, George Grenfell (*styled* Hon. 14 Dec. 1869)   *Parliamentary Secretary* 21 Dec. 1868 (AB, iv, 343).

Glyn, Richard Carr   *Supernumerary Clerk* 2 July 1772–18 March 1773 (T 29/42 p. 133). *Under Clerk* 18 March 1773–c. 10 Oct. 1775 (T 29/43 p. 1). Pd. to 10 Oct. 1775 (T 53/53 p. 80).

Goderich, Viscount *see* **Robinson,** Hon. Frederick John

Godolphin, Charles   *Clerk* occ. 25 May 1686 (*CTB,* viii, 753).

Godolphin, Sidney (cr. Lord **Godolphin** 28 Sept. 1684; Earl of **Godolphin** 26 Dec.

1706) *Commissioner* 26 March 1679– 24 April 1684. *First Lord* 9 Sept. 1684–16 Feb. 1685. *Commissioner* 4 Jan. 1687–18 March 1690. *First Lord* 15 Nov. 1690–31 Oct. 1696; 9 Dec. 1700–30 Dec. 1701. *Treasurer* 8 May 1702–10 Aug. 1710.

Golding, Edward *Commissioner* 18 Nov. 1803–16 May 1804.

Goodenough, George Trenchard *Under Clerk* 11 Nov. 1766–30 Nov. 1782 (T 29/38 p. 192). Res. 30 Nov. 1782 on app. as Secretary to Board of Taxes (T 29/52 p. 518).

Gordon, Sir Alexander Cornewall Duff, 3rd Bart. *Junior Clerk* 4 Dec. 1827–1 Jan. 1840 (T 29/276 p. 54). *Assistant Clerk* 1 Jan. 1840–24 March 1854 (T 29/421 p. 1A). *Senior Clerk* 24 March 1854–4 July 1856 (T 29/554 p. 642). *First Class Clerk* 4 July 1856–9 Jan. 1857 (T 29/564 p. 47). Res. 9 Jan. 1857 on app. as Commissioner of Inland Revenue (T 29/566 p. 8).
   Private Secretary to Chancellor of Exchequer (Lewis) 16 March 1855–9 Jan. 1857 (T 29/558 p. 760).

Gordon, Robert *Financial Secretary* 6 Sept. 1839–19 June 1841 (T 29/417 p. 76).

Gordon *see also* **Hamilton Gordon**

Gordon Lennox, Lord Henry George Charles *Commissioner* 28 Feb. 1852–4 Jan. 1853; 1 March 1858–16 March 1859.

Gore, Charles Alexander (*styled* Hon. 8 Feb. 1837) *Junior Clerk* 4 Nov. 1834–20 June 1839 (T 29/359 pp. 43–4). Res. 20 June 1839 on app. as Commissioner of Woods and Forests (T 29/414 p. 312).

Goulburn, Henry *Chancellor of Exchequer* 26 Jan. 1828–22 Nov. 1830 (*Times*, 28 Jan. 1828); 3 Sept. 1841–6 July 1846 (ibid. 6 Sept. 1841).
   Commissioner 26 Jan. 1828–24 Nov. 1830; 8 Sept. 1841–6 July 1846.

Gower *see* **Leveson Gower**

Grafton, Augustus Henry (Fitzroy) 3rd Duke of *First Lord* 2 Aug. 1766–6 Feb. 1770.

Graham, James (Graham) *styled* Marquess of *Commissioner* 26 Dec. 1783–10 Aug. 1789.

Graham, Robert *Commissioner* 14 April–22 Nov. 1834.

Graham Montgomery, Sir Graham, 3rd Bart. *Commissioner* 13 July 1866–17 Dec. 1868.

Grange, James *Junior Clerk* 5 July 1798–7 Jan. 1806 (T 29/73 p. 208). *Assistant Clerk* 7 Jan. 1806–27 Feb. 1816 (T 29/86 p. 1A). *Senior Clerk* 27 Feb. 1816–17 Oct. 1834 (T 29/139 p. 337). Ret. 17 Oct. 1834 (T 29/358 p. 329).

Granger, Miles *Under Clerk* occ. Jan. 1698 (T 1/58 f. 177); pd. from 14 June 1698 to 24 June 1712 (*CTB*, xvii, 841; ibid. xxviii, 490); widow pd. 8 Oct. 1712 for quarter 24 June to 29 Sept. 1712 (ibid. xxviii, 492). D. by 20 July 1712 (Prob 8/105).

Grant, Charles *Commissioner* 20 Dec. 1813–25 March 1819.

Grant, John *Messenger to Chancellor of Exchequer* 22 Nov. 1820–22 Dec. 1840 (T 38/552 p. 252). Ret. 22 Dec. 1840 (T 29/432 p. 473).

Grantham, Edmund *Messenger of Receipt* 22 May 1723–11 Feb. 1742 (C 66/3553, 3572). Left office 11 Feb. 1742 (app. of Oswald).

Green, Robert *Messenger* pd. from 25 Dec. 1698 to 25 Dec. 1702 (*CTB*, xvii, 876; ibid. xxviii, 407). D. by 22 Feb. 1703 (ibid. xxviii, 410).

Greene, Thomas *Messenger of Chamber* occ. 26 March 1663 (*CTB*, i, 510). D. by 5 Dec. 1663 (ibid. 560).

Greenwood, Charles *Messenger* 5 April 1814–5 March 1824 (T 41/4). *Assistant*

Keeper of Papers 5 March 1824–19 Feb. 1839 (T 29/231 p. 88). Ret. 19 Feb. 1839 (T 29/410 p. 375).

    Bookranger 8 Oct. 1822–5 March 1824 (T 29/214 p. 144).

Greenwood, John   *Assistant Solicitor* 30 Dec. 1851–5 June 1866 (T 29/545 p. 663). *Solicitor* 5 June 1866 (AB, iv, 217).

Gregory, Richard   *Messenger of Chamber* 5 Dec. 1663–c. 17 July 1677 (*CTB*, i, 560). D. by 17 July 1677 (ibid. v, 688).

Grenville, George (*styled* Hon. 13 Sept. 1749)   *Commissioner* 23 June 1747–6 April 1754. *First Lord* 15 April 1763–13 July 1765.

    Chancellor of Exchequer 16 April 1763–16 July 1765 (C 66/3689).

Grenville, Hon. James   *Commissioner* 15 Nov. 1756–19 March 1761.

Grenville, James   *Commissioner* 1 April 1782–4 April 1783.

Grenville, William Wyndham (Grenville) 1st Lord   *First Lord* 10 Feb. 1806–31 March 1807.

Greville, Algernon Frederick   *Private Secretary to First Lord* (Wellington) 28 Jan. 1828–Nov. 1830 (T 29/277 p. 350).

Grey, Charles (Grey) 2nd Earl   *First Lord* 22 Nov. 1830–16 July 1834 (*Times*, 23 Nov. 1830).

Grey, Hon. Charles   *Private Secretary to First Lord* (Grey) probably app. Aug. 1832 in place of C. Wood; occ. 1833, 1834 (*Royal Kal.* (1833), 235; ibid. (1834), 235).

Grey, Charles Samuel   *Junior Clerk* 17 Sept. 1833–27 Aug. 1841 (T 29/345 pp. 314–315). *Assistant Clerk* 27 Aug. 1841–8 Nov. 1850 (T 29/440 pp. 493–5). Res. 8 Nov. 1850 on app. as Paymaster of Civil Services, Ireland (T 29/541 p. 262).

    Private Secretary : to Financial Secretary (Baring) 8 May 1835–Aug. 1839 (T 29/365 p. 165); *to Chancellor of Exchequer* (Baring) 30 Aug. 1839–Sept. 1841 (T 29/416 p. 516); *to Assistant Secretary* (Trevelyan) 3 Feb. 1843–July 1846 (T 29/458 p. 44); *to First Lord* (Russell) 7 July 1846–8 Nov. 1850 (T 29/499 p. 144).

Grey, Ralph William   *Private Secretary to First Lord* (Russell) occ. from 1848 to 1851 (*Royal Kal.* (1848), 167; ibid. (1851), 165).

Grey *see also* **de Grey**

Grove, John   *Messenger* 12 Aug. 1836–c. 11 Aug. 1854 (T 29/380 p. 234). D. by 11 Aug. 1854 (T 29/556 p. 321).

    Messenger to Secretary 8 Feb.–12 Aug. 1853 (T 29/550 p. 325). *Messenger of Chamber* 12 Aug. 1853–c. 11 Aug. 1854 (T 29/552 p. 354).

Gunn, Arthur   *Extra Clerk* 26 Aug. 1856–24 May 1861 (T 29/564 p. 441). *Supplementary Third Class Clerk* 24 May 1861–10 May 1864 (AB, iv, 113). *Supplementary Second Class Clerk* 10 May 1864–30 March 1869 (ibid. 164). Res. 30 March 1869 (ibid. v, 1).

Gurdon, William Brampton   *Third Class Clerk* 18 April 1863–7 Dec. 1868 (AB, iv, 147). *Second Class Clerk* 7 Dec. 1868 (ibid. 327–8).

    Private Secretary : to Chancellor of Exchequer (Gladstone) 20 May 1865–July 1866 (ibid. 184–5); *to First Lord* (Gladstone) 24 Dec. 1868 (ibid. 344–5).

Guy, Henry   *Secretary* March 1679–April 1689 (Baxter, *Treasury*, 190–8); June 1691–Feb. 1695 (ibid.).

Gwyn, Francis   *Secretary for Irish Business* April 1685–Dec. 1686 (Baxter, *Treasury*, 195).

Gybbon, Phillips   *Commissioner* 16 Feb. 1742–26 Dec. 1744.

Haines, John   *Messenger of Chamber* 2 Oct. 1827–3 April 1829 (T 29/274 p. 42).

Office Keeper 3 April 1829–2 Feb. 1855 (T 29/292 p. 44). Res. 2 Feb. 1855 (T 29/558 p. 360).

Haines, Mary *Housekeeper* 7 April 1835–29 May 1851 (T 29/364 pp. 148–9). D. 29 May 1851 (T 29/543 p. 639).

Halifax, Earl of *see* **Montagu,** Charles

Halligan, Thomas *Messenger* 28 March 1817–11 July 1834 (T 29/147 p. 632). Ret. 11 July 1834 (T 29/355 pp. 279–80).

Halligan, Thomas *City Messenger* 23 April 1830–21 Aug. 1835 (T 29/304 p. 369). *Messenger to Secretary* 21 Aug. 1835–25 July 1836 (T 29/368 pp. 481–7). *Messenger of Chamber* 25 July 1836–12 Aug. 1853 (T 29/379 p. 427). *Messenger of Registry* 12 Aug. 1853–2 June 1859 (T 29/552 p. 353). *Office Keeper* 2 June 1859 (T 29/575 p. 458).

Hambling, Herbert *Messenger* 25 March 1868 (AB, iv, 318).

Hamilton, Lord Claud John *Commissioner* 6 Nov.–17 Dec. 1868.

Hamilton, George Alexander *Financial Secretary* 2 March 1852–5 Jan. 1853 (T 29/546 p. 607); 2 March 1858–21 Jan. 1859 (T 29/570 p. 579). *Assistant Secretary* 21 Jan. 1859–10 May 1867 (T 29/574 p. 23). *Permanent Secretary* 10 May 1867–1 Feb. 1870 (AB, iv, 272–6). Res. 1 Feb. 1870 (ibid. v, 20–1).

Hamilton *see also* **Baillie Hamilton**

Hamilton Gordon, Hon. Arthur *Private Secretary to First Lord* (Aberdeen) 18 Jan.–8 April 1853 (T 29/550 pp. 136, 225).

Hampden, Richard *Commissioner* 9 April 1689–3 May 1694.
   Chancellor of Exchequer 18 March 1690–10 May 1694 (C 66/3334).

Hankins, Richard *Law Clerk* 9 Jan. 1835–26 Feb. 1856 (T 29/361 p. 98). Dis. 26 Feb. 1856 (AB, iii, 304–6).

Hannam, W. *Messenger* 30 April 1861–25 Aug. 1868 (AB, iv, 111). Res. 25 Aug. 1868 (ibid. 318).
   Messenger to Secretary 14 Feb. 1866–25 Aug. 1868 (ibid. 212).

Hardinge, Nicholas *Junior Secretary* 22 April 1752–18 Nov. 1756 (T 29/32 p. 32). *Senior Secretary* 18 Nov. 1756–9 April 1758 (vac. of J. West). D. 9 April 1758 (*Gent. Mag.* (1758), xxviii, 197).

Hare, Ralph *Messenger* 12 Aug. 1791–12 April 1793 (T 29/63 p. 420). Res. 12 April 1793 (T 29/65 p. 460).

Hargrave, Francis *Parliamentary Counsel* 26 July 1781–14 Aug. 1789 (T 29/50 p. 308). Left office 14 Aug. 1789 (T 29/61 p. 52).

Harley, Robert (cr. Earl of **Oxford** 23 May 1711) *Commissioner* 10 Aug. 1710–30 May 1711.
   Chancellor of Exchequer 11 Aug. 1710–30 May 1711 (C 66/3477). *Treasurer* 30 May 1711–30 July 1714.

Harley, Thomas *Junior Secretary* 11 June 1711–30 July 1714 (T 38/438 flyleaf; ibid. 243).

Harlow, G. *Deputy Messenger of Receipt* occ. from 1785 to 1787 (*Royal Kal.* (1785), 181; ibid. (1787), 181).

Harris, James *Commissioner* 15 April 1763–13 July 1765.

Harrison, George *Assistant Secretary* 19 Aug. 1805–7 April 1826 (T 29/85 p. 351). Res. 7 April 1826 (T 29/256 p. 126).
   Auditor 29 May 1807–7 April 1826 (T 29/90 p. 317).

Harrison, Matthew *Junior Clerk* 23 Feb. 1813–11 March 1823 (T 29/121 p. 705).

Assistant Clerk 11 March 1823–3 Feb. 1843 (T 29/219 p. 151). *Senior Clerk* 3 Feb. 1843–9 May 1856 (T 29/458 p. 43). Res. 9 May 1856 (T 29/563 p. 354).

Private Secretary to Assistant Secretary (Harrison, Hill) 5 Dec. 1825–June 1828 (T 29/252 p. 63; T 38/552 p. 79).

Harrison, Thomas   *Messenger of Receipt* 21 May 1762–11 Aug. 1783 (C 66/3684). D. 11 Aug. 1783 (*Gent. Mag.* (1783), liii (2), 717).

Harrison, Thomas Charles   *Junior Clerk* 25 June 1811–10 Oct. 1820 (T 29/111 p. 753). *Assistant Clerk* 10 Oct. 1820–13 Sept. 1836 (T 29/190 p. 224). *Senior Clerk* 13 Sept. 1836–3 Feb. 1843 (T 29/381 p. 227). *Chief Clerk* 3 Feb. 1843–9 May 1856 (T 29/458 p. 43). Res. 9 May 1856 (T 29/563 p. 355).

Private Secretary to Assistant Secretary (Harrison) occ. from 14 Nov. 1817 to 5 Dec. 1825 (T 29/155 p. 264; T 29/252 p. 63).

Harrison, William   *Parliamentary Counsel* 1798–4 Oct. 1841 (*Report of Select Committee on House of Commons Offices and Fees 1833* (HC 1833, xii), 341–2). D. 4 Oct. 1841 (*Gent. Mag.* (1841), cxi (2), 555).

Harvey, Robert   *Messenger to Secretary* 5 July 1824–21 Aug. 1835 (T 41/5). *Messenger of Chamber* 21 Aug. 1835–25 July 1836 (T 29/368 pp. 481–7). *Messenger to First Lord* 25 July 1836–c. 1854 (T 29/379 p. 426). Last occ. 1854 (*Royal Kal.* (1854), 166).

Harward, John   *Junior Clerk* 29 July 1785–15 Aug. 1787 (T 29/56 p. 517). *Junior (Assistant) Clerk* 15 Aug. 1787–14 Jan. 1791 (T 29/58 p. 498). D. 14 Jan. 1791 (T 53/60 p. 145).

Hatfield, George   *Doorkeeper* 8 May 1804–July 1814 (T 29/83 p. 36). D. July 1814 (T 41/4).

Hatwell, John   *Messenger* 1793–5 April 1814 (*15th Rept. on Finance*, 294). Ret. 5 April 1814 (T 41/4).

Hayter, William Goodenough   *Financial Secretary* 22 May 1849–9 July 1850 (T 29/533 p. 356). *Parliamentary Secretary* 9 July 1850–2 March 1852 (T 29/540 p. 82); 5 Jan. 1853–2 March 1858 (T 29/550 p. 15).

Hayward, Carleton   *Solicitor* 4 Aug. 1737–9 Aug. 1744 (*CTBP 1735–8*, 456). Left office 9 Aug. 1744 (*CTBP 1742–5*, 652).

Hearns, William   *Deputy Messenger of Receipt* occ. 1744 (*Court and City Reg.* (1744), 31).

Heath, John   *Deputy Messenger of Receipt* occ. from 8 April 1746 to 1754 (T 29/30 p. 260; T 48/63; *Court and City Reg.* (1754), 108).

Herbert, George   *Under Clerk of Revenue* 5 Jan. 1758–3 Jan. 1799 (*2nd Rept. on Fees*, 72). Res. 3 Jan. 1799 (T 29/74 p. 64).

Placed on establishment 23 Feb. 1762 (T 29/34 p. 232).

Herbert, George   *Senior Clerk of Bills* 7 Jan. 1806–12 Oct. 1836 (T 29/86 p. 1). D. 12 Oct. 1836 (T 29/383 p. 58).

Hereford, George   *Supplementary Third Class Clerk* 19 Nov. 1869 (AB, v. 11).

Herries, John Charles   *Junior Clerk* 5 July 1798–3 Jan. 1799 (T 29/73 p. 208). *Under Clerk of Revenue* 3 Jan. 1799–19 Aug. 1805 (T 29/74 p. 64). *Assistant Clerk of Revenue* 19 Aug. 1805–21 June 1811 (T 29/85 p. 351). Res. 21 June 1811 (T 29/111 p. 665). *Private Secretary to First Lord* (Perceval) 31 Oct. 1809–21 June 1811 (T 41/3). *Junior Secretary* 7 Feb. 1823–4 Feb. 1827 (T 29/218 p. 77). *Chancellor of Exchequer* 3 Sept. 1827–26 Jan. 1828 (*Times*, 4 Sept. 1827).

Commissioner 8 Sept. 1827–26 Jan. 1828.

Hervey, Lord Alfred   *Commissioner* 4 Jan. 1853–8 March 1855.

Hervey, George William *Third Class Clerk* 20 Oct. 1865–30 Dec. 1869 (AB, iv, 203). *Second Class Clerk* 30 Dec. 1869 (ibid. v, 17).

Assistant Private Secretary to Parliamentary Secretary (Taylor, Noel) 14 July 1866–Dec. 1868 (ibid. iv, 236–7, 340–1).

Hicks, John *Junior Clerk of Civil List* 20 Oct. 1837–6 July 1840 (T 29/394 p. 325). Res. 6 July 1840 (T 29/427 p. 99).

Hill, Richard *Commissioner* 15 Nov. 1699–8 May 1702.

Hill, William *Junior Clerk* 17 May 1808–23 Feb. 1810 (T 29/94 p. 512). *Assistant Clerk of Revenue* 23 Feb. 1810–17 Feb. 1815 (T 29/104 p. 369). *Principal Clerk Assistant* 17 Feb. 1815–22 Oct. 1816 (T 29/133 p. 745). Left office 22 Oct. 1816 on app. as Chief Clerk, Commissariat (T 29/143 p. 725).

Superintendent of Parliamentary Returns 3 April 1812–17 Feb. 1815 (T 29/111 p. 752).

Assistant Secretary 7 April 1826–15 June 1828 (T 29/256 p. 126). D. 15 June 1828 (T 41/6).

Hislop, John Reynolds *Junior Clerk* 25 Aug. 1808–27 Oct. 1816 (T 29/96 p. 275). *Assistant Clerk* 27 Oct. 1816–8 Aug. 1823 (T 29/143 p. 726). Res. 8 Aug. 1823 (T 29/224 p. 121).

Hobhouse, Henry *Assistant Solicitor* 21 Dec. 1811–c. 2 July 1817 (T 54/52 p. 148). Res. by 2 July 1817 on app. as Under Secretary, Home Office (T 54/53 p. 372).

Hoblyn, Thomas *Junior Clerk* 7 Jan. 1797–3 Jan. 1799 (T 29/70 p. 82). *Junior (Assistant) Clerk* 3 Jan. 1799–6 March 1800 (T 29/74 p. 65). *Assistant Clerk of Minutes* 6 March 1800–19 Aug. 1805 (T 29/76 p. 18). *Assistant Clerk* 19 Aug. 1805–13 July 1808 (T 29/85 p. 348). *Senior Clerk* 13 July 1808–31 July 1818 (T 29/95 p. 387). *Chief Clerk* 31 July 1818–17 Oct. 1834 (T 29/163 p. 682). Ret. 17 Oct. 1834 (T 29/358 p. 329).

Hoby Mill *see* **Mill**

Hollier, Samuel *Messenger to First Lord* 6 May 1859 (AB, iv, 33).

Hopkins, Richard *Commissioner* 20 June 1791–3 Feb. 1797.

Horneck, Philip *Solicitor* 18 Jan. 1716–13 Oct. 1728 (*CTB*, xxx, 81; T 54/31 p. 1). D. 13 Oct. 1728 (*Hist. Reg. Chron.* (1728), xiii, 55).

Horsman, Edward *Commissioner* 30 May 1840–8 Sept. 1841.

Howard, Hon. Charles Wentworth George *Private Secretary to First Lord* (Melbourne) 15 Oct. 1839–Sept. 1841 (T 29/418 p. 267).

Howard, Lord Edward George *Private Secretary to First Lord* (Russell) 7–12 July 1846 (T 29/499 p. 144; T 41/9).

Howard, Hon. Sir Robert, kt. *Secretary* Oct. 1671–July 1673 (Baxter, *Treasury*, 181–2).

Howarth, Humphrey Maynwaring App. 'one of the Clerks of the Treasury' Aug. 1732 (*Gent. Mag.* (1732), ii, 928). Position uncertain.

Hugessen *see* **Knatchbull Hugessen**

Hughes, John *Under Clerk of Revenue* app. by Aug. 1742 (app. of W. Speer); occ. 1745 (*Court and City Reg.* (1745), 100). D. by 20 April 1749 (T 29/31 p. 196).

Hughes, T. *Messenger* 26 April 1865 (AB, iv, 180).

Humphreys, J. *Messenger to Chancellor of Exchequer* 1 April 1845–2 July 1860 (T 29/484 p. 95). Ret. 2 July 1860 (AB, iv, 88).

Hunt, George Ward *Financial Secretary* 14 July 1866–29 Feb. 1868 (AB, iv, 236).

Chancellor of Exchequer 29 Feb.–9 Dec. 1868 (*Times*, 2 March 1868).
   Commissioner 3 March–17 Dec. 1868.
Hunter, Thomas Orby   *Commissioner* 15 April 1763–13 July 1765.
Hurst, John   *Messenger* pd. from 29 Sept. 1692 to 24 June 1700 (*CTB*, x, 27; ibid. xv, 393).
Huskisson, William   *Junior Secretary* 21 May 1804–10 Feb. 1806 (T 29/86 p. 63); 1 April 1807–8 Dec. 1809 (T 29/89 p. 449).
Hyde, Sir Edward, kt.   *Chancellor of Exchequer* 19 July 1642–6 Sept. 1660 (W. H. Black, *Docquets of Letters Patent 1642–6* (London 1837), 351). Surrendered office 6 Sept. 1660 (*CTB*, i, 56).
   First Lord 19 June–8 Sept. 1660.
Hyde, Hon. Lawrence (cr. Viscount **Hyde** 23 April 1681; Earl of **Rochester** 29 Nov. 1682)   *Commissioner* 26 March–21 Nov. 1679. *First Lord* 21 Nov. 1679–9 Sept. 1684. *Treasurer* 16 Feb. 1685–4 Jan. 1687.
Jackson, J.   *Supplementary Third Class Clerk* 5 March 1863 (AB, iv, 144).
Jackson, Richard   *Commissioner* 13 July 1782–4 April 1783.
Jeffreys, John   *Junior Secretary* 30 Nov. 1742–1 May 1746 (*CTBP 1742–5*, 95).
Jenkinson, Charles   *Private Secretary to First Lord* (Bute) May 1762–April 1763 (*New Companion*, 85). *Junior Secretary* 18 April–24 Aug. 1763 (T 29/35 p. 69). *Senior Secretary* 24 Aug. 1763–15 July 1765 (ibid. p. 151). *Commissioner* 1 Dec. 1767–12 Jan. 1773.
Jephson, William   *Secretary* April 1689–7 June 1691 (Baxter, *Treasury*, 195–7). D. 7 June 1691 (ibid. 197).
Jett, Thomas   *Under Clerk* pd. from 24 June 1698 to 24 June 1713 (*CTB*, xvii, 841; ibid. xxviii, 495).
John, E. W.   *Extra Clerk* 8 Oct. 1858–c. 1859 (AB, iv, 26). Last occ. 1859 (*Royal Kal.* (1859), 169).
Johnson, Charles   *Messenger to First Lord* 19 March 1847 (T 29/507 p. 358).
Johnston, Thomas   *Messenger* app. 1788 (*15th Rept. on Finance*, 294); occ. 17 May 1797 (ibid.).
Jolliffe, Sir William George Hylton, 1st Bart.   *Parliamentary Secretary* 2 March 1858–24 June 1859 (T 29/570 p. 579).
Jones, Charles Valence   *Solicitor* 12 Dec. 1729–c. 4 Aug. 1737 (*CTBP 1729–30*, 312). D. by 4 Aug. 1737 (*CTBP 1735–8*, 456).
Jones, Hugh Valence   *Solicitor* 9 Aug. 1744–9 Jan. 1800 (*CTBP 1742–5*, 652; T 54/38 p. 95). D. 9 Jan. 1800 (T 53/62 p. 109).
   Private Secretary to First Lord (Newcastle) July 1757–May 1762 (Namier, *Structure of Politics*, 176).
Jones, John   *Doorkeeper* 10 May 1727–4 March 1735 (T 29/25 p. 295). *Messenger of Chamber* 4 March 1735–10 Feb. 1742 (*CTBP 1735–8*, 146). *Messenger of Receipt* 12 Feb. 1742–10 April 1762 (C 66/3611, 3681). D. 10 April 1762 (*Gent. Mag.* (1762), xxxii, 194).
Jones, Lewis A.   *Junior Clerk* 19 Dec. 1834–24 April 1849 (T 29/360 p. 341). *Assistant Clerk* 24 April 1849–4 July 1856 (T 29/532 pp. 423–5). *Second Class Clerk* 4 July 1856–5 Sept. 1857 (T 29/564 p. 47). *First Class Clerk* 5 Sept. 1857–4 Feb. 1868 (T 29/568 p. 446). *Superintendent and Principal Clerk of Registry* 4 Feb. 1868 (AB, iv, 297–8).
   Superintendent of Registry 5 Sept. 1857–4 Feb. 1868 (T 29/568 p. 446).

Jones, W. P. *Extra Clerk* 23 April 1858–c. 1861 (T 29/571 p. 26). Last occ. 1861 (*Royal Kal.* (1861), 169).

Kelly, Thomas *Messenger* 15 March–12 Aug. 1836 (T 29/375 p. 329). *Messenger to First Lord* 12 Aug. 1836–30 March 1838 (T 29/380 p. 234). Dis. 30 March 1838 (T 29/399 pp. 156–7).

Kelsall, Henry *Chief Clerk* Nov. 1714–10 Feb. 1762 (T 38/439 p. 28). D. 10 Feb. 1762 (*Gent. Mag.* (1762), xxxii, 93).

Kemmeter, Charles *Bag Carrier* 29 Dec. 1737–c. 1 Oct. 1747 (*CTBP 1735–8*, 354). D. by 1 Oct. 1747 (T 29/31 p. 49).

Kempe, John Arrow *Third Class Clerk* 12 Aug. 1867 (AB, iv, 283).

Kennedy, Thomas Francis *Commissioner* 26 Nov. 1832–14 April 1834.

Keppel, Hon. George Thomas *Private Secretary to First Lord* (Russell) 12 July 1846–28 July 1847 (T 41/9).

Kerrick, John *Under Clerk of Revenue* 13 Feb. 1754–10 Jan. 1755 (T 29/32 p. 177). *Under Clerk* 10 Jan. 1755–3 July 1765 (ibid. p. 266). Res. 3 July 1765 (T 29/37 p. 51).

King, Benjamin *Messenger of Receipt* 5 Sept. 1674–c. 10 July 1689 (C 66/3167). Forfeited office c. 10 July 1689 (*CTB*, ix, 184).

King, Charles *Office Keeper* 29 July 1717–3 April 1721 (*CTB*, xxxi, 476). Dis. 3 April 1721 (T 29/24, pt. ii, 43).

King, John *Messenger of Receipt* 5 Sept. 1674–c. 10 July 1689 (C 66/3167). Forfeited office c. 10 July 1689 (*CTB*, ix, 184).

King, John *Junior Secretary* 10 Feb.–2 Sept. 1806 (T 29/86 p. 113).

King, Samuel *Under Clerk* pd. from 30 Sept. 1712 to 25 Dec. 1720 (T 1/171 ff. 17, 37; *CTB*, xxviii, 497, 501; ibid. xxix, 628; T 53/28 p. 304); executors pd. 28 March 1721 for quarter 25 Dec. 1720 to 25 March 1721 (T 53/28 p. 369). D. 15/17 March 1721 (Prob 11/579 f. 52).

King, Rev. Walker *Private Secretary to First Lord* (Rockingham) June–July 1782 (*New Companion*, 85).

Kingsman, Thomas *Extra Clerk* 16 Dec. 1783–24 Dec. 1789 (T 29/54 p. 496). *Receiver of Fees* 24 Dec. 1789–c. 15 Jan. 1791 (T 29/61 p. 293). D. by 15 Jan. 1791 (T 29/62 p. 415).
    Clerk of Bills 29 July 1785–24 Dec. 1789 (T 29/56 p. 517).

Kipps, Thomas *Messenger of Receipt* 18 July 1660–c. 14 Feb. 1668 (C 66/2942). Left office by 14 Feb. 1668 (app. of Vine).

Kitchin, Joseph *Doorkeeper* 4 Feb. 1742–c. 12 April 1763 (*CTBP 1742–5*, 6). D. by 12 April 1763 (T 29/35 p. 63).

Knatchbull Hugessen, Edward Hugessen *Commissioner* 23 June 1859–7 June 1866.

Knell, Thomas *Messenger* app. 1793 (*15th Rept. on Finance*, 294); occ. 17 May 1797 (ibid.).

Laing, Samuel *Financial Secretary* 24 June 1859–2 Nov. 1860 (T 29/575 p. 482).

Langford, Samuel *Clerk* occ. 25 Oct. 1678 (*CTB*, v, 1468). *Chief Clerk* occ. July 1689, 4 Feb. 1690 (LS 13/231 p. 13; *CTB*, xvii, 553). D. by 29 Dec. 1690 (*CTB*, ix, 948–9).

Langwith, John *Messenger of Chamber* 21 July 1677–c. 14 Oct. 1692 (*CTB*, v, 694; ibid. viii, 25; ibid. ix, 177). D. by 14 Oct. 1692 (ibid. ix, 1866).

Lansdowne, Henry Charles Keith (Petty FitzMaurice) 5th Marquess of *Commissioner* 17 Dec. 1868.

Latimer, Viscount *see* **Osborne,** Viscount

Law, William   *Junior Clerk* 12 Oct. 1838–22 March 1850 (T 29/406 p. 265). *Assistant Clerk* 22 March 1850–4 July 1856 (T 29/538 p. 616). *First Class Clerk* 4 July 1856–18 Dec. 1860 (T 29/564 p. 47). *Principal Clerk* 18 Dec. 1860–10 May 1867 (AB, iv, 106). *Auditor of Civil List and Assistant to Secretaries* 10 May 1867 (ibid. 272–6).
    Private Secretary: to First Lord (Russell) 23 Nov. 1847–Feb. 1852 (T 29/515 p. 367); *to Financial Secretary* (Hamilton) 5 March 1852–Jan. 1853 (T 29/546 p. 637); (Wilson) 20 Dec. 1853–13 Feb. 1855 (T 29/553 p. 553); *to First Lord* (Palmerston) 13 Feb. 1855–Oct 1856 (T 29/558 p. 479; T 29/565 p. 29).

Lawley, Hon. Francis Charles   *Private Secretary to Chancellor of Exchequer* (Gladstone) 18 Jan. 1853–29 Aug. 1854 (T 29/550 p. 136; T 29/556 p. 455).

Lawton, William   'One of the Assistant Clerks of the Treasury'; d. 14 Dec. 1733 (*Gent. Mag.* (1733), iii, 663). Position uncertain.

Leake *see* **Martin Leake**

Legge (*later* **Bilson Legge**), Hon. Henry   *Junior Secretary* 30 April 1741–15 July 1742 (*CTBP 1739–41*, 461). *Commissioner* 27 June 1746–29 April 1749. *Chancellor of Exchequer* 6 April 1754–25 Nov. 1755 (C 66/3642); 16 Nov. 1756–13 April 1757 (C 66/3654); 2 July 1757–19 March 1761 (C 66/3658).
    Commissioner 6 April 1754–22 Nov. 1755; 15 Nov. 1756–19 March 1761.

Leheup, Peter   *Under Clerk* 20 April 1721–1 Nov. 1752 (T 29/24, pt. ii, 51). *Chief Clerk* 1 Nov. 1752–30 July 1755 (T 29/32 p. 76). Dis. 30 July 1755 (ibid. p. 333).

Leheup, Thomas   *Assistant Solicitor* 29 April 1746–10 Nov. 1747 (T 54/34 pp. 396–7). D. 10 Nov. 1747—'Peter Leheup' (*Gent. Mag.* (1747), xvii, 545).

Le Marchant, Denis   *Secretary* 19 June–8 Sept. 1841 (T 29/438 p. 381).

Lennox, Lord Arthur   *Commissioner* 23 May 1844–9 Aug. 1845.

Lennox *see also* **Gordon Lennox**

Leveson Gower, Lord Francis   *Commissioner* 30 April–8 Sept. 1827.

Leveson Gower, Lord Granville   *Commissioner* 28 July 1800–21 March 1801.

Levett, John William   *Extra Clerk* 20 Aug. 1841–16 Jan. 1850 (T 29/440 p. 341). D. 16 Jan. 1850 (T 29/538 p. 250).

Lewis, George Cornewall (succ. as 2nd Bart. 22 Jan. 1855)   *Financial Secretary* 9 July 1850–2 March 1852 (T 29/540 p. 81). *Chancellor of Exchequer* 28 Feb. 1855–26 Feb. 1858 (*Times*, 1 March 1855).
    Commissioner 8 March 1855–1 March 1858.

Lewis, Thomas Frankland   *Junior Secretary* 4 Sept. 1827–28 Jan. 1828 (T 29/273 p. 35).

Lincoln, Henry (Pelham Clinton) *styled* Earl of   *Commissioner* 31 Dec. 1834–20 April 1835.

Lingen, Ralph Robert Wheeler   *Permanent Secretary* 1 Feb. 1870 (AB, v, 20–1).

Litchfield, Charles   *Junior Clerk* 14 April 1815–13 Feb. 1824 (T 29/134 p. 876). *Assistant Clerk of Revenue* 13 Feb. 1824–17 Oct. 1834 (T 29/230 p. 224). *Assistant Clerk* 17 Oct. 1834–26 Jan. 1841 (T 29/358 p. 329). *Senior Clerk* 26 Jan. 1841–25 Feb. 1851 (T 29/433 p. 453). *Chief Clerk* 25 Feb. 1851–24 March 1854 (T 29/542 p. 398). Res. 24 March 1854 (T 29/554 p. 642).

Litchfield, Henry Charles   *Solicitor* 28 March 1806–30 Dec. 1817 (T 54/50 pp. 41–2). Res. 30 Dec. 1817 (T 29/156 pp. 615–16).

Littleton, Sir Thomas, 3rd Bart.   *Commissioner* 2 May 1696–1 June 1699.

Liverpool, Robert (Jenkinson) 2nd Earl of   *First Lord* 16 June 1812–20 April 1827.

Livingstone, Harford Charles Forbes *Junior Clerk* 17 Nov. 1840–28 Oct. 1842 (T 29/431 pp. 303–4). D. 28 Oct. 1842 (T 41/9).

Lloyd, Charles *Private Secretary to First Lord* (Grenville) June 1763–July 1765 (*Gent. Mag.* (1763), xxxiii, 315).

Under Clerk 29 Aug. 1763–22 Jan. 1773 (T 29/35 p. 156). D. 22 Jan. 1773 (*Gent. Mag.* (1773), xliii, 48).

Lloyd, Philip *Clerk* first occ. 18 June 1669 (*CTB*, iii, 327). Probably left office 16 Sept. 1674 on app. as Clerk of Privy Council (PC 2/64 p. 274).

Lloyd, Thomas *Solicitor* 8 April 1679–c. 2 March 1685 (*CTB*, vi, 16). Left office by 2 March 1685 (ibid. viii, 24).

Long, Charles *Junior Secretary* 26 Feb. 1791–9 April 1801 (T 29/62 p. 485). *Commissioner* 16 May 1804–10 Feb. 1806.

Long, Charles *Messenger* 3 Nov. 1840–c. 27 May 1863 (T 29/431 p. 47). D. by 27 May 1863 (AB, iv, 149).

Messenger to Secretary 11 Aug. 1854–21 Jan. 1862 (T 29/556 p. 321). *Superintendent of Upper Floor* 21 Jan. 1862–24 April 1863 (AB, iv, 127). *Messenger of Chamber* 24 April–c. 27 May 1863 (ibid. 145).

Long, George *Messenger* 29 March 1842–29 Sept. 1868 (T 29/447 pp. 579–84). Res. 29 Sept. 1868 (AB, iv, 322).

Messenger to Secretary 27 May 1856–24 April 1863 (T 29/563 p. 512). *Superintendent of Upper Floor* 24 April 1863–29 Sept. 1868 (AB, iv, 145).

Lovaine, George (Percy) *styled* Lord *Commissioner* 16 May 1804–10 Feb. 1806.

Lowe, Christopher *Under Clerk* 6 Sept. 1721–24 Jan. 1754 (T 29/24, pt. ii, 92). D. 24 Jan. 1754 (*Gent. Mag.* (1754), xxiv, 48).

Lowe, Robert *Chancellor of Exchequer* 9 Dec. 1868 (*Times*, 10 Dec. 1868). *Commissioner* 17 Dec. 1868.

Lowman, John *Messenger* 12 Aug. 1836–c. Sept. 1837 (T 29/380 p. 234). Left office c. Sept. 1837 (T 41/8).

Lowndes, Charles *Under Clerk* pd. from 25 Dec. 1721 to 5 July 1755 (T 53/29 p. 428; T 53/45 p. 100). *Chief Clerk* 30 July 1755–23 Feb. 1762 (T 29/32 p. 333). Res. 23 Feb. 1762 (T 29/34 p. 232).

Keeper of Papers 6 June 1757–15 July 1765 (T 54/36 p. 443).

Junior Secretary 15 July–30 Sept. 1765 (T 29/37 p. 67). *Senior Secretary* 30 Sept. 1765–18 Aug. 1767 (ibid. p. 151).

Lowndes, John *Under Clerk* pd. from 29 Sept. 1699 to 25 Dec. 1711 (*CTB*, xvii, 869; ibid. xxviii, 479).

Lowndes, Robert 'Supernumerary Clerk'; occ. from 1704 to 1707 (Chamberlayne, *Present State* (1704), 557; ibid. (1707), 590). Position uncertain.

Lowndes, Thomas *Under Clerk* pd. from 25 March 1695 to 24 June 1698 (*CTB*, xvii, 759, 834).

Lowndes, Thomas *Under Clerk* pd. from 25 Dec. 1711 to 25 Dec. 1721 (*CTB*, xxviii, 490, 501; ibid. xxix, 628; T 53/29 p. 153). Res. 20 Nov. 1721 (T 29/24, pt. ii, 152).

Lowndes, Wendover *Messenger* pd. from 3 April 1683 to 29 March 1686 (*CTB*, vii, 750; ibid. viii, 674).

Lowndes, William *Clerk* app. c. 1675 (T 64/126 p. 247). *Chief Clerk* occ. from July 1689 to 1693 (LS 13/231 p. 13; Miège, *New State* (1693), pt. iii, 404). *Secretary* Feb. 1695–11 June 1711 (T 64/126 p. 247; *CTB*, x, 1369). *Senior Secretary* 11 June 1711–20 Jan. 1724 (T 38/438 flyleaf). D. 20 Jan. 1724 (*Hist. Reg. Chron.* (1724), ix, 7).

Lowndes, William *Under Clerk* pd. from 25 Dec. 1703 to 25 Dec. 1717 (*CTB*, xxviii, 423, 501; ibid. xxix, 628; ibid. xxxi, 728). *Chief Clerk* Jan. 1718–31 July 1759 (T 38/440 p. 92). Ret. 31 July 1759 (T 29/33 p. 218).

Lowndes, William *Parliamentary Counsel* 14 Aug. 1789–1798 (T 29/61 p. 52). Left office 1798 on app. as Chairman of Board of Taxes (*Report of Select Committee on House of Commons Offices and Fees 1833* (HC 1833, xii), 341–2).

Lowry Corry, Montagu William *Private Secretary: to Chancellor of Exchequer* (Disraeli) 14 July 1866–March 1868 (AB, iv, 236–7); *to First Lord* (Disraeli) 5 March–Dec. 1868 (ibid. 300).

Lowther, Sir John, 2nd Bart. *First Lord* 18 March–15 Nov. 1690. *Commissioner* 15 Nov. 1690–21 March 1692.

Lowther, Thomas *Deputy Messenger of Receipt* occ. 17 Oct. 1715 (*CTB*, xxix, 297). *Messenger of Receipt* 14 Feb. 1718–20 July 1743 (C 66/3524, 3572). Res. 20 July 1743 (*CTBP 1742–5*, 298).

Lowther, William (Lowther) *styled* Viscount *Commissioner* 25 Nov. 1813–30 April 1827.

Luff, W. W. *Supplementary Third Class Clerk* 4 Nov. 1867 (AB, iv, 293).

Lushington, Stephen Rumbold *Junior Secretary* 7 Jan. 1814–7 Feb. 1823 (T 29/127 p. 85). *Senior Secretary* 7 Feb. 1823–19 April 1827 (vac. of C. Arbuthnot).

Luttrell, Francis Wynne *Junior Clerk* 22 Jan. 1819–3 May 1820 (T 29/169 p. 494). D. 3 May 1820 (T 41/5).

Lyle, William *Extra Clerk* 1 Feb. 1850–c. 4 April 1857 (T 29/538 p. 250). D. by 4 April 1857 (T 29/567 p. 3).

Lymington, Viscount *see* **Wallop,** John

Lyttleton, George (succ. as 5th Bart. 14 Sept. 1751) *Commissioner* 26 Dec. 1744–6 April 1754; 22 Nov. 1755–15 Nov. 1756.
    Chancellor of Exchequer 25 Nov. 1755–16 Nov. 1756 (C 66/3649).

Macalpine, John *Receiver of Fees* 1 Feb. 1791–c. 20 Aug. 1794 (T 29/62 p. 415). D. by 20 Aug. 1794 (T 29/67 p. 183).

Macaulay, Henry George *Third Class Clerk* 26 June 1860–21 June 1867 (AB, iv, 86). *Second Class Clerk* 21 June 1867–7 May 1869 (ibid. 277–8). D. 7 May 1869 (ibid. v, 1).

McCulloch, John Ramsay *Junior Clerk of Civil List* 6 July–10 Aug. 1840 (T 29/427 p. 99). Declined app. 10 Aug. 1840 (T 29/428 p. 152).

Macfarlane, John *Office Keeper* 20 March 1801–16 Oct. 1802 (T 29/77 p. 335). D. 16 Oct. 1802 (T 41/2).

Mackenzie *see* **Forbes Mackenzie**

Mackintosh, John *Extra Clerk* occ. 30 Nov. 1782 (T 29/53 p. 183). Dis. 7 Jan. 1797 (T 29/70 p. 82).
    Clerk of Bills 30 Nov. 1782–7 Jan. 1797 (T 29/53 p. 183).

Maclean, Henry Charles *Extra Clerk* app. 6 July 1832 (T 29/331 p. 144). No further occ.

MacNaughten, Edmund Alexander *Commissioner* 25 March 1819–31 July 1830.

Macrae, Kenneth *Extra Clerk* 2 Dec. 1823–24 Dec. 1852 (T 29/510 pp. 529–34). Res. 24 Dec. 1852 (T 29/549 p. 690).

Maddams, George *Messenger* 2 Oct. 1856 (AB, iii, 319).
    Doorkeeper 10 Jan. 1861–21 Jan. 1862 (ibid. iv, 109). *Messenger to Secretary* 27

May 1863–11 April 1865 (ibid. 149). *Messenger of Registry* 11 April 1865 (ibid. 178–80).

Maguire, Robert Hugh *Messenger* 26 June 1865 (AB, iv, 185).

Makins, George *Extra Clerk* pd. from 10 Oct. 1820 to 13 March 1824 (T 38/552 pp. 26, 69). D. 13 March 1824 (ibid. p. 252).

Mann, Christopher *Bookranger* 27 May 1801–13 Nov. 1802 (T 29/77 p. 472). *Office Keeper* 13 Nov. 1802–19 April 1812 (T 29/79 p. 523). D. 19 April 1812 (T 41/4).

Mann, Thomas *Office Keeper* 17 Oct. 1715–29 July 1717 (*CTB*, xxix, 297). App. determined 29 July 1717 (ibid. xxxi, 476); 4 April 1721–c. 5 March 1752 (T 54/26 p. 38). Left office by 5 March 1752 (T 54/35 p. 329).

Manning, William *Messenger* 18 Nov. 1822–15 Dec. 1829 (T 41/4). Res. 15 Dec. 1829 (T 41/6).

Mansell, Sir Thomas, 5th Bart. *Commissioner* 10 Aug. 1710–30 May 1711.

Marchant *see* **Le Marchant**

Martin, Samuel *Junior Secretary* 18 Nov. 1756–30 April 1757 (T 29/32 p. 415); 31 May 1758–29 May 1762 (T 29/33 p. 48). *Senior Secretary* 29 May 1762–13 May 1763 (T 29/34 p. 295).

Martin, Stephen *Under Clerk* 20 Nov. 1721–16 March 1722 (T 29/24, pt. ii, 152). Dis. 16 March 1722 (ibid.).

Martin Leake, John *Under Clerk* 7 April 1763–30 Nov. 1782 (T 29/35 p. 63). *Chief Clerk* 30 Nov. 1782–29 July 1785 (T 29/52 p. 517). Res. 29 July 1785 on app. as Commissioner of Audit (T 29/56 p. 516).

Martin Leake, John *Junior Clerk* 16 Oct. 1846–6 Oct. 1854 (T 29/502 p. 246). *Assistant Clerk* 6 Oct. 1854–4 July 1856 (T 29/557 p. 23). *Second Class Clerk* 4 July 1856–20 May 1857 (T 29/564 p. 47). Ret. 20 May 1857 (T 29/567 p. 519).

Martin Leake, Stephen Ralph *Supernumerary Clerk* 20 May 1803–19 Aug. 1805 (T 29/81 p. 89). *Junior Clerk* 19 Aug. 1805–3 April 1812 (T 29/85 p. 348). *Assistant Clerk* 3 April 1812–17 Oct. 1834 (T 29/116 p. 455). *Chief Clerk* 17 Oct. 1834–26 Jan. 1841 (T 29/358 p. 330). *Principal Clerk Assistant* 26 Jan. 1841–20 Feb. 1852 (T 29/433 p. 451). Res. 20 Feb. 1852 (T 29/546 p. 529).
  Private Secretary to First Lord (Grey, Melbourne) 31 Dec. 1830–Nov. 1834 (T 29/312 p. 486; T 29/357 p. 25).

Maryborough, Lord *see* **Wellesley Pole,** Hon. William

Masser, Thomas William *Messenger to First Lord* 20 May–c. 25 July 1836 (T 54/56 p. 423; T 29/379 pp. 427–8). D. by 25 July 1836 (T 29/379 p. 426).

Matthews, James *Sorter of Books* occ. from Sept. 1782 to 31 July 1784 (T 29/53 p. 183; T 29/55 p. 389).

Maule, George *Assistant Solicitor* 2 July 1817–1 Jan. 1818 (T 54/53 p. 372). *Solicitor* 1 Jan. 1818–14 Nov. 1851 (ibid. p. 461). D. 14 Nov. 1851 (T 29/545 p. 310).

Maxwell Barry, John *Commissioner* 7 Jan. 1817–3 May 1823.

May, — App. 'a clerk of the Treasury' May 1751 (*Gent. Mag.* (1751), xxi, 237); occ. as Clerk 1752 (*Court and City Reg.* (1752), 109). Position uncertain.

Medley, Thomas *Under Clerk* pd. from 24 June 1698 to 25 Dec. 1703 (T 1/58 f. 229; *CTB*, xvii, 860; ibid. xxviii, 421). Left office by 21 Feb. 1704 (*CTB*, xxviii, 421).

Melbourne, William (Lamb) 2nd Viscount *First Lord* 16 July–17 Nov. 1834 (*Times*, 17 July 1834); 18 April 1835–3 Sept. 1841 (ibid. 20 April 1835).

Mellish, William   *Senior Secretary* 15 July–30 Sept. 1765 (T 29/37 p. 67).

Metcalfe, J.   *Extra Clerk* 1807–26 April 1844 (T 29/472 p. 475). Res. 26 April 1844 (ibid.).

Methuen, Paul   *Commissioner* 13 Oct. 1714–15 April 1717.

Micklethwaite, Thomas   *Commissioner* 15 April 1717–20 March 1718.

Middlesex, Charles (Sackville) *styled* Earl of   *Commissioner* 23 Dec. 1743–23 June 1747.

Mill (from 1766 **Hoby Mill**), John (succ. as 7th Bart. 17 March 1770)   *Under Clerk* 11 Feb. 1746–22 Feb. 1776 (T 29/30 p. 239). Ret. 22 Feb. 1776 (T 29/45 p. 54).

Miller, J. T.   *Extra Clerk* 27 Jan. 1859–24 March 1861 (T 29/574 p. 30). *Supplementary First Class Clerk* 24 May 1861–9 May 1864 (AB, iv, 113). Res. 9 May 1864 (ibid. 160–4).

Mills, Edwin   *Extra Clerk* 1 Oct. 1857–c. 1860 (T 29/569 p. 36). Last occ. 1860 (*Royal Kal.* (1860), 169).

Mills, Richard   *Extra Clerk* 27 Nov. 1855–15 Aug. 1859 (T 29/561 p. 467). *Accountant* 15 Aug. 1859 (T 29/576 p. 243).

Milnes Gaskell, James   *Commissioner* 8 Sept. 1841–11 March 1846.

Minet, James Wacker   *Messenger* 5 March 1824–3 April 1854 (T 41/5). Res. 3 April 1854 (T 29/555 p. 95).
  Messenger to Secretary 18 Feb. 1831–8 Feb. 1853 (T 29/314 p. 347; T 29/550 p. 325).

Mitchell, Samuel   *Messenger to Secretary* 29 Jan. 1829–20 April 1835 (T 41/6). Dis. 20 April 1835 (T 29/364 p. 333).

Mitford, Robert   *Extra Clerk* 28 July 1796–7 Jan. 1797 (T 29/69 p. 341). *Junior Clerk* 7 Jan. 1797–14 Nov. 1800 (T 29/70 p. 82). *Junior (Assistant) Clerk* 14 Nov. 1800–19 Aug. 1805 (T 29/77 p. 60). *Assistant Clerk* 19 Aug. 1805–3 April 1812 (T 29/85 p. 348). *Senior Clerk* 3 April 1812–22 Oct. 1816 (T 29/116 p. 455). *Principal Clerk Assistant* 22 Oct. 1816–11 March 1823 (T 29/143 p. 725). Res. 11 March 1823 on app. as Chairman of Board of Taxes (T 29/219 p. 151).

Mitford, William   *Supernumerary Clerk* 21 May 1762–3 July 1765 (T 29/34 p. 286). *Under Clerk* 3 July 1765–30 Nov. 1782 (T 29/37 p. 51). *Senior Clerk* 30 Nov. 1782–16 Dec. 1783 (T 29/52 p. 520). *Chief Clerk* 16 Dec. 1783–24 March 1807 (T 29/54 p. 496). Res. 24 March 1807 (T 29/89 p. 397).

Monck, Charles Stanley (Monck) 4th Viscount   *Commissioner* 8 March 1855–1 March 1858.

Monck, Sir George, kt. (cr. Duke of **Albemarle** 7 July 1660)   *Commissioner* 19 June–8 Sept. 1660. *First Lord* 24 May 1667–3 Jan. 1670. D. 3 Jan. 1670.

Moner, C.   *Sorter of Books* occ. 1802 (*Royal Kal.* (1802), 251).

Monmouth, Earl of *see* **Mordaunt**, Viscount

Montagu, Charles (cr. Lord **Halifax** 13 Dec. 1700; Earl of **Halifax** 19 Oct. 1714)   *Commissioner* 21 March 1692–1 May 1697. *First Lord* 1 May 1697–15 Nov. 1699. *Chancellor of Exchequer* 10 May 1694–2 June 1699 (C 66/3369). *First Lord* 13 Oct. 1714–19 May 1715. D. 19 May 1715.

Montagu, Sir Edward, kt. (cr. Earl of **Sandwich** 12 July 1660)   *Commissioner* 19 June–8 Sept. 1660.

Montagu, Frederick   *Commissioner* 1 April–13 July 1782; 4 April–26 Dec. 1783.

Montagu *see also* **Wortley Montagu**

Montgomery *see* **Graham Montgomery**

Mordaunt, Charles (Mordaunt) 2nd Viscount (cr. Earl of **Monmouth** 9 April 1689) *First Lord* 9 April 1689–18 March 1690.

More O'Ferrall, Richard *Commissioner* 20 May 1835–30 Aug. 1839. *Secretary* 9 June–8 Sept. 1841 (T 29/438 p. 181).

Morgan, Algernon H. V. *Extra Clerk* 15 Dec. 1856–17 July 1857 (T 29/565 p. 551). Res. 17 July 1857 on app. as Assistant Examiner, Audit Office (T 29/568 p. 15; *Royal Kal.* (1858), 168).

Morin (from 10 Nov. 1787 **Tirel Morin**), John *Private Secretary to First Lord* (Shelburne) Oct. 1782–April 1783 (*New Companion*, 85).
    Keeper of Papers 5 Jan. 1783–20 May 1806 (T 54/44 p. 112). Ret. 20 May 1806 (T 29/87 p. 33).

Mornington, Richard (Wesley *later* Wellesley) 2nd Earl of *Commissioner* 19 Sept. 1786–3 Aug. 1797.

Morrice, Sir William, kt. *Commissioner* 19 June–8 Sept. 1660.

Morten, Louis *Messenger* 6 March 1820–c. 27 May 1856 (T 41/4). D. by 27 May 1856 (T 29/563 p. 512).
    Doorkeeper 21 Aug. 1835–c. 27 May 1856 (T 29/368 pp. 481–7).

Mount Charles, Francis Nathaniel (Conyngham) *styled* Earl of *Commissioner* 13 June 1826–24 April 1830.

Mowatt, Francis *Junior Clerk* 2 May–4 July 1856 (T 29/563 p. 314). *Third Class Clerk* 4 July 1856–29 June 1860 (T 29/564 p. 47). *Second Class Clerk* 29 June 1860 (AB, iv, 87).

Muckworthy, Joseph *Messenger to Secretary* first occ. 1810 (*Royal Kal.* (1810), 254). Left office 1 March 1822 (T 38/552 p. 39).

Murray, David Rodney *Serjeant at Arms* 10 Aug. 1810–27 Jan. 1832 (C 66/4104). Office abolished 27 Jan. 1832 (T 29/325 pp. 565–6).

Murray, Herbert Harley *Junior Clerk* 3 Dec. 1852–4 July 1856 (T 29/549 p. 457). *Second Class Clerk* 4 July 1856–30 Dec. 1869 (T 29/564 p. 47). *First Class Clerk* 30 Dec. 1869 (AB, v, 17).
    Private Secretary : to First Lord (Derby) 14 July 1866–March 1868 (ibid. iv, 236); *to Chancellor of Exchequer* (Hunt) 5 March–Dec. 1868 (ibid. 300).

Napier, Robert *Junior Clerk* 4 Sept. 1835–28 Aug. 1838 (T 29/369 p. 118). Res. 28 Aug. 1838 (T 29/404 p. 657).

Nash, E. *Extra Clerk* 7 Oct. 1842–24 May 1861 (T 29/454 p. 92). *Supplementary Second Class Clerk* 24 May–25 June 1861 (AB, iv, 113). *Senior Clerk of Civil List* 25 June 1861 (ibid. 116).

Nelson, Henry *Keeper of Papers* 2 June 1726–c. 25 March 1727 (T 52/34 pp. 181–2). Pd. to 25 March 1727 (T 53/33 p. 118).

Neville, Ralph *Commissioner* 11 March–6 July 1846.

Newcastle, Thomas (Pelham Holles) 1st Duke of *First Lord* 18 March 1754–15 Nov. 1756; 2 July 1757–28 May 1762.

Newman, John *Office Keeper* 2 Feb. 1855–c. 2 June 1859 (T 29/558 p. 360). D. by 2 June 1859 (T 29/575 p. 458).

Newport, Hon. Thomas (cr. Lord **Torrington** 20 June 1716) *Commissioner* 11 Oct. 1715–20 March 1718.

Nicholas, Sir Edward, kt. *Commissioner* 19 June–8 Sept. 1660.

Nicol, Henry *Extra Clerk* 3 April 1849–4 July 1856 (T 28/532 p. 78). *Second Class*

Clerk 4 July 1856–6 Jan. 1860 (T 29/564 p. 47). Left office 6 Jan. 1860 on app. as Superintendent, County Court Department (AB, iv, 88–90).

Nicolay, F. G. *Extra Clerk* pd. from 10 Oct. 1820 to 5 Jan. 1827 (T 38/552 pp. 26, 82).

Nicolay, Frederick *Supernumerary Clerk* 27 May–24 Dec. 1789 (T 29/60 p. 384). *Junior Clerk* 24 Dec. 1789–9 Nov. 1791 (T 29/61 p. 292). *Junior (Assistant) Clerk* 9 Nov. 1791–3 Jan. 1795 (T 29/63 p. 549). *Assistant Clerk of Minutes* 3 Jan. 1795–28 Feb. 1798 (T 29/67 p. 371). *Clerk of Minutes* 28 Feb. 1798–3 Jan. 1799 (T 29/72 p. 187). *Senior Clerk* 3 Jan. 1799–13 July 1808 (T 29/74 p. 64). *Senior Clerk of Minutes* 13 July 1808–3 April 1812 (T 29/95 p. 386). *Chief Clerk* 3 April 1812–11 Feb. 1818 (T 29/116 p. 455). D. 11 Feb. 1818 (T 41/4).

Nicoll, John *Commissioner* 19 March–20 April 1835.

Noel, Hon. Gerard James *Commissioner* 13 July 1866–6 Nov. 1868. *Parliamentary Secretary* 11 Nov.–21 Dec. 1868 (AB, iv, 333).

North, Hon. Sir Dudley, kt. *Commissioner* 26 July 1684–16 Feb. 1685.

North, Frederick (North) *styled* Lord *Commissioner* 2 June 1759–13 July 1765. *Chancellor of Exchequer* 6 Oct. 1767–27 March 1782 (C 66/3714). *Commissioner* 12 Oct. 1767–6 Feb. 1770. *First Lord* 6 Feb. 1770–1 April 1782.

Northcote, Sir Stafford Henry, 8th Bart. *Financial Secretary* 21 Jan.–24 June 1859 (T 29/574 p. 23).

Nugent, George (Nugent Grenville) 2nd Lord *Commissioner* 24 Nov. 1830–26 Nov. 1832.

Nugent, Robert *Commissioner* 6 April 1754–20 Dec. 1759.

Nuthall, Thomas *Solicitor* 30 July 1765–7 March 1775 (T 54/40 p. 15). D. 7 March 1775 (T 53/53 p. 278).

O'Beirne, Rev. Thomas Lewis *Private Secretary to First Lord* (Portland) April–Dec. 1783 (*New Companion*, 85).

O'Brien *see* Wyndham O'Brien

O'Connor, Dennis (*styled* The O'Connor Don) *Commissioner* 6 July 1846–6 Aug. 1847.

O'Dell, William *Commissioner* 7 Jan. 1817–25 March 1819.

O'Ferrall *see* More O'Ferrall

Oldnal, John *Messenger of Receipt* 4 Aug. 1743–17 Oct. 1764 (C 66/3613, 3681). D. 17 Oct. 1764 (*Gent. Mag.* (1764), xxxiv, 499).

Oliver, Joseph *Messenger* 18 Feb. 1831–25 Sept. 1835 (T 29/314 p. 347). Dis. 25 Sept. 1835 (T 29/369 pp. 531–2).

Oneby, John (ktd. 14 Aug. 1672) *Messenger of Receipt* 18 Nov. 1668–29 June 1674 (C 66/3103). Surrendered office 29 June 1674 (C 75/6).

Onslow, George (cr. Lord **Cranley** 20 May 1775; succ. as 4th Lord **Onslow** 8 Oct. 1776) *Commissioner* 13 July 1765–15 Dec. 1777.

Onslow, Sir Richard, 2nd Bart. *Chancellor of Exchequer* 13 Oct. 1714–12 Oct. 1715 (C 66/3508). *Commissioner* 13 Oct. 1714–11 Oct. 1715.

Ord, William Henry *Commissioner* 20 April 1835–22 Aug. 1836.

Orde, Thomas *Senior Secretary* 15 July 1782–5 April 1783 (T 29/52 p. 259).

Orford, Earl of *see* Walpole, Robert

Ormond, James (Butler) 1st Marquess of *Commissioner* 19 June–8 Sept. 1660.

Osborne, Thomas (Osborne) Viscount (cr. Viscount **Latimer** 15 Aug. 1673; Earl of **Danby** 27 June 1674) *Treasurer* 24 June 1673–26 March 1679.

O'Shaughnessy, J. *Messenger* 14 Feb. 1866 (AB, iv, 212).

Oswald, George *Messenger of Receipt* 11 Feb.–c. 7 Dec. 1742 (C 66/3611). D. by 7 Dec. 1742 (*CTBP 1742–5*, 98).

Oswald, James *Commissioner* 20 Dec. 1759–15 April 1763.

Ouney *see* **de Ouney**

Oxenden, Sir George, 5th Bart. *Commissioner* 28 July 1727–22 June 1737.

Oxford, Earl of *see* **Harley,** Robert

Paget, Hon. Berkeley *Commissioner* 26 June 1810–13 June 1826.

Paget, Hon. Henry *Commissioner* 10 Aug. 1710–30 May 1711.

Palmer, Charles *Office Keeper* 5 March 1752–26 Oct. 1769 (T 54/35 p. 329). D. 26 Oct. 1769 (T 53/51 p. 370).

Palmerston, Henry (Temple) 2nd Viscount *Commissioner* 15 Dec. 1777–1 April 1782.

Palmerston, Henry John (Temple) 3rd Viscount *First Lord* 8 Feb. 1855–26 Feb. 1858 (*Times,* 9 Feb. 1855); 18 June 1859–18 Oct. 1865 (ibid. 20 June 1859). D. 18 Oct. 1865.

Parker, John *Commissioner* 22 Aug. 1836–25 June 1841. *Financial Secretary* 7 July 1846–22 May 1849 (T 29/499 p. 144).

Parratt, George Frederick *Junior Clerk* 10 March 1841–8 Nov. 1850 (T 29/435 p. 245). *Assistant Clerk* 8 Nov. 1850–4 July 1856 (T 29/541 p. 262). *Second Class Clerk* 4 July 1856 (T 29/564 p. 47).

Parsons, Edward *Messenger to Chancellor of Exchequer* 29 April 1825–c. 1 April 1845 (T 29/244 p. 384). D. by 1 April 1845 (T 29/484 p. 95).

Paxton, Nicholas *Assistant Solicitor* 20 Dec. 1722–24 Dec. 1730 (T 53/30 p. 126; T 54/30 p. 396). *Solicitor* 24 Dec. 1730–27 July 1742 (*CTBP 1729–30*, 498). Left office 27 July 1742 (*CTBP 1742–5*, 59).

Pearson, Henry Robert *Junior Clerk* 23 March 1810–31 July 1818 (T 29/104 p. 574). *Assistant Clerk* 31 July 1818–30 April 1835 (T 29/163 p. 682). *Senior Clerk* 30 April 1835–21 Jan. 1845 (T 29/364 pp. 417–18). *Chief Clerk* 21 Jan. 1845–3 April 1849 (T 29/481 p. 424). Ret. 3 April 1849 (T 29/532 p. 78).

Peel, Frederick *Financial Secretary* 2 Nov. 1860–19 Aug. 1865 (AB, iv, 91).

Peel, Sir Robert, 2nd Bart. *First Lord* 10 Dec. 1834–18 April 1835 (*Times,* 11 Dec. 1834).
    Chancellor of Exchequer 10 Dec. 1834–18 April 1835 (ibid.).
    First Lord 3 Sept. 1841–6 July 1846 (ibid. 4 Sept. 1841).

Peel, William Yates *Commissioner* 31 July–24 Nov. 1830; 31 Dec. 1834–20 April 1835.

Peirce, John *Messenger* occ. 4 Feb. 1690 (*CTB*, xvii, 554).

Pelham, Hon. Henry *Commissioner* 3 April 1721–2 April 1724. *First Lord* 25 Aug. 1743–6 March 1754. D. 6 March 1754 (*Gent. Mag.* (1754), xxiv, 142).
    Chancellor of Exchequer 12 Dec. 1743–6 March 1754 (C 66/3613).

Pelham, James *Under Clerk* pd. from 25 March 1702 to 29 Sept. 1707 (*CTB*, xxviii, 402, 451).

Pelham, Thomas *Commissioner* 18 March 1690–21 March 1692; 1 May 1697–1 June 1699; 29 March 1701–8 May 1702.

Pemberton, Christopher Robert *Junior Clerk* 12 Jan. 1821–11 Aug. 1826 (T 29/193 p. 320). *Assistant Clerk of Revenue* 11 Aug. 1826–17 Oct. 1834 (T 29/260 p. 192). *Assistant Clerk* 17 Oct. 1834–19 March 1850 (T 29/358 p. 329). Res. 19 March 1850 (T 29/538 pp. 591–2).

Private Secretary : to Junior Secretary (Herries) 24 Aug. 1824–Sept. 1827 (T 29/236 p. 314); (Dawson) 8 Feb. 1828–Nov. 1830 (T 29/278 p. 148); *to Chancellor of Exchequer* (Goulburn) 8 Sept. 1841–July 1846 (T 29/441 p. 77).

Pembroke, William   *Under Clerk of Revenue* 6 July 1779–19 Aug. 1805 (T 29/48 p. 326). *Senior Clerk of Revenue* 19 Aug. 1805–23 Feb. 1810 (T 29/85 p. 351). Res. 23 Feb. 1810 (T 29/104 p. 399).

Pennington, George James   *Auditor of Civil List* 22 Jan. 1836–15 Nov. 1850 (T 29/373 p. 392). Res. 15 Nov. 1850 (T 29/541 p. 286).

Pennington, John (succ. as 3rd Bart. 3 Dec. 1744)   *Under Clerk* 18 Sept. 1732–c. 29 Sept. 1744 (*Hist. Reg. Chron.* (1732), xvii, 37). Pd. to 29 Sept. 1744 (T 53/41 p. 122).

Perceval, Alexander   *Commissioner* 8–20 Sept. 1841.

Perceval, Hon. Spencer   *Chancellor of Exchequer* 26 March 1807–11 May 1812 (E 197/8 p. 57). D. 11 May 1812 (*Gent. Mag.* (1812), lxxxii (1), 499).
   Commissioner 31 March 1807–6 Dec. 1809. *First Lord* 6 Dec. 1809–11 May 1812.

Pettit, Thomas   *Bookranger* 1 Feb. 1811–4 April 1820 (T 29/109 p. 402). *Assistant Keeper of Papers* 4 April 1820–14 Feb. 1824 (T 29/184 p. 99; T 41/4). D. 14 Feb. 1824 (T 41/5).

Petty, Lord Henry   *Chancellor of Exchequer* 5 Feb. 1806–26 March 1807 (E 197/8 p. 39).
   Commissioner 10 Feb. 1806–31 March 1807.

Philp, E.   *Extra Clerk* 13 April 1859–24 May 1861 (T 29/475 p. 49). *Supplementary Third Class Clerk* 24 May 1861–19 Nov. 1869 (AB, iv, 113). *Supplementary Second Class Clerk* 19 Nov. 1869 (ibid. v, 11a).

Pickering, Danby   *Parliamentary Counsel* 28 Nov. 1769–24 March 1781 (T 29/40 p. 117). D. 24 March 1781 (*Gent. Mag.* (1781), li, 148).

Pinney, J.   *Extra Clerk* pd. from 10 Oct. 1820 to 5 Jan. 1821 (T 38/552 p. 26). Dis. 9 Feb. 1821 (T 29/194 p. 322).

Pitt, William   *Under Clerk* 23 Jan. 1718–20 April 1721 (*CTB*, xxxii, 7). Res. 20 April 1721 (T 29/24, pt. ii, 51).

Pitt, Hon. William   *Chancellor of Exchequer* 10 July 1782–2 April 1783 (T 90/142); 19 Dec. 1783–14 March 1801 (ibid.); 10 May 1804–23 Jan. 1806 (T 90/144). D. 23 Jan. 1806 (*Gent. Mag.* (1806), lxxvi (1), 644).
   Commissioner 13 July 1782–4 April 1783. *First Lord* 26 Dec. 1783–21 March 1801; 16 May 1804–23 Jan. 1806.

Planta, Joseph   *Senior Secretary* 19 April 1827–26 Nov. 1830 (T 29/268 p. 261). *Commissioner* 22 Nov.–31 Dec. 1834.

Plaxton, William   *Under Clerk of Revenue* 20 April 1749–13 Feb. 1754 (T 29/31 p. 196). *Under Clerk* 13 Feb. 1754–10 July 1758 (T 29/32 p. 177). Dis. 10 July 1758 (T 29/33 p. 66).

Plunkett, Hon. Edmond Luke   *Junior Clerk* 17 Dec. 1850–4 July 1856 (T 29/541 p. 519). *Second Class Clerk* 4 July 1856–21 June 1867 (T 29/564 p. 47). *First Class Clerk* 21 June 1867–30 Dec. 1869 (AB, iv, 277). Res. 30 Dec. 1869 (ibid. v, 17).

Pococke, Augustus Frederick   *Junior Clerk* 1 Sept. 1818–27 Feb. 1824 (T 29/165 p. 32). Res. 27 Feb. 1824 (T 29/230 pp. 440–1).

Pole *see* **Wellesley Pole**

Ponsonby, Hon. George   *Commissioner* 24 Nov. 1830–22 Nov. 1834.

Ponsonby, Hon. Gerald Henry Brabazon   *Junior Clerk* 24 Feb. 1852–4 July 1856

(T 29/546 p. 553). *Second Class Clerk* 4 July 1856–20 May 1867 (T 29/564 p. 47). Res. 20 May 1867 (AB, iv, 270).

Private Secretary to First Lord (Palmerston) 13 Nov. 1857–Feb. 1858 (T 29/569 p. 245).

Ponsonby, Robert Wentworth *Junior Clerk* 23 Sept. 1836–28 Sept. 1840 (T 29/381 p. 368). D. 28 Sept. 1840 (Burke, *Peerage* (1900), 146).

Poole, Ferdinando (succ. as 4th Bart. 8 July 1767) *Under Clerk* 1 Nov. 1752–23 Feb. 1762 (T 29/32 p. 76). *Chief Clerk* 23 Feb. 1762–30 Nov. 1782 (T 29/34 p. 232). Res. 30 Nov. 1782 (T 29/52 pp. 516–17).

Portland, William Henry (Cavendish Bentinck) 3rd Duke of *First Lord* 4 April–26 Dec. 1783; 31 March 1807–30 Oct. 1809. D. 30 Oct. 1809.

Postlethwaite, James *Chief Clerk* 31 July 1759–6 Sept. 1761 (T 29/33 p. 218). D. 6 Sept. 1761 (*Lond. Mag.* (1761), xxx, 505).

Potter, Hanbury *Doorkeeper* 12 April 1763–10 Jan. 1798 (T 29/35 p. 67). Ret. 10 Jan. 1798 (T 29/71 p. 537).

Poulett, John (Poulett) 1st Earl *First Lord* 10 Aug. 1710–30 May 1711.

Powell, Thomas *Assistant Keeper of Papers* 5 July 1798–1 Aug. 1810 (T 29/73 p. 212). D. 1 Aug. 1810 (T 41/3).

Power, Benjamin *Under Clerk of Revenue* occ. 17 Oct. 1715 (*CTB*, xxix, 297). *Under Clerk* pd. from 25 March to 25 Dec. 1721 (T 53/29 pp. 42, 153). D. 16 Jan. 1722 (*Hist. Reg. Chron.* (1722), vii, 7).

Powys, Richard *Clerk* occ. 31 July 1687 (*CTB*, viii, 1489). *Under Clerk* occ. July 1689, 4 Feb. 1690 (LS 13/231 p. 13; *CTB*, xvii, 553). *Chief Clerk* received dividend of fees from April 1695 to Feb. 1724 (T 1/35 f. 204; T 38/442 p. 92). D. 16 Feb. 1724 (T 38/442 p. 92).

Poyntz, William Dean *Supernumerary Clerk* 26 Jan. 1768–2 July 1772 (T 29/39 p. 63). *Under Clerk* 2 July 1772–30 Nov. 1782 (T 29/42 p. 133). *Junior Clerk* 30 Nov. 1782–16 Dec. 1783 (T 29/52 p. 520). *Senior Clerk* 16 Dec. 1783–29 Oct. 1789 (T 29/54 p. 496). D. 29 Oct. 1789 (T 60/28 p. 170).

Pratt, Thomas *Under Clerk* 4 March 1724–16 Nov. 1769 (*Hist. Reg. Chron.* (1724), ix, 13). *Chief Clerk* 16 Nov. 1769–5 July 1798 (T 29/40 p. 102). Res. 5 July 1798 (T 29/73 pp. 207–8).

Keeper of Papers 17 Sept. 1765–5 Jan. 1783 (T 54/40 p. 35; T 54/44 p. 112).

Pretyman, Rev. George *Private Secretary to First Lord* (Pitt) Dec. 1783–March 1787 (*New Companion*, 85).

Primrose, Henry William *Third Class Clerk* 13 Oct. 1869 (AB, v, 9).

Pringle, Alexander *Commissioner* 8 Sept. 1841–28 April 1845.

Puller, Christopher Cholmeley *Third Class Clerk* 12 June 1865–12 May 1869 (AB, iv, 182). *Second Class Clerk* 12 May 1869 (ibid. v, 2).

Purvis, Robert *Messenger* 16 Sept. 1853–1 March 1860 (T 29/552 p. 591). Dis. 1 March 1860 (AB, iv, 76).

Pybus, Charles Small *Commissioner* 3 Aug. 1797–18 Nov. 1803.

Ramsey, John *Serjeant at Arms* 6 Nov. 1674–27 May/26 Sept. 1684 (C 66/3162; *CTB*, viii, 137). D. between 27 May and 26 Sept. 1684 (*CTB*, vii, 1136; ibid. viii, 137; Prob 6/59).

Solicitor 15 July 1676–c. 8 April 1679 (*CTB*, v, 274). Dis. by 8 April 1679 (ibid. vi, 16).

Ramus, George Edward *Supernumerary Clerk* 7 April 1763–29 July 1766 (T 29/35

p. 63). *Under Clerk* 29 July 1766–30 Nov. 1782 (T 29/38 p. 98). *Senior Clerk* 30 Nov. 1782–29 July 1785 (T 29/52 p. 521). *Chief Clerk* 29 July 1785–13 May 1808 (T 29/56 p. 516). D. 13 May 1808 (T 41/3).

Ray, W. S. *Supplementary Third Class Clerk* 7 July 1868 (AB, iv, 314).

Ready, William *Office Keeper* 24 April 1812–8 Oct. 1822 (T 29/116 p. 777). Dis. 22 Oct. 1822 (T 29/214 p. 143). *Messenger* 22 Oct. 1822–2 May 1834 (ibid.). Left office 2 May 1834 (T 29/353 p. 53).

Reeve, John *Messenger of Chamber* occ. 4 Sept. 1660 (*CTB*, i, 54). D. by 7 Dec. 1662 (ibid. 520).

Reymann, J. F. *Messenger* app. by 12 Dec. 1809 (app. of Emmans); pd. from 5 Jan. 1814 to 17 Nov. 1822 (T 41/4). Res. 17 Nov. 1822 (T 41/5).

Reynolds, Frederick *Under Clerk* 26 Sept. 1753–22 Feb. 1776 (T 29/32 p. 153). *Chief Clerk* 22 Feb. 1776–16 Dec. 1783 (T 29/45 p. 53). Res. 16 Dec. 1783 (T 29/54 p. 495).

Reynolds, Henry Revell *Assistant Solicitor* 22 Nov. 1842–30 Dec. 1851 (T 29/455 pp. 413–14). *Solicitor* 30 Dec. 1851–1 June 1866 (T 29/545 p. 663). Res. 1 June 1866 (AB, iv, 216).

Reynolds, John Stuckey *Junior Clerk* 13 July 1808–27 Feb. 1816 (T 29/95 p. 386). *Assistant Clerk* 27 Feb. 1816–7 April 1826 (T 29/139 p. 337). Left office 7 April 1826 on app. as Senior Clerk, Commissariat (T 29/256 p. 127).

Private Secretary to Junior Secretary (Lushington) pd. from 10 Oct. 1820 to 4 March 1823 (T 38/552 pp. 26, 46).

Rice *see* **Spring Rice**

Rich, Henry *Commissioner* 6 July 1846–28 Feb. 1852.

Richards, John *Messenger* 8 March 1824–4 June 1844 (T 41/5). Ret. 4 June 1844 (T 29/474 p. 58).

Richards, Joseph *Messenger of Receipt* 29 Aug. 1689–1 Feb. 1732 (C 66/3329, 3434, 3502, 3572). D. 1 Feb. 1732 (*Gent. Mag.* (1732), ii, 630).

Richards, William *Deputy Messenger of Receipt* occ. 1718 (Chamberlayne, *Present State* (1718), pt. ii, 53); remained in office until d. D. by 15 Jan. 1736 (*CTBP 1735–8*, 158).

Messenger pd. from 30 Sept. 1729 to 25 Dec. 1735 (*CTBP 1729–30*, 145; T 53/38 p. 163).

Ricketts, Edward Woodville *Junior Clerk* 21 April 1826–30 April 1835 (T 29/256 p. 353). *Assistant Clerk* 30 April 1835–3 April 1849 (T 29/364 pp. 417–18). Res. 3 April 1849 (T 29/532 pp. 57–8).

Superintendent of Registry 3 Feb. 1843–3 April 1849 (T 29/458 p. 43).

Ridout, John Christopher *Junior (Assistant) Clerk* 30 Nov. 1782–15 Aug. 1787 (T 29/52 pp. 517–18, 521). Res. 15 Aug. 1787 on app. as Deputy Searcher, Port of London (T 29/58 p. 498).

Robartes, John (Robartes) 2nd Lord *Commissioner* 19 June–8 Sept. 1660.

Roberts, John *Private Secretary to First Lord* (Pelham, Newcastle) Aug. 1743–Nov. 1756 (Namier, *Structure of Politics*, 175).

Roberts, W. B. *Extra Clerk* 22 Feb. 1850–8 March 1852 (T 29/438 p. 397). Left office 8 March 1852 (T 41/9).

Robinson, Frederick J. *Junior Clerk of Civil List* 20 Aug. 1851 (T 29/544 pp. 447–8). *Supplementary Second Class Clerk* 9 Aug. 1861 (AB, iv, 119–20).

Robinson, Hon. Frederick John (cr. Viscount **Goderich** 28 April 1827) *Commis-*

sioner 5 Oct. 1812–25 Nov. 1813. *Chancellor of Exchequer* 31 Jan. 1823–20 April 1827 (E 197/8 p. 215).

    Commissioner 10 Feb. 1823–30 April 1827. *First Lord* 3 Sept. 1827–26 Jan. 1828 (*Times*, 4 Sept. 1827).

Robinson, John   *Under Clerk* pd. from 24 June 1720 to 24 June 1723 (T 53/28 p. 304; T 53/30 p. 162).

Robinson, John   *Junior Secretary* 16 Oct. 1770–29 March 1782 (T 29/40 p. 380).

Rochester, Earl of *see* **Hyde,** Hon. Lawrence

Rockingham, Charles (Watson Wentworth) 2nd Marquess of   *First Lord* 13 July 1765–2 Aug. 1766; 1 April–1 July 1782. D. 1 July 1782.

Rodney, Hon. William   *Junior Clerk* 10 Nov. 1818–4 Dec. 1827 (T 29/167 p. 191). Res. 4 Dec. 1827 on app. as Secretary to Comptrollers of Army Accounts (T 29/276 p. 54).

Rogers, G.   *Messenger* 4 July 1866 (AB, iv, 232).

Roome, Edward   *Solicitor* 22 Oct. 1728–8 Dec. 1729 (T 54/31 p. 106). D. 8 Dec. 1729 (*CTBP 1731–4*, 154).

Rose, Edward   *Messenger to Secretary* 6 March 1822–13 Jan. 1829 (T38/552 p. 39). D. 13 Jan. 1829 (T 41/6).

Rose, George   *Junior Secretary* 15 July 1782–5 April 1783 (T 29/52 p. 259). *Senior Secretary* 27 Dec. 1783–24 March 1801 (T 29/54 p. 209).

Rose, James   *Messenger* 22 Aug. 1836–25 May 1837 (T 29/380 p. 443). Res. 25 May 1837 (AB, ii, 219).

Rosenhagen, Anthony   *Extra Clerk* 1 April 1795–5 July 1798 (T 29/67 p. 518). *Junior Clerk* 5 July 1798–19 Aug. 1805 (T 29/73 p. 208). *Assistant Clerk* 19 Aug. 1805–19 May 1815 (T 29/85 p. 348). Res. 19 May 1815 on app. as Joint Comptroller of Army Accounts (T 29/135 p. 311).

    Clerk of Bills 7 Jan. 1797–7 Jan. 1806 (T 29/70 p. 82).

    Private Secretary to Chancellor of Exchequer (Perceval, Vansittart) 21 June 1811–19 May 1815 (T 29/111 p. 666; T 29/135 pp. 311–12).

Rosier, John   *Parliamentary Agent* 28 Nov. 1769–13 Aug. 1796 (T 29/40 p. 118). D. 13 Aug. 1796 (*Gent. Mag.* (1796), lxvi (2), 708).

Ross, Charles   *Commissioner* 31 Dec. 1834–20 April 1835.

Ross, William   *Messenger of Receipt* 29 June 1765–c. 23 May 1801 (C 66/3701). D. by 23 May 1801 (app. of Betty).

Ross, William   *Deputy Messenger of Receipt* occ. from 1785 to 1792 (*Royal Kal.* (1785), 181; ibid. (1792), 181).

Rossiter, William   *Messenger* 15 Feb. 1865 (AB, iv, 177).

Rosslyn, James (St. Clair Erskine) 2nd Earl of   *Commissioner* 22 Nov.–31 Dec. 1834.

Rowe, Milward   *Under Clerk* pd. from 24 June 1742 to 10 Oct. 1761 (T 53/41 p. 122; T 53/48 p. 10). *Supernumerary Chief Clerk* 22 Dec. 1761–23 Feb. 1762 (T 29/34 p. 207). *Chief Clerk* 23 Feb. 1762–30 Nov. 1782 (ibid. p. 232). Res. 30 Nov. 1782 (T 29/52 pp. 516–17).

Royer, James   *Under Clerk* 17 Dec. 1755–21 May 1762 (T 29/32 p. 360). *Under Clerk of Revenue* 21 May 1762–22 Feb. 1776 (T 29/34 p. 286). *Under Clerk* 22 Feb. 1776–30 Nov. 1782 (T 29/45 pp. 55, 57). *Senior Clerk* 30 Nov. 1782–16 Dec. 1783 (T 29/52 p. 520). Res. 16 Dec. 1783 (T 29/54 p. 496).

Ruffe, William   *Messenger of Receipt* 29 Sept. 1825–2 May 1836 (C 66/4297; T 54/56 p. 84). Res. 2 May 1836 (T 29/377 pp. 40–1).

Rumsey, Lacy *Assistant Clerk of Bills* 2 Dec. 1808–1 Nov. 1836 (T 29/98 p. 62). *Senior Clerk of Bills* 1 Nov. 1836–22 Dec. 1854 (T 29/383 p. 51). Left office 22 Dec. 1854 on transfer to office of Paymaster General (T 29/557 p. 484).

Rushout, Sir John, 4th Bart. *Commissioner* 16 Feb. 1742–23 Dec. 1743.

Rushworth, Home *Extra Clerk* 3 April 1840–10 Dec. 1841 (T 29/424 pp. 76–7). *Junior Clerk* 10 Dec. 1841–17 June 1845 (T 29/444 pp. 205–7). Res. 17 June 1845 (T 29/486 pp. 316, 369).

    Private Secretary to Financial Secretary (Cardwell) 4 Feb.–23 May 1845 (T 29/482 p. 47; T 29/485 p. 404).

Rushworth, John *Solicitor* occ. from 28 Feb. 1661 to 11 Jan. 1665 (*CTB*, i, 215–16, 645).

Russell, Arthur John Edward *Private Secretary to First Lord* (Russell) 13 Dec. 1850–Feb. 1852 (T 29/541 p. 501).

Russell, George *Junior Clerk* 2 Dec. 1851–23 May 1856 (T 29/545 p. 459). Res. 23 May 1856 on app. as Assistant Secretary to Board of Works (T 29/563 p. 466).

    Private Secretary to Financial Secretary (Wilson) 13 Feb. 1855–23 May 1856 (T 29/558 p. 479).

Russell, Lord John (cr. Earl **Russell** 30 July 1861) *First Lord* 6 July 1846–27 Feb. 1852 (*Times*, 7 July 1846); 3 Nov. 1865–6 July 1866 (ibid. 4 Nov. 1865).

Ryan, Charles Lister *Junior Clerk* 24 Feb. 1852–4 July 1856 (T 29/546 p. 553). *Second Class Clerk* 4 July 1856–10 May 1865 (T 29/564 p. 47). Res. 10 May 1865 on app. as Secretary to Board of Audit (AB, iv, 181).

    Private Secretary: to Chancellor of Exchequer (Disraeli) 22 March 1858–March 1859 (T 29/570 p. 602); *to Financial Secretary* (Northcote) 14 March–June 1859 (AB, iv, 27); *to Chancellor of Exchequer* (Gladstone) 24 June 1859–10 May 1865 (T 29/575 p. 482).

Ryder, George Lisle *Third Class Clerk* 1 Sept. 1857–21 June 1867 (T 29/568 p. 429). *Second Class Clerk* 21 June 1867 (AB, iv, 277–8).

    Private Secretary to Financial Secretary (Ayrton) 24 Dec. 1868–Nov. 1869 (ibid. 344–5).

Ryder, Hon. Richard *Commissioner* 16 Sept.–2 Dec. 1807.

Ryley, Philip (ktd. 26 April 1728) *Serjeant at Arms* 27 Nov. 1684–20 Aug. 1702 (C 66/3248, 3285, 3327). Left office 20 Aug. 1702 (app. of R. Ryley); 28 Feb. 1706–25 Jan. 1733 (C 66/3452, 3505, 3566). D. 25 Jan. 1733 (*Gent. Mag.* (1733), iii, 47).

Ryley, Reginald *Serjeant at Arms* 20 Aug. 1702–28 Feb. 1706 (C 66/3455). Left office 28 Feb. 1706 (app. of P. Ryley).

Sadleir, John *Commissioner* 4 Jan. 1853–8 March 1854.

St. John, Charles William *Junior Clerk* 3 March 1829–23 Aug. 1833 (T 29/291 p. 39). Dis. 23 Aug. 1833 (T 29/344 pp. 468–70).

St. Quintin, Sir William, 3rd Bart. *Commissioner* 13 Oct. 1714–15 April 1717.

Salter, Richard *Messenger of Receipt* 22 July 1805–14 July 1836 (C 66/4041; T 54/56 p. 84). Res. 14 July 1836 (T 29/379 p. 207).

Salwey, Arthur *Junior Clerk* 23 Feb. 1813–29 Oct. 1823 (T 29/121 p. 705). *Assistant Clerk* 29 Oct. 1823–12 Oct. 1832 (T 29/226 pp. 397–8). Res. 12 Oct. 1832 (T 29/334 pp. 178–9).

Samways, James *Messenger to First Lord* 2 Aug. 1838–19 Feb. 1847 (T 29/404 p. 43). Ret. 19 Feb. 1847 (T 29/506 p. 388).

Sandwich, Earl of *see* **Montagu**, Sir Edward, kt.

Sandys, Samuel *Chancellor of Exchequer* 12 Feb. 1742–12 Dec. 1743 (C 66/3608). *Commissioner* 16 Feb. 1742–23 Dec. 1743.

Sanford, Henry *Junior Clerk* 23 May 1799–7 Jan. 1806 (T 29/74 p. 400). *Assistant Clerk* 7 Jan. 1806–27 Oct. 1816 (T 29/86 p. 1). *Senior Clerk* 27 Oct. 1816–17 Oct. 1834 (T 29/143 p. 726). *Chief Clerk* 17 Oct. 1834–13 Sept. 1836 (T 29/358 p. 329). Res. 13 Sept. 1836 (T 29/381 pp. 227–8).

Auditor 17 Oct. 1834–13 Sept. 1836 (T 29/358 p. 333).

Sargent, Frederick *Junior Clerk* 4 Nov. 1817–21 Aug. 1832 (T 29/155 p. 53). *Assistant Clerk* 21 Aug. 1832–18 Feb. 1848 (T 29/332 p. 474). Res. 18 Feb. 1848 (T 29/518 p. 323).

Sargent, John *Junior Secretary* 8 July 1802–21 May 1804 (T 29/79 p. 224).

Sargent, William *Supernumerary Clerk* July/Oct. 1803–19 Aug. 1805 (T 41/3). *Junior Clerk* 19 Aug. 1805–14 April 1815 (T 29/85 p. 348). *Assistant Clerk* 14 April 1815–31 July 1818 (T 29/134 p. 875). Left office 31 July 1818 on app. as Senior Clerk, Commissariat (T 29/163 p. 680).

Private Secretary to Chancellor of Exchequer (Vansittart) 19 May 1815–31 July 1818 (T 29/135 p. 312).

Saunders, E. *Senior Clerk of Civil List* 22 Feb. 1831–27 April 1837 (T 29/314 pp. 439–42). D. 27 April 1837 (T 41/8).

Sawyer, E. *Junior Clerk of Civil List* 22 Feb. 1831–5 May 1837 (T 29/314 pp. 439–442). *Senior Clerk of Civil List* 5 May 1837–19 June 1861 (AB, ii, 218). D. 19 June 1861 (ibid. iv, 116).

Schaller, Benedict *Messenger of Receipt* 25 Feb. 1767–27 Nov. 1769 (C 66/3712). *Office Keeper* 14 Nov. 1769–23 Dec. 1796 (T 54/41 p. 80). D. 23 Dec. 1796 (T 41/2).

Schutz, Charles *Supernumerary Clerk* 17 Feb. 1757–8 Feb. 1758 (T 29/32 p. 442). *Under Clerk* 8 Feb. 1758–22 Feb. 1776 (T 29/33 p. 15). Ret. 22 Feb. 1776 (T 29/45 p. 54).

Sclater Booth, George *Financial Secretary* 4 March–21 Dec. 1868 (AB, iv, 299).

Scorey, John *Messenger* 9 March 1840–16 June 1841 (T 29/423 p. 168). Left office 16 June 1841 (T 29/438 p. 307).

Scott, Charles *Messenger* 29 March 1842–7 July 1848 (T 29/447 pp. 579–84). D. 7 July 1848 (T 41/9).

Scrivenor, G. H. *Extra Clerk* 7 Feb. 1851–10 March 1852 (T 29/542 p. 257). Left office 10 March 1852 (T 41/9).

Scrope, John *Senior Secretary* Jan. 1724–9 April 1752 (T 38/442 p. 87). D. 9 April 1752 (*Gent. Mag.* (1752), xxii, 192).

Segar, Anthony *Office Keeper* first occ. 16 Sept. 1667 (*CTB*, i, 543). D. by 27 Feb. 1694 (ibid. x, 514).

Segar, Henry *Under Clerk* pd. from 25 March 1695 to 24 June 1710 (*CTB*, xvii, 759; ibid. xxviii, 474).

Serjeant, Edmund *Deputy Messenger of Receipt* occ. 17 Oct. 1715, 1716 (*CTB*, xxix, 297; Chamberlayne, *Present State* (1716), 494).

Seton, Wilmot *Junior Clerk* 2 Dec. 1834–18 Feb. 1848 (T 29/360 p. 37). *Assistant Clerk* 18 Feb. 1848–4 July 1856 (T 29/518 p. 325). *Principal Clerk* 4 July 1856–18 July 1860 (T 29/564 p. 47). D. 18 July 1860 (*Gent. Mag.* (1860), cxlvii, 218).

Seymour, Edward *Messenger of Receipt* 7 Dec. 1665–28 Oct. 1668 (letters patent not traced but recited in grant to Oneby). Surrendered office 28 Oct. 1668 (surrender recited in grant to Oneby).

Seymour, Sir Edward, 3rd Bart.   *Commissioner* 21 March 1692–3 May 1694.

Seymour, Edward Adolphus (Seymour) *styled* Lord   *Commissioner* 20 April 1835–6 Nov. 1839.

Seymour, Horace Alfred Damer   *Third Class Clerk* 16 Oct. 1867 (AB, iv, 289).
     Assistant Private Secretary to Parliamentary Secretary (Glyn) 24 Dec. 1868 (ibid. 344–5).

Shaftesbury, Earl of *see* **Ashley**, Anthony Lord

Sharpe, John   *Solicitor* 27 July 1742–22 Oct. 1756 (*CTBP 1742–5*, 59). D. 22 Oct. 1756 (AO 3/1102).

Shaw, Edward   *Bag Carrier* 1 Oct. 1747–8 Dec. 1769 (T 29/31 p. 49). D. 8 Dec. 1769 (T 53/51 p. 409).
     Housekeeper of Levée Rooms 21 May 1762–10 July 1765 (T 29/34 p. 286; T 29/37 p. 66).

Shaw, Elizabeth   *Housekeeper of Levée Rooms* 10 July 1765–c. 15 Nov. 1787 (T 29/37 p. 66). D. by 15 Nov. 1787 (T 29/59 p. 26).

Shaw, William   *Clerk* occ. 19 Nov. 1680 (*Secret Service Expenses*, 20). *Chief Clerk* first occ. 1693 (Miège, *New State* (1693), pt. iii, 404); received dividend of fees from April 1695 to Dec. 1696 (T 1/35 f. 204; T 1/42 f. 129). D. by 1 May 1697 (Prob 11/438 f. 103).

Sheen, John   *Messenger of Receipt* 16 Dec. 1742–20 Oct. 1749 (C 66/3612). D. 20 Oct. 1749 (*Lond. Mag.* (1749), xviii, 481).

Shelburne, Henry (Petty FitzMaurice) *styled* Earl of   *Commissioner* 24 Dec. 1847–15 Aug. 1848.

Shelburne, William (Petty) 2nd Earl of   *First Lord* 13 July 1782–4 April 1783.

Shelley, Spencer   *Junior Clerk* 29 Oct. 1830–26 Jan. 1841 (T 29/310 p. 431). *Assistant Clerk* 26 Jan. 1841–24 March 1854 (T 29/433 p. 454). *Senior Clerk* 24 March 1854–4 July 1856 (T 29/544 p. 642). *First Class Clerk* 4 July 1856–24 Dec. 1859 (T 29/564 p. 47). *Principal Clerk* 24 Dec. 1859–10 May 1867 (T 29/577 p. 432). Ret. 10 May 1867 (AB, iv, 276).
     Private Secretary to Financial Secretary (Gordon) 18 Sept. 1839–June 1841 (T 29/417 p. 247).
     Clerk of Parliamentary Accounts 15 Nov. 1850–24 March 1854 (T 29/541 p. 316). *Clerk of Estimates* 24 March 1854–4 July 1856 (T 29/554 p. 642).

Shepherd, John   *Bookranger* pd. from 29 Sept. 1724 to 24 June 1745 (T 53/31 p. 350; T 53/42 p. 46).
     Deputy Messenger of Receipt occ. 1743, 1745 (T 48/63).

Shepherd, Mary   *Housekeeper* first occ. 1742 (T 48/67). D. c. May 1768 (*Gent. Mag.* (1768), xxxviii, 302).

Sheridan, Richard Brinsley   *Junior Secretary* 5 April–27 Dec. 1783 (T 29/54 p. 1).

Shrewsbury, Charles (Talbot) 1st Duke of   *Treasurer* 30 July–13 Oct. 1714.

Sidebotham, Henry   *Extra Clerk* 24 Aug. 1857–24 May 1861 (T 29/568 p. 253). *Supplementary Third Class Clerk* 24 May–3 Oct. 1861 (AB, iv, 113). Res. 3 Oct. 1861 (ibid. 127).

Simpson, James   *Extra Clerk* 28 Nov. 1856–24 May 1861 (T 29/565 p. 276). *Supplementary Third Class Clerk* 24 May 1861–7 Feb. 1867 (AB, iv, 113). *Supplementary Second Class Clerk* 7 Feb. 1867–19 Nov. 1869 (ibid. 252). *Supplementary First Class Clerk* 19 Nov. 1869 (ibid. v, 11).

Skinner, George Edward   *Supplementary Third Class Clerk* 24 Jan. 1862–23 April

1868 (AB, iv, 128). *Supplementary Audit Clerk* 23 April 1868–19 Nov. 1869 (ibid. 305). *Supplementary Second Class Clerk* 19 Nov. 1869 (ibid. v, 11).

Smeaton, Thomas *Messenger* 1660–25 March 1687 (*CTP 1557–1696*, 38). Res. 25 March 1687 (ibid.).

Smith, Aaron *Solicitor* 20 April 1689–c. 11 Sept. 1696 (*CTB*, ix, 88). Dis. by 11 Sept. 1696 (ibid. xi, 31, 265).

Smith, John *Commissioner* 3 May 1694–29 March 1701.
Chancellor of Exchequer 2 June 1699–27 March 1701 (C 66/3409); 22 April 1708–11 Aug. 1710 (C 66/3464).

Smith, John *Clerk of Irish Revenue* 28 March 1817–30 Nov. 1830 (T 29/147 p. 630). Res. 30 Nov. 1830 on app. as Vice-Treasurer of Ireland (T 29/311 p. 444).

Smith, Joseph *Junior Clerk* 30 Nov. 1782–25 Feb. 1783 (T 29/52 p. 518). *Junior (Assistant) Clerk* 25 Feb. 1783–15 Aug. 1787 (T 29/53 p. 183). *Junior Clerk* 15 Aug. 1787–25 Nov. 1794 (T 29/58 p. 499). Res. 25 Nov. 1794 (T 29/67 p. 295).
Private Secretary to First Lord (Pitt) March 1787–March 1801 (*New Companion*, 85).

Smith, Robert Vernon *Commissioner* 24 Nov. 1830–22 Nov. 1834.

Smith, Samuel *Messenger* app. by 12 Dec. 1809 (app. of Emmans); pd. from 5 Jan. 1814 (T 41/4). D. 19 Jan. 1831 (T 29/313 pp. 388–9).

Smith, W. B. *Extra Clerk* pd. from 10 Oct. 1820 (T 38/552 p. 26). Res. 24 Aug. 1841 (T 29/440 p. 417).

Smith, William Edward *Supernumerary Clerk* 16 Nov. 1769–2 July 1772 (T 29/40 p. 102). *Under Clerk* 2 July 1772–22 Feb. 1776 (T 29/42 p. 133). *Under Clerk of Revenue* 22 Feb. 1776–12 Dec. 1797 (T 29/45 p. 57). D. 12 Dec. 1797 (*Gent. Mag.* (1797), lxvii (2), 1077).

Smyth, John *Commissioner* 7 May 1794–5 July 1802.

Somerset, Lord Granville Charles Henry *Commissioner* 25 March 1819–30 April 1827; 26 Jan. 1828–24 Nov. 1830.

Somerset, Raglan George Henry *Junior Clerk* 28 March 1854–4 July 1856 (T 29/554 p. 657). *Third Class Clerk* 4 July 1856–c. 1857 (T 29/564 p. 47). Last occ. 20 April 1857 (AB, iii, 336).

Southampton, Thomas (Wriothesley) 4th Earl of *Commissioner* 19 June–8 Sept. 1660. *Treasurer* 8 Sept. 1660–16 May 1667. D. 16 May 1667.

Southworth, Samuel *Clerk* occ. 4 Feb. 1690 (*CTB*, xvii, 553).

Sparry, Elizabeth *Housekeeper of Levée Rooms* 15 Nov. 1787–25 July 1793 (T 29/59 p. 26). Res. 25 July 1793 on app. as Housekeeper, Excise Office (T 29/66 p. 107).

Spearman, Alexander Young *Assistant Clerk of Revenue* 13 Feb. 1824–22 Feb. 1831 (T 29/230 p. 224). *Auditor of Civil List* 22 Feb. 1831–22 Jan. 1836 (T 29/314 pp. 439–42). *Assistant Secretary* 22 Jan. 1836–21 Jan. 1840 (T 29/373 p. 392). Res. 21 Jan. 1840 (T 29/421 p. 350).
Clerk of Parliamentary Accounts 13 Feb. 1824–17 Oct. 1834 (T 29/230 p. 224; T 29/358 p. 326).
Private Secretary to Chancellor of Exchequer (Herries) 13 Sept. 1827–Jan. 1828 (T 29/273 p. 164).

Spearman, Alexander Young *Junior Clerk* 25 Feb. 1851–27 Nov. 1855 (T 29/542 p. 399). Res. 27 Nov. 1855 (T 29/561 p. 467).
Private Secretary to Chancellor of Exchequer (Disraeli) 18 Sept.–Dec. 1852 (AB, iii, 194).

Speer, Edward *Junior Clerk* 19 May 1815–6 Jan. 1826 (T 29/135 p. 312). *Assistant Clerk* 6 Jan. 1826–3 Feb. 1843 (T 29/253 pp. 153–4). *Senior Clerk* 3 Feb. 1843–27 May 1856 (T 29/458 p. 43). Res. 27 May 1856 (T 29/563 p. 512).

    Private Secretary to Financial Secretary (Spring Rice) 31 Dec. 1830–June 1834 (T 29/312 p. 486).

    Superintendent of Registry 3 Feb. 1835–3 Feb. 1843 (T 29/362 pp. 55–9); 24 Aug. 1852–27 May 1856 (T 29/548 p. 333).

Speer, William *Under Clerk of Revenue* Aug. 1742–5 Jan. 1758 (*2nd Rept. on Fees*, 71). *Chief Clerk of Revenue* 5 Jan. 1758–3 Jan. 1799 (ibid.). Res. 3 Jan. 1799 (T 29/74 pp. 63–4).

    Placed on establishment as *Under Clerk* 27 July 1757 (T 29/32 p. 475). Res. as such 23 Aug. 1783 (T 29/54 p. 332).

Speer, William *Junior Clerk* 23 Aug. 1783–29 July 1785 (T 29/54 p. 332). *Junior (Assistant) Clerk* 29 July 1785–5 July 1798 (T 29/56 p. 517). *Senior Clerk* 5 July 1798–17 May 1808 (T 29/73 p. 209). *Chief Clerk* 17 May 1808–17 Oct. 1834 (T 29/94 p. 512). Ret. 17 Oct. 1834 (T 29/358 p. 329).

    Auditor 2 Jan. 1821–17 Oct. 1834 (T 29/193 p. 79).

Spence, Thomas *Under Clerk* pd. from 29 Sept. 1707 to 25 March 1714 (*CTB*, xxviii, 453, 500).

Spencer, Earl *see* **Althorp**, John Charles Viscount

Spiegel *see* **van der Spiegel**

Spring Rice, Stephen Edward *Private Secretary to Chancellor of Exchequer* (Spring Rice) April 1835–30 Aug. 1838 (T 41/8).

Spring Rice, Thomas *Financial Secretary* 26 Nov. 1830–6 June 1834 (T 29/311 p. 381). *Chancellor of Exchequer* 18 April 1835–26 Aug. 1839 (*Times*, 20 April 1835). *Commissioner* 20 April 1835–30 Aug. 1839.

Squibb, Robert *Clerk* occ. 23 March 1681 (*CTB*, vii, 95). *Chief Clerk* occ. from July 1689 to 1693 (LS 13/231 p. 13; Miège, *New State* (1693), pt. iii, 404). D. c. 11 Sept. 1694 (Luttrell, *Hist. Relation*, iii, 368).

Stafford, John *Messenger* 3 Feb. 1862 (AB, iv, 128).

    Messenger to Secretary 25 Aug. 1868 (ibid. 318).

Stanhope, Charles *Junior Secretary* April 1717–April 1721 (T 38/440 p. 1).

Stanhope, Edward *Under Clerk of Revenue* 23 May 1718–22 May 1724 (*CTB*, xxxii, 58). D. 22 May 1724 (*Hist. Reg. Chron.* (1724), ix, 29).

Stanhope, James (cr. Viscount **Stanhope** 3 July 1717) *First Lord* 15 April 1717–20 March 1718.

    Chancellor of Exchequer 15 April 1717–20 March 1718 (C 66/3520).

Stanley, Edward John (*styled* Hon. 9 May 1839) *Parliamentary Secretary* 21 April 1835–9 June 1841 (T 29/364 p. 337).

Stansfeld, James *Third Lord* 17 Dec. 1868–9 Nov. 1869. *Financial Secretary* Nov. 1869 (AB, v, 10).

Stapleton, Augustus George *Private Secretary to First Lord* (Canning) 30 April–Aug. 1827 (T 41/6).

Stapleton, Hon. Thomas *Junior Clerk* app. 4 Nov. 1817 (T 29/155 p. 53). Last occ. 14 Nov. 1817 (ibid. p. 263).

Starck, Henry Savile *Junior (Assistant) Clerk* 30 Nov. 1782–1 Nov. 1789 (T 29/52 pp. 517, 521). *Senior Clerk* 1 Nov. 1789–5 July 1798 (T 29/61 pp. 291–2). Res. 5 July 1798 (T 29/73 p. 208).

Steele, — App. 'a clerk of the Treasury' Sept. 1731 (*Gent. Mag.* (1731), i, 404). Position uncertain.

Steele, Thomas *Junior Secretary* 27 Dec. 1783–26 Feb. 1791 (T 29/54 p. 509).

Stephens, Francis *Serjeant at Arms* first occ. 8 Aug. 1663 (*CTB*, i, 540). Surrendered office 12 Jan. 1674 (surrender recited in grant to Ramsey).

Stephenson, Augustus Frederick William Keppel *Assistant Solicitor* 19 June 1866 (AB, iv, 220).

Stephenson, Benjamin Charles *Third Class Clerk* 1 Sept. 1857–2 Feb. 1865 (T 29/568 p. 429). Res. 2 Feb. 1865 (AB, iv, 176).
    Assistant Private Secretary to Parliamentary Secretary (Hayter, Jolliffe) 26 Sept. 1857–June 1859 (AB, iii, 352; T 29/575 p. 482).

Stephenson, Francis Charles *Supplementary Third Class Clerk* 7 Dec. 1864 (AB, iv, 174).

Stephenson, John *Extra Clerk* 23 Feb. 1824–31 May 1850 (T 38/552 p. 54). Ret. 31 May 1850 (T 29/539 p. 467).

Stephenson, William Henry *Junior Clerk* 23 March 1827–22 May 1838 (T 29/267 p. 422). *Assistant Clerk* 22 May 1838–25 Feb. 1851 (T 29/401 p. 495). *Senior Clerk* 25 Feb. 1851–20 Feb. 1852 (T 29/542 p. 398). *Principal Clerk Assistant* 20 Feb. 1852–4 July 1856 (T 29/546 p. 529). *Principal Clerk* 4 July 1856–9 Dec. 1862 (T 29/564 p. 47). Res. 9 Dec. 1862 on app. as Chairman of Board of Inland Revenue (AB, iv, 134).
    Private Secretary : to First Lord (Peel) 8 Sept. 1841–July 1846 (T 29/441 p. 77); *to Chancellor of Exchequer* (Wood) 15 Nov. 1850–12 Aug. 1851 (T 29/541 p. 316; T 29/544 pp. 340–1).
    Clerk of Parliamentary Accounts 22 March–15 Nov. 1850 (T 29/538 p. 615).

Steuart, Robert *Commissioner* 20 April 1835–30 May 1840.

Stevenson, William *Keeper of Papers* 20 May 1806–22 March 1829 (T 29/87 pp. 33–4). D. 22 March 1829 (T 41/6).

Stewart, Hon. James Henry Keith *Assistant Secretary* 4 July 1828–22 Jan. 1836 (T 29/283 p. 94). Res. 22 Jan. 1836 (T 29/373 p. 392).

Stonehewer, Richard *Private Secretary to First Lord* (Grafton) Aug. 1766–Jan. 1770 (*New Companion*, 85).

Stormont, William David (Murray) *styled* Viscount *Commissioner* 31 Dec. 1834–20 April 1835.

Strachey, Henry *Senior Secretary* 1 April–15 July 1782 (T 29/52 p. 1).

Strickland, Sir William, 4th Bart. *Commissioner* 27 May 1725–28 July 1727.

Stronge, Charles Walter *Junior Clerk* 20 Dec. 1833–21 Jan. 1845 (T 29/348 p. 401). *Assistant Clerk* 21 Jan. 1845–4 July 1856 (T 29/481 p. 424). *First Class Clerk* 4 July 1856–9 Dec. 1862 (T 29/564 p. 47). *Principal Clerk* 9 Dec. 1862 (AB, iv, 134–135).
    Private Secretary to First Lord (Derby) 5 March–Dec. 1852 (T 29/546 p. 637).
    Clerk of Parliamentary Accounts 24 March 1854–24 Dec. 1860 (T 29/554 p. 642).

Stuart Wortley, Hon. James Frederick *Private Secretary to Chancellor of Exchequer* (Gladstone) Jan. 1860–15 May 1865 (AB, iv, 78, 183–4).

Stuckey, Vincent *Extra Clerk* 5 April 1791–3 Jan. 1795 (T 29/63 p. 70). *Junior Clerk* 3 Jan. 1795–5 July 1798 (T 29/67 p. 372). *Assistant Clerk of Minutes* 5 July 1798–3 Jan. 1799 (T 29/73 p. 209). *Clerk of Minutes* 3 Jan. 1799–19 Aug. 1805 (T 29/74 p. 65). *Senior Clerk of Minutes* 19 Aug. 1805–13 July 1808 (T 29/85 p. 348). Res.

13 July 1808 (T 29/95 p. 386). *Clerk of Expiring Laws and Revenue Bills* 13 July 1808–5 Jan. 1822 (ibid.). Ret. 5 Jan. 1822 (T 29/200 p. 243).
   Clerk of Bills 8 Feb. 1794–5 July 1798 (T 29/66 p. 308).

Sturgeon, John   *Messenger of Receipt* 3 Aug. 1660–12 Nov. 1662 (C 66/2946). Surrendered office 12 Nov. 1662 (C 75/2).

Sturges Bourne, William   *Senior Secretary* 21 May 1804–10 Feb. 1806 (T 29/86 p. 63). *Commissioner* 31 March 1807–6 Dec. 1809.

Sunderland, Charles (Spencer) 3rd Earl of   *First Lord* 20 March 1718–3 April 1721.

Sundon, Lord *see* **Clayton,** William

Surrey, Charles (Howard) *styled* Earl of   *Commissioner* 4 April–26 Dec. 1783.

Sutton, —   'A Clerk of the Treasury'; d. c. Oct. 1743 (*Gent. Mag.* (1743), xiii, 554). Position uncertain.

Sutton, Sir Richard, 1st Bart.   *Commissioner* 12 Sept. 1780–1 April 1782.

Talbot, Hon. Wellington Patrick Manvers Chetwynd   *Private Secretary to First Lord* (Derby) 13 March–Dec. 1852 (T 41/9); 22 March 1858–June 1859 (T 29/570 p. 602).

Tankerville, Ford (Grey) 1st Earl of   *Commissioner* 1 June–15 Nov. 1699. *First Lord* 15 Nov. 1699–9 Dec. 1700.

Taylor, John   *Messenger of Receipt* 30 July 1689–5 Nov. 1690 (C 66/3328). Left office 5 Nov. 1690 (app. of S. Clerke).

Taylor, John   *Under Clerk* occ. 4 Feb. 1690 (*CTB*, xvii, 553). *Chief Clerk* received dividend of fees from April 1695 to Nov. 1714 (T 1/35 f. 204; T 38/439 p. 18). *Junior Secretary* Nov. 1714–12 Oct. 1715 (T 38/439 p. 28).
   Chief Clerk of Revenue pd. from 25 Dec. 1688 to 25 March 1695 (*CTB*, ix, 19; ibid. x, 979).

Taylor, Thomas   *Messenger* first occ. July 1822 (T 41/1). Ret. 21 Aug. 1835 (T 29/368 p. 487).

Taylor, Thomas Edward   *Commissioner* 1 March 1858–23 June 1859. *Parliamentary Secretary* 14 July 1866–11 Nov. 1868 (AB, iv, 236).

Teare, Edward   *Messenger* pd. from 1669 to 1682 (*CTB*, iii, 93; ibid. vii, 474).

Thomas, William   *Chief Clerk* Oct. 1713–Nov. 1714 (T 1/171 f. 58). Left office Nov. 1714 (T 38/439 pp. 18, 28).

Thorpe, Mary   *Housekeeper* 18 July 1799–7 April 1835 (T 29/74 p. 491). Res. 7 April 1835 (T 29/364 pp. 148–9).

Thring, Henry   *Parliamentary Counsel* 8 Feb. 1869 (T 29/614 pp. 276–80).

Thurkettle, John   *Messenger of Chamber* 27 Feb. 1694–14 Sept. 1720 (*CTB*, x, 514; ibid. xvii, 234; ibid. xxix, 201). D. 14 Sept. 1720 (T 53/28 p. 12).

Thurkettle, Thomas   *Deputy Messenger of Receipt* occ. 27 May 1718 (*CTB*, xxxii, 59). *Messenger of Chamber* 4 Oct. 1720–3 March 1735 (T 54/26 p. 143; T 54/31 p. 425). D. 3 March 1735 (T 53/38 p. 39).

Thynne, Lord George   *Commissioner* 21 March 1801–16 May 1804.

Thynne, Henry Frederick   *Commissioner* 26 July 1684–16 Feb. 1685.

Tilson, Christopher   *Clerk* app. 1684 (*Commons Journals*, xxiv, 296). *Under Clerk* occ. 4 Feb. 1690 (*CTB*, xvii, 553); pd. from 25 March 1695; payment continued after app. as Chief Clerk to 24 June 1710 (ibid. 759; ibid. xxviii, 473). *Chief Clerk* probably unnamed recipient of dividend of fees from Jan. 1698 (T 1/58 f. 177); certainly in office 6 April 1699 (*CTB*, xvii, 852). D. 25 Aug. 1742 (*Gent. Mag.* (1742), xii, 444).

Chief Clerk of Revenue pd. from 25 March 1695 to 29 Sept. 1714 (*CTB*, x, 1125; ibid. xxix, 107).

Tirel Morin *see* **Morin**

Titchfield, William Henry (Cavendish Bentinck) *styled* Marquess of *Commissioner* 31 March–16 Sept. 1807.

Tomlins, Alfred *Clerk of Irish Revenue* 28 March 1817–10 March 1840 (T 29/147 p. 360). Ret. 10 March 1840 (T 29/423 p. 219).

Tomlins, Sir Thomas Edlyne, kt. *Assistant Parliamentary Counsel* 1817–Jan. 1831 (T 41/4). Res. Jan. 1831 (*Gent. Mag.* (1841), cxi (2), 321).

Tompkins, Thomas *Under Clerk* 29 April 1742–22 Feb. 1776 (*CTBP 1742–5*, 33). Ret. 22 Feb. 1776 (T 29/45 p. 54).

Torrington, Lord *see* **Newport**, Hon. Thomas

Townshend, Hon. Charles *Chancellor of Exchequer* 2 Aug. 1766–4 Sept. 1767 (C 66/3708). D. 4 Sept. 1767 (*Gent. Mag.* (1767), xxxvii, 479).
  Commissioner 2 Aug. 1766–4 Sept. 1767.

Townshend, Charles *Commissioner* 6 Feb. 1770–16 June 1777.

Townshend, Hon. John Thomas *Commissioner* 22 June 1793–28 July 1800.

Townshend, Thomas *Commissioner* 13 July 1765–1 Dec. 1767.

Treby, George *Commissioner* 20 Oct. 1740–16 Feb. 1742.

Trevelyan, Charles Edward (ktd. 27 April 1848) *Assistant Secretary* 21 Jan. 1840–21 Jan. 1859 (T 29/421 p. 350). Res. 21 Jan. 1859 on app. as Governor of Madras (T 29/574 p. 23).

Trollope, John (succ. as 6th Bart. 13 May 1789). *Junior Clerk* 16 Dec. 1783–15 Aug. 1787 (T 29/54 p. 496). *Junior (Assistant) Clerk* 15 Aug. 1787–27 May 1789 (T 29/58 p. 498). Res. 27 May 1789 (T 29/60 p. 384).

Trumbull, Sir William, kt. *Commissioner* 3 May 1694–1 Nov. 1695.

Tufnell, Henry *Commissioner* 6 Nov. 1839–8 Sept. 1841. *Parliamentary Secretary* 7 July 1846–9 July 1850 (T 29/499 p. 144).

Tufton, Alfred *Under Clerk* 10 June–30 Nov. 1782 (T 29/52 p. 184). *Junior (Assistant) Clerk* 30 Nov. 1782–25 Feb. 1783 (ibid. p. 520). Res. 25 Feb. 1783 (T 29/53 p. 183).

Turner, C. G. *Assistant Accountant* 19 Nov. 1869 (AB, v, 11).

Turner, Sir Charles, kt. (cr. Bart. 27 April 1727) *Commissioner* 11 June 1720–11 May 1730.

Turner, Sir John, 3rd Bart. *Commissioner* 28 May 1762–13 July 1765.

Turner, Thomas *Messenger to Chancellor of Exchequer* 23 Nov. 1864 (AB, iv, 174).

Turner, Sir William, kt. *Solicitor* first occ. Jan. 1673 (*CTB*, iv, 49). Dis. by 15 July 1676 (ibid. v, 274).

Turnor, Algernon *Third Class Clerk* 31 Aug. 1867 (AB, iv, 286).

Twiss, Quintin William Francis *Third Class Clerk* 29 Aug. 1856–6 Jan. 1860 (AB, iii, 316). Left office 6 Jan. 1860 on app. as Assistant Superintendent, County Court Department (ibid. iv, 88–90).
  Assistant Private Secretary to Parliamentary Secretary (Brand) 24 June 1859–6 Jan. 1860 (T 29/575 p. 482).

Tyler, John *Messenger* app. 29 July 1836 (T 29/379 p. 535). *Messenger to First Lord* app. not traced; in office on res. Res. 2 Aug. 1838 (T 29/404 p. 43).

Tyrconnel, Earl of *see* **Carpenter**, John Delaval

Unwin, John *Supernumerary Clerk* 20 Nov. 1799–20 March 1801 (T 29/75 p. 230).

Junior Clerk 20 March 1801–24 March 1807 (T 29/77 p. 335). *Assistant Clerk* 24 March 1807–21 Feb. 1817 (T 29/89 p. 397). *Senior Clerk* 21 Feb. 1817–13 Sept. 1836 (T 29/146 p. 451). *Chief Clerk* 13 Sept. 1836–26 Dec. 1839 (T 29/381 p. 227). Res. 26 Dec. 1839 (T 29/420 p. 387).

van der Spiegel, Adolphus   *Supernumerary Clerk* 20 March 1801–July/Oct. 1803 (T 29/77 p. 355). *Junior Clerk* July/Oct. 1803–13 July 1808 (T 41/3). *Assistant Clerk* 13 July 1808–10 Oct. 1820 (T 29/95 p. 387). *Senior Clerk* 10 Oct. 1820–17 Oct. 1834 (T 29/190 pp. 223–4). *Chief Clerk* 17 Oct. 1834–21 Jan. 1845 (T 29/358 p. 329). Res. 21 Jan. 1845 (T 29/481 p. 323).

   Auditor 13 Sept. 1836–21 Jan. 1845 (T 29/381 p. 227).

Vandiest, Frederick George   *Junior Clerk* 13 April 1824–2 Jan. 1829 (T 29/232 p. 185). *Assistant Clerk of Revenue* 2 Jan. 1829–17 Oct. 1834 (T 29/289 pp. 48–9). Ret. 17 Oct. 1834 (T 29/358 p. 329).

Vandinande, Cornelius   *Supernumerary Clerk* 1 June 1736–c. 29 Sept. 1738 (*CTBP 1735–8*, 169). Pd. to 29 Sept. 1738 (T 53/39 p. 39).

Vane, Hon. Henry (succ. as 3rd Lord **Barnard** 27 April 1753; cr. Earl of **Darlington** 3 April 1754)   *Commissioner* 29 April 1749–22 Dec. 1755.

Vansittart, Nicholas   *Junior Secretary* 9 April 1801–8 July 1802 (T 29/77 p. 364). *Senior Secretary* 8 July 1802–21 May 1804 (vac. of J. H. Addington); 10 Feb. 1806– 1 April 1807 (T 29/86 p. 113). *Chancellor of Exchequer* 23 May 1812–31 Jan. 1823 (E 197/8 p. 125).

   Commissioner 16 June 1812–10 Feb. 1823.

Varey, James   *Under Clerk* pd. from 25 Dec. 1700 to 29 Sept. 1710 (T 1/77 f. 182; T 1/111 f. 92; *CTB*, xxviii, 456, 477). D. by 8 Dec. 1710 (Prob 8/103).

Venables, Thomas   *Private Secretary to First Lord* (Peel) Dec. 1834–April 1835 (T 41/8).

Vernon, Joseph   *Receiver of Fees* 20 Aug. 1794–31 Dec. 1834 (T 29/67 p. 183). Ret. 31 Dec. 1834 (T 29/358 p. 329; T 29/360 p. 145).

   Supernumerary Clerk 4 Dec. 1802–19 Aug. 1805 (T 29/80 p. 45). *Junior Clerk* 19 Aug. 1805–7 Jan. 1806 (T 29/85 p. 348; T 29/86 p. 1; T 41/3).

Vesey, Edward Agmondesham   *Junior Clerk* 18 Aug. 1825–13 Oct. 1830 (T 29/248 p. 289). D. 13 Oct. 1830 (*Gent. Mag.* (1830), c (2), 380).

Vesey Fitzgerald *see* **Fitzgerald**

Vincent, George   *Messenger of Receipt* grant in reversion 5 Sept. 1674 (C 66/3167); in office by 30 Jan. 1689 (*CTB*, viii, 2161). Forfeited office by 10 July 1689 (ibid. ix, 184).

Vincent, Henry William   *Junior Clerk* 23 Feb. 1813–11 March 1823 (T 29/121 p. 705). *Assistant Clerk* 11 March 1823–24 Aug. 1824 (T 29/219 p. 151). Res. 24 Aug. 1824 (T 29/236 p. 213).

   Private Secretary to Junior Secretary (Herries) 11 March 1823–24 Aug. 1824 (T 29/219 pp. 153–4).

Vine, George   *Messenger of Receipt* 14 Feb. 1668–c. 22 Aug. 1673 (C 66/3098). D. by 22 Aug. 1673 (*CTB*, iv, 383).

Vivian, Hon. John Cranch Walker   *Commissioner* 17 Dec. 1868.

Walker, Augustus Henry   *Extra Clerk* 3 April 1849–7 Feb. 1851 (T 29/532 p. 78). Res. 7 Feb. 1851 (T 29/542 p. 257).

Walker, John   *Messenger of Receipt* 21 Nov. 1749–17 Oct. 1791 (C 66/3628, 3681). D. 17 Oct. 1791 (*Gent. Mag.* (1791), lxi (2), 975).

Waller, Alfred *Junior Clerk* 29 Nov. 1833–3 Feb. 1843 (T 29/347 p. 618). *Assistant Clerk* 3 Feb. 1843–4 July 1856 (T 29/458 p. 43). *First Class Clerk* 4 July 1856–30 Aug. 1857 (T 29/564 p. 47). D. 30 Aug. 1857 (T 29/568 p. 446).

Superintendent of Registry app. not traced but probably occ. at time of reorganisation 4 July 1856; first occ. 1857 (*Royal Kal.* (1857), 166); remained in office until d.

Wallop, John (cr. Viscount **Lymington** 11 June 1720) *Commissioner* 15 April 1717–11 June 1720.

Walpole, Edward *Junior Secretary* 24 June 1730–1 June 1739 (*CTBP 1729–30*, 396).

Walpole, Edward *Junior Clerk* 25 Aug. 1808–17 Feb. 1815 (T 29/96 p. 275). *Assistant Clerk of Revenue* 17 Feb. 1815–2 Jan. 1829 (T 29/133 p. 747). *Senior Clerk of Revenue* 2 Jan. 1829–17 Oct. 1834 (T 29/289 p. 48). *Senior Clerk* 17 Oct. 1834–3 Feb. 1843 (T 29/358 p. 333). Res. 3 Feb. 1843 (T 29/458 p. 52).

Private Secretary : to Junior Secretary (Lewis) 13 Sept. 1827–Jan. 1828 (T 29/273 p. 164); *to Chancellor of Exchequer* (Goulburn) 8 Feb. 1828–Nov. 1830 (T 29/278 p. 148).

Walpole, Horatio *Junior Secretary* 12 Oct. 1715–April 1717 (*CTB*, xxix, 295); April 1721–24 June 1730 (T 38/441 p. 98).

Walpole, Robert (ktd. 27 May 1725; cr. Earl of **Orford** 6 Feb. 1742) *First Lord* 11 Oct. 1715–15 April 1717; 3 April 1721–16 Feb. 1742.

Chancellor of Exchequer 12 Oct. 1715–15 April 1717 (C 66/3511); 3 April 1721–12 Feb. 1742 (C 66/3542, 3570).

Warner, Thomas *Serjeant at Arms* 13 July 1660–1663 (C 66/2942). Left office 4 Feb./8 Aug. 1663 (*CTB*, i, 497, 540).

Warwick, Sir Philip, kt. *Secretary* June 1660–May 1667 (Baxter, *Treasury*, 174–5).

Waters, C. *Supplementary Third Class Clerk* 19 Nov. 1869 (AB, v, 11).

Watford, John *Messenger* app. 1793 (*15th Rept. on Finance*, 294); occ. 17 May 1797 (ibid.).

Watkins, John *Deputy Messenger of Receipt* occ. from 18 Dec. 1744 to 1761 (*CTBP 1742–5*, 541; *Court and City Reg.* (1761), 110).

Watkins, John *Supernumerary Clerk* 8 Nov. 1756–27 July 1757 (T 29/32 p. 414). *Under Clerk* 27 July 1757–22 Feb. 1776 (ibid. p. 475). Ret. 22 Feb. 1776 (T 29/45 p. 54).

Watson, William *Bookranger* 19 April 1766–26 May 1801 (T 29/37 p. 421). D. 26 May 1801 (T 41/2).

Bag Carrier 12 Jan. 1770–26 May 1801 (T 29/40 p. 169).

Weaver, Robert *Under Clerk of Revenue* 18 Aug. 1722–15 Nov. 1725 (*Hist. Reg. Chron.* (1722), vii, 40; BM Add. MS 34736 f. 105). D. 15 Nov. 1725 (*Hist. Reg. Chron.* (1725), x, 47).

Webb, Isaac *Under Clerk of Revenue* D. 11 Aug. 1722 (*Hist. Reg. Chron.* (1722), vii, 38).

Webb, Philip Carteret *Solicitor* 4 Nov. 1756–30 July 1765 (E 403/2478 p. 70; T 54/38 p. 84). Left office 30 July 1765 (T 54/40 p. 15).

Webster, Edward *Under Clerk* app. c. 1691 (*CTB*, xxxi, 16); pd. from 25 March 1695 to 5 Jan. 1755 (ibid. xvii, 759; ibid. xxviii, 501; ibid. xxix, 628; T 53/45 p. 100). D. by 10 Jan. 1755 (T 29/32 p. 266).

Webster, Henry *Under Clerk* 18 March 1773–30 Nov. 1782 (T 29/43 p. 1). Dis. 30 Nov. 1782 (T 29/52 p. 518).

Wekett, William   *Messenger* pd. from 3 April 1683 to 13 Jan. 1693 (*CTB*, vii, 750; ibid. xvii, 687). *Messenger of Chamber* 14 Oct. 1692–27 Feb. 1694 (ibid. ix, 1866). *Office Keeper* 27 Feb. 1694–17 Oct. 1715 (ibid. x, 514; ibid. xvii, 234; ibid. xxix, 374). Left office 17 Oct. 1715 (ibid. xxix, 297).

    Messenger of Receipt 30 July 1689–3 Feb. 1718 (C 66/3328, 3434, 3504). D. 3 Feb. 1718 (*Hist. Reg. Chron.* (1718), iii, 6).

Welby, Reginald Earle   *Third Class Clerk* 26 Aug. 1856–18 Dec. 1860 (AB, iii, 316). *Second Class Clerk* 18 Dec. 1860 (ibid. iv, 106).

    Private Secretary: to Financial Secretary (Laing, Peel, Childers, Hunt, Sclater Booth) 24 June 1859–Dec. 1868 (T 29/575 p. 482; AB, iv, 91, 198, 237, 300); *to Third Lord* (Stansfeld) 24 Dec. 1868–Nov. 1869 (AB, iv, 344–5); *to Financial Secretary* (Stansfeld) 10 Nov. 1869 (ibid. v, 11).

Weller, James   *Messenger to Secretary* 10 June 1824–18 Feb. 1831 (T 41/5). *Book-ranger* 18 Feb. 1831–21 Aug. 1835 (T 29/314 p. 347). *Messenger* 21 Aug. 1835–2 Oct. 1837 (T 29/368 pp. 481–7). D. 2 Oct. 1837 (T 29/399 p. 496).

Wellesley, Hon. Henry   *Commissioner* 16 May–7 Aug. 1804. *Senior Secretary* 1 April 1807–5 April 1809 (T 29/89 p. 449).

Wellesley, Richard   *Commissioner* 6 Jan.–16 June 1812.

Wellesley Pole, Hon. William (cr. Lord **Maryborough** 17 July 1821)   *Commissioner* 6 Jan.–16 June 1812; 22 Nov.–31 Dec. 1834.

Wellington, Arthur (Wellesley) 1st Duke of   *First Lord* 26 Jan. 1828–22 Nov. 1830 (*Times*, 28 Jan. 1828); 17 Nov.–10 Dec. 1834 (ibid. 18 Nov. 1834).

West, Algernon Edward   *Private Secretary to First Lord* (Gladstone) 24 Dec. 1868 (AB, iv, 344–5).

West, Gilbert   *Junior Clerk* 5 July 1798–19 Aug. 1805 (T 29/73 p. 208). *Assistant Clerk* 19 Aug. 1805–14 April 1815 (T 29/85 p. 348). *Senior Clerk* 14 April 1815–17 Oct. 1834 (T 29/134 p. 875). Ret. 17 Oct. 1834 (T 29/358 p. 329).

West, James   *Junior Secretary* 1 May 1746–9 April 1752 (T 29/30 p. 272). *Senior Secretary* 9 April 1752–18 Nov. 1756 (d. of Scrope; *Gent. Mag.* (1752), xxii, 193). *Junior Secretary* 5 July 1757–9 April 1758 (T 29/32 p. 470). *Senior Secretary* 9 April 1758–29 May 1762 (d. of Hardinge).

West, John Balchen   *Supernumerary Clerk* 3 July 1765–26 Jan. 1768 (T 29/37 p. 51). *Under Clerk of Revenue* 26 Jan. 1768–6 July 1779 (T 29/39 p. 63). Res. 6 July 1779 (T 29/48 p. 326).

West, Temple   *Supernumerary Clerk* 1 Feb.–9 Nov. 1791 (T 29/62 p. 415). *Junior Clerk* 9 Nov. 1791–3 Jan. 1795 (T 29/63 p. 549). *Junior (Assistant) Clerk* 3 Jan. 1795–19 Aug. 1805 (T 29/67 p. 372). *Assistant Clerk* 19 Aug. 1805–7 Jan. 1806 (T 29/85 p. 348). *Senior Clerk* 7 Jan. 1806–18 April 1809 (T 29/86 p. 1). Ret. 18 April 1809 (T 29/100 pp. 333–4).

Westcote, William Henry (Lyttleton) 1st Lord   *Commissioner* 16 June 1777–1 April 1782.

Wharton, Richard   *Junior Secretary* 8 Dec. 1809–7 Jan. 1814 (T 29/103 p. 361).

Whately, Thomas   *Junior Secretary* 24 Aug. 1763–15 July 1765 (T 29/35 p. 151).

Wheeler, F. G.   *Extra Clerk* 8 Oct. 1858–c. 1859 (AB, iv, 26). Last occ. 1859 (*Royal Kal.* (1859), 169).

White, H. A.   *Extra Clerk* pd. from 1 April 1824 to 21 Jan. 1825 (T 38/552 pp. 57, 61).

White, Joseph   *Assistant Solicitor* 1 Aug. 1781–1 July 1794 (T 54/43 p. 391). *Solicitor*

1 July 1794–21 Feb. 1806 (T 54/47 p. 254). Ret. 21 Feb. 1806 (T 29/85 pp. 490–1; T 29/86 p. 173).

White, Luke (*styled* Hon. 19 Aug. 1863) *Commissioner* 26 March 1862–7 June 1866.

Whiting, William *Messenger* 12 Feb. 1839–9 March 1840 (T 29/410 p. 235). Left office 9 March 1840 (T 41/8).

Whitmore, Henry *Commissioner* 1 March 1858–23 June 1859; 13 July 1866–17 Dec. 1868.

Wickens, T. E. *Extra Clerk* 13 Dec. 1836–24 May 1861 (T 29/384 pp. 248–9). *Supplementary First Class Clerk* 24 May 1861–c. 1869 (AB, iv, 113). Last occ. 1869 (*Royal Kal.* (1869), 171).

   Assistant Accountant 27 Feb. 1855–19 Nov. 1869 (T 29/558 p. 578).

Wickham, Henry Lewis *Private Secretary to Chancellor of Exchequer* (Althorp) 31 Dec. 1830–28 June 1833 (T 29/312 p. 486).

Wickham, William *Commissioner* 10 Feb. 1806–31 March 1807.

Wilbraham, Roger William *Junior Clerk* 22 May 1838–22 March 1850 (T 29/401 pp. 495–6). *Assistant Clerk* 22 March 1850–4 July 1856 (T 29/538 p. 616). *First Class Clerk* 4 July 1856 (T 29/564 p. 47).

   Private Secretary: to Financial Secretary (Parker, Hayter, Lewis) 7 July 1846–Feb. 1852 (T 29/499 p. 144; T 29/533 p. 356; T 29/540 pp. 81–2); *to Chancellor of Exchequer* (Gladstone) 18 Jan. 1853–March 1855 (T 29/550 p. 136).

   Clerk of Parliamentary Accounts 24 Dec. 1860–31 Dec. 1869 (AB, iv, 105).

Wilbraham *see also* **Bootle Wilbraham**

Wilkin, Thomas *Under Clerk of Revenue* occ. 30 June 1742, 1745 (*Commons Journals*, xxiv, 299; Chamberlayne, *Present State* (1745), pt. ii, 61). *Chief Clerk of Revenue* 11 Oct. 1752–26 Dec. 1757 (T 29/32 p. 71). D. 26 Dec. 1757 (*Gent. Mag.* (1757), xxvii, 578).

   Placed on establishment 27 July 1757 (T 29/32 p. 475).

Williams, Edward *Messenger* pd. from 29 Sept. 1703 to 24 June 1714 (*CTB*, xxviii, 427, 502).

Williams, Elizabeth *Housekeeper* occ. 27 Nov. 1712, 17 Oct. 1715 (*CTB*, xxvi, 87; ibid. xxix, 297).

Williams, John *Messenger* app. Nov. 1780 (*2nd Rept. on Fees*, 81); occ. 4 May 1786 (ibid.).

Willimot, Robert *Private Secretary to First Lord* (Liverpool) 16 June 1812–April 1827 (T 41/4).

Wilmington, Spencer (Compton) 1st Earl of *First Lord* 16 Feb. 1742–2 July 1743. D. 2 July 1743.

Wilson, Charles Rivers *Junior Clerk* 26 Feb.–4 July 1856 (T 29/562 p. 512). *Third Class Clerk* 4 July 1856–30 June 1857 (T 29/564 p. 47). *Second Class Clerk* 30 June 1857 (T 29/567 p. 519).

   Private Secretary: to Financial Secretary (Wilson, Hamilton) 30 May 1856–Jan. 1859 (AB, iii, 314; T 29/570 p. 583); *to Assistant and Permanent Secretary* (Hamilton) 12 May 1859–Dec. 1868 (T 29/475 pp. 250–1); *to Chancellor of Exchequer* (Lowe) 24 Dec. 1868 (AB, iv, 344–5).

Wilson, James *Financial Secretary* 5 Jan. 1853–2 March 1858 (T 29/550 p. 15).

Windsor, Henry M. *Junior Clerk of Civil List* 10 Aug. 1840–8 Aug. 1851 (T 29/428 p. 152). Res. 8 Aug. 1851 (AB, iii, 163).

Winkley, W.   *Extra Clerk* 14 May 1806–5 Aug. 1851 (T 41/9). Res. 5 Aug. 1851 (T 29/544 p. 282).

Winnington, Thomas   *Commissioner* 20 May 1736–28 April 1741.

Winter, John   *Messenger to Chancellor of Exchequer* 1 Jan. 1841–4 Nov. 1864 (T 29/ 433 p. 1). Res. 4 Nov. 1864 (AB, iv, 168).

Winter, Matthew   *Extra Clerk* Dec. 1777–16 Dec. 1783 (*2nd Rept. on Fees*, 70). *Junior Clerk* 16 Dec. 1783–15 Aug. 1787 (T 29/54 p. 496). *Junior (Assistant) Clerk* 15 Aug. 1787–3 Jan. 1795 (T 29/58 p. 498). *Junior Clerk* 3 Jan. 1795–28 Feb. 1798 (T 29/67 p. 371). Res. 28 Feb. 1798 on app. as Secretary to Board of Taxes (T 29/72 p. 187).

Clerk of Minutes April 1782–28 Feb. 1798 (T 29/54 p. 538).

Wolfe, Lewis   *Extra Clerk* occ. 30 Nov. 1782 (T 29/53 pp. 183–4). Res. 18 Feb. 1789 on app. as Comptroller of Accounts, Stationery Office (T 29/60 pp. 218–19).

Clerk of Bills 30 Nov. 1782–29 July 1785 (T 29/53 pp. 183–4; T 29/56 p. 517).

Wolseley, Robert   *Clerk* occ. from 7 Nov. 1671 to 3 July 1673 (*CTB*, iii, 957; ibid. iv, 187). Left office c. June 1673 on app. as Commissioner of Wine Licences (*Letters to Sir Joseph Williamson 1673–4*, ed. W. D. Christie (Camden 2nd ser., viii, ix, 1874), i, 117).

Wood, Charles (succ. as 3rd Bart. 31 Dec. 1846)   *Private Secretary to First Lord* (Grey) 31 Dec. 1830–10 Aug. 1832 (T 29/312 p. 486). *Parliamentary Secretary* 10 Aug. 1832–19 Dec. 1834 (T 29/332 p. 226). *Chancellor of Exchequer* 6 July 1846–27 Feb. 1852 (*Times*, 7 July 1846).

Commissioner 6 July 1846–28 Feb. 1852.

Wood, Edward   *Supernumerary Clerk* 1 April 1795–7 Jan. 1797 (T 29/67 p. 518). *Junior Clerk* 7 Jan. 1797–3 Jan. 1799 (T 29/70 p. 82). *Assistant Clerk of Minutes* 3 Jan. 1799–6 March 1800 (T 29/74 p. 65). Res. 6 March 1800 (T 29/76 p. 18).

Wood, Frederick   *Junior Clerk* 6 March 1800–20 May 1803 (T 29/76 p. 18). Res. 20 May 1803 (T 29/81 p. 89).

Wood, Joseph   *Messenger of Receipt* 11 Dec. 1798–c. 23 May 1801 (C 66/3954). D. by 23 May 1801 (app. of Andrews).

Wood, Thomas   *Messenger of Chamber* 5 July 1795–26 July 1807 (T 54/47 p. 361). D. 26 July 1807 (T 41/3).

Woodford, Charles   *Under Clerk of Revenue* 14 Feb. 1799–19 Aug. 1805 (T 29/74 p. 65). *Assistant Clerk of Revenue* 19 Aug. 1805–2 Jan. 1821 (T 29/85 p. 351). *Senior Clerk of Revenue* 2 Jan. 1821–17 Oct. 1834 (T 29/193 p. 77). Ret. 17 Oct. 1834 (T 29/358 p. 329).

Private Secretary to Junior Secretary (Wharton) occ. 19 May 1812 (T 29/117 p. 293).

Woodger, Thomas   *Messenger of Chamber* 27 July 1807–2 Oct. 1827 (T 54/50 p. 267). Ret. 2 Oct. 1827 (T 29/274 pp. 41–2).

Woods, W. W.   *Extra Clerk* 4 April 1857–27 Jan. 1859 (T 29/567 p. 3). Res. 27 Jan. 1859 on app. to post in Colonial Office (T 29/574 p. 30).

Worsfold, W.   *Messenger* 15 Dec. 1829–c. 10 Jan. 1861 (T 41/6). D. by 10 Jan. 1861 (AB, iv, 109).

Messenger to Secretary first occ. 1837 (*Royal Kal.* (1837), 235); remained in office until 27 May 1856. *Doorkeeper* 27 May 1856–c. 10 Jan. 1861 (T 29/563 p. 512).

Wortley *see* **Stuart Wortley**

Wortley Montagu, Edward   *Commissioner* 13 Oct. 1714–11 Oct. 1715.

Wright, Ezechiel *Messenger of Receipt* 5 Sept. 1674–c. 10 July 1689 (C 66/3167). Forfeited office c. 10 July 1689 (*CTB*, ix, 184).

Wright, James *Messenger of Receipt* 23 Feb. 1732–14 March 1746 (C 66/3584). D. 14 March 1746 (T 53/42 p. 46).

Wright, Nathaniel *Messenger of Receipt* 5 Sept. 1674–c. 10 July 1689 (C 66/3167). Forfeited office c. 10 July 1689 (*CTB*, ix, 184).

Wright, Richard *Assistant Solicitor* 17 Nov. 1747–c. 30 May 1750 (T 54/34 p. 502). D. by 30 May 1750 (T 54/35 p. 200).

Wyatt, William *Under Clerk* pd. from 25 March 1715 to 25 March 1723 (*CTB*, xxix, 628; T 53/30 p. 146). D. 13 April 1723 (*Hist. Reg. Chron.* (1723), viii, 19).

Wyndham, Sir William, 3rd Bart. *Chancellor of Exchequer* 21 Aug. 1713–13 Oct. 1714 (C 66/3493).

Wyndham, William *Under Clerk* 29 Nov. 1725–c. 24 June 1733 (T 29/25 p. 127). Pd. to 24 June 1733 (T 53/37 p. 69).

Wyndham, William Wadham *Supernumerary Clerk* 9 Nov. 1791–April/July 1792 (T 29/63 p. 549). *Under Clerk of Revenue* April/July 1792–19 Aug. 1805 (T 53/60 p. 145). *Senior Clerk of Revenue* 19 Aug. 1805–1 March 1808 (T 29/85 p. 351). Res. 1 March 1808 (T 29/93 pp. 421–2).

Wyndham O'Brien, Percy *Commissioner* 22 Dec. 1755–15 Nov. 1756.

Wynne, William *Junior Clerk* 24 Dec. 1852–11 Jan. 1856 (T 29/549 p. 702). Res. 11 Jan. 1856 (T 41/9).

Wyse, Thomas *Commissioner* 30 Aug. 1839–8 Sept. 1841.

Yeates, Robert *Chief Clerk* 31 July 1759–27 May 1769 (T 29/33 p. 218). D. 27 May 1769 (*Gent. Mag.* (1769), xxxix, 271).

Yonge, William (ktd. 1725; succ. as 4th Bart. 18 July 1731) *Commissioner* 2 April 1724–28 July 1727; 11 May 1730–19 May 1735.

Yorke, Joseph *Supernumerary Clerk* 16 Aug. 1790–1 Feb. 1791 (T 29/62 p. 220). *Junior Clerk* 1 Feb. 1791–3 Jan. 1795 (ibid. p. 415). *Junior (Assistant) Clerk* 3 Jan. 1795–14 Nov. 1800 (T 29/67 pp. 371–2). *Senior Clerk* 14 Nov. 1800–18 Feb. 1817 (T 29/77 p. 60). Ret. 18 Feb. 1817 (T 29/146 pp. 389–90).

Young, John *Commissioner* 20 Sept. 1841–21 May 1844. *Parliamentary Secretary* 21 May 1844–7 July 1846 (T 29/473 p. 389).

Young, Thomas *Private Secretary to First Lord* (Melbourne) 2 Sept.–Nov. 1834 (T 29/357 p. 25).

Young, Thomas *Messenger* 12 Feb. 1839–c. 21 Jan. 1862 (T 29/410 p. 235). D. by 21 Jan. 1862 (AB, iv, 127).

    Messenger to Secretary 12 Aug. 1853–1 Oct. 1856 (T 29/552 p. 354). *Superintendent of Upper Floor* 1 Oct. 1856–c. 21 Jan. 1862 (AB, iii, 322).